ROYAL HISTORICAL SOCIETY
STUDIES IN HISTORY
SERIES
No. 31

MERCHANT SHIPPING AND WAR

A Study of Defence Planning in Twentieth-Century Britain

S0-BXL-627

Recent volumes published in this series include

For a complete list of the series please see pp. 219-20

MERCHANT SHIPPING AND WAR

A Study in Defence Planning in Twentieth-Century Britain

Martin Doughty

LONDON: Royal Historical Society
NEW JERSEY: Humanities Press Inc.
1982

© Martin Doughty
Swift Printers Ltd ISBN: 0 901050 83 0
Humanities Press ISBN: 0 391026 88 7
All rights reserved

ALLEN COUNTY PUBLIC LIBRARY
FORT WAYNE, INDIANA

The Society records its gratitude to the following, whose generosity made possible the initiation of this series: The British Academy; The Pilgrim Trust; The Twenty-Seven Foundation; The United States Embassy bicentennial funds; The Wolfson Trust; several private donors.

The publication of this volume was assisted by a grant from the late Miss Isobel Thornley's bequest to the University of London.

British Library Cataloguing in Publication Data

Doughty, Martin
Merchant shipping and war.
(Royal Historical Society studies in history series; no. 31)
1. Great Britain – Commerce – History
I. Title   II. Series
382'.0941   HF3505

First published in Great Britain in 1982 by Swift Printers (Publishing) Ltd, London EC1
for The Royal Historical Society
and in the U.S.A. by Humanities Press Inc., Atlantic Highlands, NJ 07716

Printed in England by Swift Printers Ltd. London EC1

PREFACE

7052121

This book is concerned with a neglected aspect of British defence policy in the first half of the twentieth century. Its subject is, broadly speaking, merchant shipping, but it is concerned with aspects of the role of merchant shipping in the war effort which have hitherto been largely ignored by historians. The crucial importance of merchant shipping in maintaining a continuous supply of imports to this country is, of course, a cliché of the military history of the period. Analysis of the role of merchant shipping has, however, been almost entirely concerned with the problems of preventing the interruption of this flow of imports by enemy action against the ships themselves, and with the activities of naval forces in the defence of seaborne trade. The history of the two major wars in which Britain has been involved in this century suggests that this concentration on the military aspects provides only a limited appreciation of the problems Britain faced in ensuring the uninterrupted importation of essential supplies. On occasion in both world wars, the success of British efforts to safeguard seaborne imports to this country by the employment of naval forces in the defence of trade was prejudiced by the effects of inefficient organisation both of the merchant ships themselves, and of the arrangements made to receive and distribute imported goods in this country. It is these latter problems which this book investigates.

The events of the 1914-18 War clearly demonstrated that technological advances during the previous century of peace had so transformed both the nature of war itself and the organisation of the shipping industry and its associated services, that peacetime methods of commercial organisation had become entirely inadequate for the preservation of imports in a war situation. It became necessary for government — for the state — to take over control of every aspect of the problem of imports — of the ships, the ports, and the commodities themselves — and to coordinate their activities together in a coherent effort to maintain essential supplies at a satisfactory level. This experience was repeated during the Second World War. A large part of what follows in this book is therefore concerned with the relationship between the shipping industry and the state in wartime, and with the various forms of state intervention which were adopted to ensure efficient utilisation of the resources available. There is, however, no attempt to provide a narrative history of the organisation of merchant shipping during these two wars. Such histories have already appeared in the various volumes of the Official Histories of the war years. My main objective is to analyse the problems of organisation involved and the responses adopted to them, and so to elucidate the alternatives open to the state in its attempts at control. This objective can most effectively be attained through the consideration of the plans made in Britain in the period between the wars to ensure that problems comparable to those of 1914-18 should not recur in a future conflict. These years of increasingly uneasy peace provided an opportunity for the mature consideration of such problems, drawing on wartime experience, and for the investigation of alternative solutions to them. With the exact details of the future conflict uncertain, the planning process cast its net widely, considering aspects which proved of only marginal importance in the actual conditions of war in 1939. The plans in themselves thus provide a more comprehensive assessment of the problems which the British felt were likely to occur regarding imports than did wartime experience itself, and also provide an illuminating commentary on the state of British preparedness in 1939. Consequently, they form the major focus of this book.

With the experience of the 1914-18 War as a guide, both to the problems and to possible responses to them, the plans produced in the inter-war years represent a fascinating compromise between the desire, frequently expressed in Whitehall, to adopt efficient solutions involving thorough-going state intervention in control of imports and their transport, and what was regarded as the impracticability of imposing such restraints on the free market system without forfeiting the absolutely essential cooperation of the commercial interests involved. Any consideration of these plans thus becomes to some extent an attempt to explain how it was that, in 1940-41, Britain faced almost identical problems regarding imports as those she had faced in 1916-18. As such, the subject necessitates some investigation of the specific nature of the problems of the early years of the Second World War, to enable an assessment of the origins of the crisis, and of the relevance of pre-war planning to it.

Apart from the volumes of the Official History series referred to above, and one or two works of personal reminiscence by the principal figures involved in shipping control in the war years, there has been little published material dealing with the subject. This book is therefore largely based on original research into the official archives of the period, located in the Public Record Office, London. I am indebted to the Keeper of the Public Record Office for permission to quote from these documents, and to his staff for their courtesy and assistance throughout several years of visits to the Office. I should also like to thank Professors D.C. Watt and M. Howard for their advice and encouragement during the gestation of the thesis on which this book is based, and Mr. H.G. Pitt, and Worcester College, Oxford, where it all started. For what remains I am, of course, solely responsible.

CONTENTS

ABBREVIATIONS

A.T.B.	Advisory Committee on Trading and Blockade in Time of War (est. 1924). Sub-Committee of C.I.D. Re-titled Advisory Committee on Trade Questions in Time of War, 1929.
B.O.T.	Board of Trade.
B.S.W.R.I.O.C.	British Shipping War Risks Insurance Organising Committee, (1924). Sub-Committee of C.I.D.
C.I.D.	Committee of Imperial Defence, (1902).
C.O.S.	Chiefs of Staff Committee, (1923). Sub-Committee of C.I.D.
D.E.M.S.	Defensive Equipment of Merchant Ships.
D.I.C.	Distribution of Imports Committee, (1933). Sub-Committee of C.I.D.
D.O.P.	Director of Plans Division, Admiralty.
D.P.R.C.	Defence Policy and Requirements Committee, (1935).
F.(D.P.)D.	Food (Defence Plans) Department, Board of Trade, (1936).
I.B.S.	Insurance of British Shipping: Papers of B.S.W.R.I.O.C.
M.M.D.	Mercantile Marine Department, Board of Trade, (1921).
M.O.E.W.	Ministry of Economic Warfare, (1939).
M.O.S.	Ministry of Shipping, (1916-21; 1939).
M.O.W.T.	Ministry of War Transport, (1941).
M.T.	Ministry of Transport, (1919).
P.E.C.	Port Emergency Committee.
P.T.A.C.	Port and Transit Advisory Committee, (1937).
P.T.E.C.	Port and Transit Executive Committee, (1915).
P.T.O.	Port and Transit Organisation, (1937).
P.T.S.C.	Port and Transit Standing Committee, (1937).

R.P.D.	Regional Port Director.
R.U.S.I.	Royal United Services Institution.
S.D.A.C.	Shipping Defence Advisory Committee, (1937).
T.I.S.C.	Treasury Inter-Services Committee, (1936).

INTRODUCTION

In the economic life of the United Kingdom the shipping industry occupies a position of unique importance. To its operations all other industries are indebted for their access to foreign markets, and most of them for the whole, or a large proportion, of their supply of raw materials; of the normal food supply, two thirds is brought from overseas. On the labours of those who go down to the sea in ships, on the skill and enterprise with which those ships are managed, depends not only the wealth and prosperity, but the very existence of the British people.

C.E. Fayle, *The War and the Shipping Industry*, (Oxford, 1927), 1.

From the moment when man attained the ability to undertake voyages on the open sea, the dangers of naval warfare have been added to the perils of the deep which originally confronted him. The advantages which man obtained from the sea in peacetime — cheapness of transport, and speed and freedom of movement — were no less advantageous for military operations, and once such advantages had been recognised, they could only be denied to an enemy by the use of seaborne forces. Thus naval conflict developed as an inevitable consequence of man's initial conquest of the oceans for peaceful purposes.

The character of naval warfare was conditioned by the nature of the medium on which it took place. In itself, the sea has no value. Unlike the land, it cannot be possessed or divided, and mere occupancy of it provides little advantage or accession of power. It is, in Mahan's classic description, 'a wide common', featureless and in perpetual motion. Its importance lies in its utility as a medium for transport and communication, both in peace and war. Indeed, the growth of seaborne trade between nations has, in the modern world, reached such a peak that naval theorists have stressed the role of the attack upon — or defence of — such trade as more important in naval warfare than conventional military operations at sea, such as the transport of invasion forces or the capture of colonial possessions. For such theorists, exemplified by Mahan and Corbett, even the destruction of the enemy's naval forces is important only in regard to the freedom it provides to prey on his seaborne commerce. Thus, in Mahan's words, 'the necessity of a navy, in the restricted sense of the word, springs, therefore, from the existence of a peaceful shipping, and disappears with it, except in the case of a nation which has aggressive tendencies, and keeps up a navy merely as a branch of the military establishment.'[1]

Such analysis gave rise to a body of naval theory, perhaps best exemplified by the work of Sir Julian Corbett, which asserted that, since the mere destruction of the enemy's naval forces brought little direct advantage to the victor, the proper objective of naval warfare was to secure control of the communications the sea afforded. Naval warfare was not an end in itself, and success in battle was only important in so far as it enabled the use of sea communications for one's own purposes, and denied similar use to the enemy. Corbett enshrined such doctrines in the phrase 'Command of the Sea' — control of seaborne communications, which it was the objective of naval warfare to achieve. The advantages such control afforded were obvious: 'By occupying [an enemy's] maritime communications and closing the points of distribution in which they terminate, we destroy that national life afloat and thereby check the vitality of that life ashore, as far as the one is dependent on the other.'[2]

It is evident that only in the very unusual circumstances of an overwhelming superiority of power on the part of one belligerent would a nation be able to exercise total command of the sea. Indeed, Corbett's theory stressed that the normal condition of naval warfare finds command in dispute between the belligerents, each being able to obtain certain advantages from his limited command of the sea, but being unable to deny comparable advantages to the enemy. Such advantages included the freedom to mount invasions or foreign expeditions, and, of course, the freedom to protect one's own trade and to harass that of the enemy. In such circumstances of disputed command, each of these aspects of naval activity will require the attention of a proportion of the naval forces available, distributed in accordance with the objectives of national policy. The extent to which such theory deprecated the importance of the actual physical conflict of naval forces is shown by Corbett's theory of the fleet in being. He argued that all, or some, of the advantages of command could be exercised without actually achieving it by the destruction of the enemy's main fleet, since it was only necessary to achieve control over those communications you wished to use yourself or to deny to the enemy. For such purposes, provided one's own naval forces represented a sufficiently serious threat to prevent the enemy from successfully contesting the exercise of control, it was not necessary to

---

[1] A.T. Mahan, *The Influence of Sea Power upon History 1660-1783* (London, 1965 ed.), 26.

[2] J.S. Corbett, *Some Principles of Maritime Strategy* (London, 1911), 80.

destroy his naval power. Unlike Mahan, who had insisted on the necessity for a decisive naval battle to decide the issue of command, Corbett's theory thus asserted the essentially pragmatic doctrine that the proper objective of naval warfare was to secure the ability to make use of the sea, regardless of the means by which that ability was achieved. Success or failure in a maritime struggle could thus be assessed in relation to the freedom to use maritime communications, rather than in simple terms of ships lost or sunk — a lesson which the battle of Jutland, among others, was to drive home. Command of the sea was thus defined in terms of the success achieved in the utilisation of the advantages of maritime power — in forwarding one's own objectives, or in hindering those of the enemy.

Since the period of the wars against the Dutch, Britain has been, in Mahan's terms, a nation which has felt 'the necessity of a navy.' The Royal Navy, in consequence, has always included the defence of British seaborne trade among its multifarious duties, Nelson himself noting, 'I consider the protection of our trade the most essential service that can be performed.'[3] But while the defence of trade has been a legitimate operation of war for as long as men have engaged in trading enterprises at sea, it has come in the last century to occupy a peculiarly significant position in British naval philosophy and defence planning — a significance expressed in Churchill's admission that 'the only thing that ever really frightened me during the war was the U-boat peril.'[4]

It is a cliché of military history that Britain's national existence during the twentieth century has come to depend on a continuous supply of imports, particularly of food, from overseas, but it is nevertheless true. It had not, of course, always been so. Britain had become a net importer of wheat as early as the 1760s, although such imports did not form a significant proportion of total consumption until just before the French Revolution, when imports appear to have approached a figure of 5 per cent of total consumption.[5] Whether or not such a level of imports rendered Britain theoretically dependent on foreign food supplies,[6] it remains the case that it was not beyond the capacity of British agriculture to support the total food require-ments of the population without importation. That is to say that Britain retained the capacity for agricultural self-sufficiency. And

[3] Quoted in S.W. Roskill, *The War at Sea,* I (London, 1954), 111.

[4] W.S. Churchill, *The Second World War,* II (London, 1949), 598.

[5] This estimate is based on figures given in M. Olson, *The Economics of the Wartime Shortage* (Durham, N.C., 1963), 69.

[6] As Olson appears to maintain, *ibid.,* 5.

although food shortages were occasionally severe during the wars against France, 'the scarcity does not appear to have made national survival doubtful, or seriously interfered with the prosecution of the war'.[7]

This was emphatically not the case in later wars. By 1914 a century of developing industrialisation had abolished any possibility of Britain attaining self-sufficiency, not only in food, but in most primary products. Industrial development, a rapidly growing population, adherence to the free-trade system and improvements in transportation had combined to fundamentally alter the balance of British economic life. Where 1880 represents 100, the volume of net imports to Britain in 1811 had been seven. In 1911 it was 203.6.[8] When the twentieth century dawned Britain was the commercial and trade centre of the world, dependent as no other nation on overseas trade for her survival. Furthermore, between 1811 and 1911, Britain's population had expanded from twelve to nearly forty-one millions, creating an enormous increase in the demand for food. British agriculture alone could not have coped with such a demand, but in the last thirty years of the nineteenth century the combination of free-trade economics and the steamship had opened the British market to a flood of cheap foreign grain. The depression in British agriculture which resulted increased the dependence on imports until, in 1905, some four-fifths of British wheat consumption was imported. In the thirty years before 1914, British food imports generally grew at a rate of two per cent each year.[9] At the same time, the demands of British industry for raw materials created a dependence on foreign imports greater, if anything, than in the case of food. In the thirty years before 1914, raw material imports grew at an average rate of 1.8 per cent per annum.[10] By 1913, seven-eighths of Britain's raw material supplies were imported. Thus, by 1914, trade from overseas was an essential precondition, both for national survival, and for the development of the national war effort.

This vast increase in the volume of imports had been matched by an increase in the size of the mercantile marine required to bring in the goods. Between 1813 and 1913, the net tonnage of British registered merchant shipping quintupled from 2,349,000 to 12,120,000, the

[7]*Ibid.*, 50-51.

[8]B.R. Mitchell and P. Deane, *Abstract of British Historical Statistics* (Cambridge, 1962), Ch. XI.

[9]D.H. Aldcroft and H.W. Richardson, *The British Economy, 1870-1939* (London, 1969), 80.

[10]*Ibid.*

latter figure being composed of some 20,938 individual vessels. Of this gigantic total only something under 4,000 could be regarded as ocean going vessels engaged in the importation of overseas products.[11] Even so, the size of the problem which the defence of these ships presented was apparent, for as a prominent merchant service officer put it in 1905: 'If any naval power decided upon hostilities with Great Britain it will be as far as our mercantile marine is concerned, a war of extermination.'[12] Such a target was both too vulnerable, and too vital to British power, to be overlooked.

The extent of Britain's dependence on overseas imports, and thus on her merchant fleet, had first become a matter of general recognition in the mid 1880s. From that point, the problems of the defence of trade generated an increasing volume of debate, a debate which was to be finally subsumed into the more general discussion of all aspects of naval policy which characterised the years immediately preceding the 1914-18 War. While the importance of the submarine as a threat to trade had clearly been underestimated by most of the contributors to this debate, it is not possible to accuse the Royal Navy, or the governments of the day, of overlooking the seriousness of the problem of the defence of Britain's overseas trade.

From the point of view of Britain's national survival, however, these debates on the defence of trade only undertook a partial investigation of the problem of ensuring a continuous flow of imports to this country in wartime. Throughout these discussions, as throughout contemporary naval theory, the security of imports was viewed solely as a problem in the defence of merchant ships against enemy attack — in the strategic and tactical disposition of one's own naval forces in the attempt to hinder or prevent the enemy's efforts to harass trade. It was assumed that national survival could be ensured by the arrival of the ships in the ports of this country. Such had been the case in the Napoleonic Wars, but, as the events of 1914-18 were to show, the processes of industrialisation which Britain had undergone in the intervening period had so complicated the operation of her economy that such an analysis was no longer appropriate.[13] In modern circumstances other factors had to be taken into account — factors concerning the efficiency with which the ships were used, the arrange-

---

[11]C.E. Fayle, *The War and the Shipping Industry* (Oxford, 1927), 8.

[12]Quoted in B. McL. Ranft, 'The Naval Defence of British Seaborne Trade, 1860-1905' (unpublished D.Phil. thesis, Oxford, 1967), 67.

[13]This is not to suggest that pre-war planning had overlooked the economic implications of Britain's dependence on imports as such. The Committee of Imperial Defence conducted numerous investigations before the war into questions such as the insurance of shipping and cargo in wartime, the possible effects of the closure of ports

ments made to receive and distribute their cargoes and so on. In the pre-war discussions it had been assumed that the normal processes of peacetime commerce would be adequate to achieve these objectives in war also. Experience proved this assumption to be false. Inefficient use of transport facilities, congestion of the ports and other related factors proved as effective as enemy attack on the merchantmen themselves in restricting the flow of imports to this country. For the moment, one example may suffice:

> Between 1914 and 1917 the times spent in port had been so much extended that, as a result of the difference, the United Kingdom almost certainly lost more imports, in any single year than the submarines sank . . . In the first four months [of 1917], at the peak of the U-boat effort, cargoes were being sunk at the rate of about five million tons a year. At the same time the loss from delays in port, taking peacetime performance as a standard, was between four and five million tons.[14]

During the 1914-18 War it became evident that the importation of a continuous supply of food and raw materials could not be secured solely by the defence of the merchant ships in which they were transported. Despite the success of British efforts to safeguard the merchantmen by the employment of naval forces to dispute the command of the sea, the experience of the 1914-18 War demonstrated that the flow of imports could be impeded by the effects of a failure to organise the physical constituents of the trade in the most efficient manner. In short, Britain's survival depended not only on the protection of the merchantmen, but also, in Fayle's phrase, on the 'skill and enterprise with which those ships were managed'. It had become clear that, under wartime conditions in a modern industrialised society, special arrangements would have to be made to ensure efficient management of those sectors of the economy concerned with imports, just as special measures had to be taken to protect imports against enemy attack.

on the east coast of Britain by enemy action, the effect of our dependence on Germany for sugar supplies and on Baltic nations for imports such as timber, and other factors which reflected an awareness of the difficulties which Britain would face in wartime because of her trading position. The point is, however, that these investigations were concerned only with the effect of military or naval action by our enemies on British trade, and overlooked the possibility that the economic management of the trade might also be a limiting factor. It was not appreciated that the conditions of modern warfare would undermine the ability of the normal commercial processes of the capitalist market place to provide efficient management of our import trade. Consequently, no preparations to deal with such problems were made before the war.

[14]W.K. Hancock and M.M. Gowing, *British War Economy* (London, 1952), 124.

With reference to Britain's situation in the twentieth century, it might be permissible to suggest an extension of Corbett's theory of command of the sea beyond the purely military sphere, to take account of the factors just described. Command of the sea is described as the control of the communications afforded by the sea. But control of the sea is not an end in itself — it implies the utilisation of the advantage so gained, the use of the sea for one's own purposes, and its denial to the enemy. As regards trade defence, the object of naval warfare is to enable the national trade to continue unhampered by enemy action. So far as naval forces are concerned, this objective is achieved by the safe and regular arrival of the merchant ships carrying the trade at the ports of this country. From the national point of view, however, it is the arrival of the trade itself which is the crucial objective. The merchant ships are merely a means to this end, and the objective of naval warfare therefore becomes the arrival of the imports themselves on the quays of Britain's docks and harbours. To the extent that such arrivals are hindered by inefficient organisation of the ships carrying the imports, of the ports receiving imports, or, indeed, of the imports themselves, then to that extent the nation has failed to make full use of its command of the sea, or has denied to itself some of the advantages attainable from command of the sea.

Expressed simply, in wartime merchant ships are only a means to achieve the importation of the essential commodities which the nation requires to survive and to further its war effort. If inefficient organisation of shipping prevents the importation of sufficient commodities to secure these objectives, then the nation will be defeated just as surely as if the shortage of commodities was caused by the enemy's success in sinking the ships in which they are transported. In these circumstances the efficiency of the protection against enemy action given by naval forces is a marginal factor in the situation, since the mere survival of the merchantmen or their cargoes will not sustain the nation if the imports are not delivered.

Shipping has been used as an example of this mechanism, but it is necessary to stress that similar restrictions in the flow of essential imports could, and did, arise as a result of inefficiencies in the ports, in the purchase of the imports themselves, and in the internal distribution of the imports after they had arrived in this country. As a convenient shorthand for the purposes of this enquiry, the term 'import system' has been adopted to define in their entirety the transport facilities involved in the carriage of overseas commodities from their country of origin to their destination in this country — the ships, the ports, and the inland transport facilities. In the two world wars of this century, Britain faced the effects of inefficiencies in, as well as enemy attack upon, each of these areas. Britain's response to such pressure on the import system is the subject of this book.

One aspect of this subject has already been exhaustively investigated by historians — that of the design, provision and employment of naval forces to provide direct physical protection to British trade at sea. There seems little justification for a further enquiry into this aspect of naval history. Instead this book deals with the other side of the coin, with the merchant ships themselves, and with the efforts made to ensure their most efficient use in wartime.[15] Certain aspects of this subject border very closely on traditional naval history: for example, the provision of defensive armament for merchantmen, and the control of their movements to avoid known concentrations of enemy forces, both of which were the responsibility of the Admiralty. But their inclusion here is justified solely by the fact that they affected the economic performance of the ships involved, by reducing the amount of cargo carrying space available, or by altering the normal routes between ports. Apart from these aspects, this book is entirely concerned with what may be described as British attempts to achieve the most efficient organisation of the import system under war conditions.

As such, it concentrates very heavily on the inter-war period. The paradox this seems to imply is, in fact, more apparent than real. As was suggested above, the occurrence of a severe crisis in the import system during the 1914-18 War was almost entirely unexpected. The real causes of the crisis were only dimly perceived during the war itself, and the measures devised to deal with it were adopted in an ad hoc and incoherent fashion. After the war accurate analysis of the causes of the crisis became available and considerable attention was given, in both official and commercial circles, to devising arrangements to ensure that such problems did not recur in any future conflict. It is with this planning process that this book is mainly concerned. The plans naturally involved consideration of the earlier war, and their effectiveness can only be assessed in relation to the experience of the Second World War, but it is the planning process itself which

[15] For present purposes it has regrettably been necessary to restrict the definition of the term 'merchant shipping' exclusively to dry-cargo tonnage. As the dependence of the economy on oil increased in the inter-war period, so the importance of oil tankers within the British fleet increased, to the point where, in 1926, a separate organisation, the Oil Board, was set up to consider both the supply of oil, and the provision of tankers to transport it. Questions of the supply and organisation of tankers cannot be divorced from the general problems of the oil requirements of the nation as a whole, and it would not be possible to deal adequately with such subjects within the limits of an investigation centred on the problems of dry-cargo tonnage. Therefore, and bearing in mind that an entirely autonomous organisation had been created to consider the problem of tanker tonnage, I decided to omit the subject entirely.

illuminates the alternative strategies available, and elucidates the nuances of the problems involved.

Although close cooperation with commercial interests was always maintained, the major responsibility for the preparation of plans for the control of the wartime import system inevitably devolved onto the state, and thus the Civil Service, inevitably, because the experience of the 1914-18 War had shown that the essential character of the crisis lay in the inability of existing commercial structures to function adequately under war conditions. In large measure the various features of the problem were considered by the Civil Service within the structure of department responsibilities which had emerged after the 1914-18 War — the Admiralty and Board of Trade concerned with the ships, the Ministry of Transport with the ports and inland transport systems. There was no coordinating authority as such, although certain aspects of the problem came before the Committee of Imperial Defence. This lack of interdepartmental coordination was a serious handicap to the creation of satisfactory proposals in this area, and contributed greatly to the recurrence of a crisis in the import system in the early years of the Second World War.

So far as the British import programme was concerned, this crisis had been overcome by the winter of 1941-2, and the entry of the United States into the war thus provides a convenient terminal date for this study. American participation entirely transformed the shipping situation, although it did not in all respects improve it. By midsummer 1941, the British had identified both the problems and the countermeasures necessary to resolve them, and largely spent the rest of the war trying to get the Americans to adopt them also. In the latter half of the war shipping remained in short supply, but not because of inefficiencies in the operation of the British import system. Subsequent shortages resulted from the decision to pursue an amphibious strategy against the Axis powers. Ships for the import programme were scarce, but only because it was chosen to employ them in supporting military activity, not because the British import system was badly managed.

The recurrence of a crisis in the import system in the early years of the Second World War, despite the experience of the earlier conflict, clearly raises serious questions concerning the quality of the plans designed in the inter-war period to prevent such a repetition. In attempting to assess the performance of the British bureaucracy in devising suitable measures to control the import system in a future war, it is hoped that this book will illuminate the details of an important, but hitherto neglected, aspect of Britain's exercise of maritime power.

1

THE IMPORT SYSTEM AND ITS RESPONSE TO WAR

The nineteenth century saw a revolution in Britain's trading position as the progress of industrialisation destroyed her self-sufficiency and rendered her continued existence dependent on regular supplies of commodities imported from overseas. At the same time technological advances virtually revolutionised the organisation of the import system, and particularly the structure of its most important constituent, the shipping industry.[1] The development of steam propulsion and the introduction of the electric telegraph were seminal in creating the organisational backbone of the industry in the twentieth century. It was not until the middle years of this century — after the Second World War — that the industry broke free from the framework imposed on it in the later nineteenth century by such inventions. The following remarks on the organisation of the industry may therefore be regarded as applicable throughout the period with which this book is concerned.

The essential contribution of late nineteenth-century technological developments was to regularise the shipping industry. In the days of sail ships were small, and their movements, depending on the fluctuations of the wind, were unpredictable. There could be no regular services and the industry was organised on an opportunist basis. Once the vessel had delivered its export cargo from Britain, the master was responsible for finding further employment. He was therefore frequently the owner or part owner of the vessel. Given his expertise there was no need to follow a pre-arranged route, and it was the custom for vessels to sail in search of trade. Control of both the shipping and merchandising aspects of shipping operation was thus concentrated in one person.

The developments of the nineteenth century split these functions into distinct responsibilities. By 1900 the telegraph and, increasingly, the radio, enabled the employment of the ship to be supervised, and if necessary adjusted, by managers remaining in the vessel's home port. The master's concerns were restricted to the running of the vessel. Secondly, the introduction of steam propulsion enabled vessels to proceed without reference to local weather conditions. It became

[1]Numerous secondary sources have been employed in the account of the import system. Among the most important are: A. Kircaldy, *British Shipping* (London, 1914); S.G. Sturmey, *British Shipping and World Competition* (London, 1962); G. Alexandersson and G. Norstrom, *World Shipping* (New York, 1963); and R.H. Thornton, *British Shipping* (Cambridge, 1959).

possible to establish regular services between specific ports, and ships built specifically for such services, known as liners, were introduced. The older methods of operating shipping survived, since it was impracticable to serve every requirement for sea transport by a system of regular voyages. This method of ship operating became known as tramping, and the tramp steamer developed to engage in it. (These distinctions will be considered in more detail later.)

The essential characteristic of the industry as a whole remained the system of allocating available tonnage to the commodities requiring transport on the basis of supply and demand economics. The strength of the demand for transportation was assessed on the basis of the price which a commodity was capable of paying to secure that transportation. Freight rates — the prices paid for the services of the shipping industry — were thus determined solely by the competition of the market place. The stronger the demand for the commodity, the greater the price it would fetch on sale. The higher selling price would enable the owner to recoup the extra cost of transport. The industry was thus self-regulating, for when too high a freight rate was demanded, the goods would not be able to bear the cost of shipment, and the trade would cease. The safeguard against shipowners charging an excessive rate of freight was found in the competition within the industry for cargoes, and the readiness of owners to undercut each other to secure cargoes. Freight rates were thus determined automatically by the operation of market forces. (The only exception to this is the case of the liner conferences, which is discussed below.)

Once a freight had been agreed, the shipowner and the cargo owner or shipper signed or 'fixed' an agreement, or Charter Party. Such charters could be taken out for individual voyages, or for a number of voyages over a period of time — voyage charter, or time charter. With the predictability of voyages under steam, it became customary to arrange such charters some time — often many months — in advance of the actual date at which shipment was required. Such 'forward engagements' enabled the most efficient use of the ship, since its employment could be foreseen many months in advance and could be arranged in the most economical manner. It provided security of shipment at the appropriate date for the cargo, so preventing delays attending the fixing of a charter. The system thus ensured the most efficient relation of ships to cargo.

Thus far, tramp shipping and liner services operated in a similar manner. But at this point the differences begin to emerge. Despite the growth of the liner system, there remained many cargoes which could not be adequately served by a system of regular voyages, or for which the establishment of such a system would prove uneconomic. Seasonal crops, and the inevitable unusual individual shipments are the obvious examples. These demands were met by the tramp. The tramp has been described as the weathercock of demand. It is free to seek employment anywhere in the globe where remuneration is available. Where there is trade without a suitable liner service, or where an existing liner service proves inadequate, is the tramp's opportunity.

Tramp cargoes were usually arranged on one of the great shipping exchanges of the world, through brokers acting for the owners. This was necessary because of the structure of ownership of tramps — there were few tramp companies, and ships were often owned by consortia of small shareholders, or even single persons. Chartering was habitually on a trip, or voyage basis, and almost always for a bulk cargo. The paramount advantage of the tramp was its flexibility. It could go where there was cargo to be shifted, if necessary making the trip in ballast. Being employed in no regular trade, it had no specialised cargo handling equipment, and could carry any kind of bulk cargo. It was, however, rare for a tramp to carry other than bulk cargoes, for the very reason that it did not possess specialised handling equipment to enable the efficient loading of such cargoes. The tramp represented the basic cargo-carrying ship, with the lowest practicable technical complexity, and the smallest possible shore organisation to control it. It formed the cheapest level of investment in ocean-going cargo carrying, and it was entirely subject to the vagaries of the economic process in the determination of rates for its services. Tramping was a cut-throat business, and combinations of owners to determine rates were rare.

The contrast with the liner is complete. There were passenger-carrying liners where the need for regularity and predictability of sailing is obvious. But by far the majority of liners in recent times were of the combined passenger and cargo carrying type, which had developed after the market for regular services dealing with cargo had become apparent. These cargo liners retained the organisational structure characteristic of their passenger-carrying counterparts, and it is this, and the regularity of their voyages, which distinguished them from tramps.

Essentially, liners ply a fixed schedule of sailings between specified ports at regular intervals. They do not generally transport bulk cargoes, but provide shipment for general cargo of all types and in all quantities, short of a shipload. They thus served the small cargo shipper, who could not afford the cost of hire of a vessel exclusively for his own trade. As such, the liner relied on a widespread local organisation in the ports at which it called to arrange its cargoes and to fix its contracts. The cost of maintaining such local agents was obviously great, one estimate putting organisational overheads at 35 to 40 per cent of operating costs.[2] Consequently liners were generally owned by large companies, which could better defray the costs involved. Liner costs were generally higher than those for tramps. Calling at more ports, the liner had to pay more port dues. To maintain a regular service it was generally constructed to a higher mechanical standard, and to deal efficiently with part-cargoes in ports with varying cargo handling equipment, liners were generally provided with their own unloading equipment. The capital cost of a new liner was thus higher than that of a tramp, and this was yet another reason for the concentration of liner ownership in the hands of large companies, rather than the smaller organisations characteristic of the tramp sector.

This extensive investment in the physical and organisational assets of their industry also made the liner companies vulnerable to the effects of uncontrolled competition in rates. Once placed in a particular trade, the liner is obliged to continue in that trade to retain its regular customers. At this point all the operating costs of the voyage, except the cost of actually loading and unloading the cargo carried, became overhead costs, and would have to be met whether the ship carried a full cargo, or no cargo at all. The owner receives compensation in proportion to the amount by which his receipts in rates exceed the cost of handling the cargo. (This compensation does not become profit until the overhead costs are also exceeded.) Clearly, if the rates are only just sufficient to cover the cost of cargo handling, the company cannot survive long. Yet in a system of free competition, and with a sufficiency of tonnage in the trade, rates would be forced down to this level by attempts to secure more cargo by undercutting rates. The lines would not long survive, and the cargo could cease to be shipped.

To prevent the occurrence of this situation, which would benefit no one, the liner companies formed the so-called 'liner conferences'. Conferences were associations of the companies involved in each trade (trade being defined by route). The object of the conferences was to maintain and regulate the rates in the trade, by foreswearing competition, and by agreeing to a mutual schedule of rates for every class of traffic. Additional clauses regulating the sailings according to an agreed pattern were often included. The first conference was set up

---

[2] Sturmey, 246.

in 1875, on the United Kingdom-Calcutta route, which was suffering from excess competition following the opening of the Suez Canal.[3]

Since conferences only regulated the affairs of their own members, they were, naturally, vulnerable to the intervention of outside lines which might cut rates below conference levels. To guard against this danger, conferences developed a number of techniques aimed at preventing attempts by outsiders to break into the conference trade. In particular, the most common form involved the granting of a rebate to the cargo owner if he shipped only in vessels entered with the conference. Payment of such rebates was generally deferred for an agreed period after they became due, to ensure the allegiance of the shipper during that period.

The rates charged by the conferences were usually assessed secretly by the members of the conference with regard to what the trade could stand. Thus, although the shipper might not derive advantage from the reduction of rates caused by competition among owners, he was assured that any competitors he might have in the trade did not receive more favourable rates. Obviously, excessive rates would discourage trade and lead to serious attempts to break the hold of the conference, so the shipowners also had an inducement to maintain rates at a broadly competitive market level. Nonetheless, the question of the desirability of the restriction of competition by conferences is hotly debated, though it is not important here.

During the present century the importance of the liner has continued to grow. In 1914, tramps formed some 60 per cent of all British shipping, but the figure declined steadily thereafter.[4] The causes of the decline of the tramp were complex. Among them was the decline of certain bulk trades, particularly British coal exports, which had formed an important proportion of tramp employment before the First World War. Also British tramps were generally less efficient than their foreign rivals as British owners showed less inclination to adopt new technical advances to offset higher crew costs. Finally, as we have seen, tramp owners had no organisational structure which could be used to protect them from the worst effects of the general slump in shipping which occurred in the inter-war period.

While the physical constituents and organisational structure of the shipping industry had thus undergone extensive modification as a result of technological advances during the nineteenth century, its economic philosophy remained fundamentally unaltered. The technological developments were not matched by any revision of

[3]*Ibid.*, 323-4.

[4]*Ibid.*, 35, 68 and 87-8.

shipowners' attitudes to the principles upon which the industry functioned, or to the principles which determined its relationship to the government.[5] The shipping industry relied completely on the uncontrolled operation of market forces in determining its pricing structure. The industry was conceived as self-regulating, its efficiency being guaranteed by its responsiveness to the constraints of the capitalist market place. Any form of state intervention in the economic organisation of the industry would, it was held, unbalance this system, and so create, rather than ameliorate, inefficiencies.

Such attitudes reflected the traditional fierce independence of shipowners and seafaring men, and the cut-throat competition which characterised so much of the operation of their industry. One example of the violence of this competitiveness may be found in the institution known as fighting ships. Fighting ships were employed by conferences when an attempt was being made to break their monopoly. Essentially, the idea was to place a conference ship alongside every ship trying to break into the market, and to offer lower rates for the same services, the conference defraying the inevitable losses until the interloper was forced to withdraw.

If there was fierce competition within the British shipping industry, this was as nothing compared with the resistance of the industry to interference from without by the government. Before the First World War owners had little to fear from government interference, which was largely restricted to regulating the constructional standards and crew conditions of ships. The war years, however, brought considerable state interference concerning the operations of the ships themselves, and the industry showed itself prepared to go to extreme lengths to reverse this trend in the post-war period, and to re-assert its independence. Thus it spent £55,000,000 on acquiring captured German ships after the war rather than have them operated by the government in competition with commercial tonnage.[6]

[5] The most concise statement of the industry's attitude to state intervention was given by an insurance underwriter in evidence before the Royal Commission on the Defence of British Possessions and Commerce Abroad (the Carnarvon Commission), in 1881, when he noted; 'Commerce has no sense of patriotism; such an element is not regarded in commerce. . . My own opinion is that the best thing that Government can do is to leave us alone. I have a strong personal opinion that commerce is a thing that regulates itself and that it requires no Government aid whatsoever, and that the less they meddle with us the better we shall get on.' Quoted in Ranft, 178.

[6] Sturmey, 58. On the general attitude of shipowners to state intervention, see also R.H. Tawney 'The Abolition of Economic Controls, 1918-1921', *Economic History Review*, XIII (1943), republished in an extended version in *History and Society: Essays by R.H. Tawney*, (ed.) J.M. Winter, (London, 1978). Page references below are to the *Economic History Review*. See also, below 31-36.

As a corollary of this desire to restrict the intervention of government in its concerns, the industry clothed as much of its operations as possible in secrecy. Thus, apart from the simple figures of the numbers of ships registered and owned in Britain, there were few statistics available concerning the normal operations of the industry at any time before the end of the Second World War. Government intervention remained as limited as before the previous conflict, and the industry had settled into a self-satisfied frame of mind which contributed greatly to its poor performance in the inter-war years in comparison with its foreign rivals. But the economic condition of the industry in the 1930s is not immediately relevant here.

British ports in the period reflected a similar competitive structure to that of shipping. The ports were managed by their individual authorities, and to a certain extent all ports could be said to be in competition with each other for the available trade. The ports maintained a variety of statistics concerning their operations, and so far as these statistics were comparable, a national picture could be established through a simple summation. In a manner broadly similar to that with the ships, the ports were subject to various statutory regulations concerning the storage and handling of goods, navigational aids and so on. Ports derived revenue by charging ships and cargoes dues or tolls for the use of their facilities, and their freedom in the fixing of such rates was complete, except in respect of the necessity to make them broadly comparable with those of their competitors. The normal daily operations of the ports were not subject to any outside interference.

Similarly, the transport facilities concerned with the distribution of goods from the ports were entirely free to organise their operations solely in response to commercial considerations. The reorganisation of the railway structure which had occurred after the 1914-18 War did not interfere with the commercial freedom of the operators, although it was responsible for an improvement in the efficiency of the industry, and in the comprehensiveness of its statistics. Arrangements for the pooling of rolling stock and the interchangeability of working practices had been made. Road transport was regulated only in respect of the licensing of vehicles, and there were absolutely no statistics or bodies concerned with the national situation in regard to road transport as a whole. The canals were increasingly unimportant in inland transport, and they too maintained their traditional independence of any form of national coordinating structure.[7]

[7] The best general description of British transport facilities in this period is to be found in H.J. Dyos and D.H. Aldcroft, *British Transport* (Leicester, 1969). For the reorganisation of the railways after the First World War see D.H. Aldcroft, *Studies in*

In broad terms this was the structure of the British import system after it had absorbed the technological advances of the nineteenth century. This structure functioned adequately under peacetime conditions, albeit subject to the periodic fluctuations characteristic of the trade cycle. That is to say, that the system of allocating available shipping space to the demand for transport on the basis of the rate that the cargo was able to support functioned efficiently under contemporary peacetime conditions. The first significant test of the effectiveness of such a system in wartime came in 1914. It is also necessary to stress that the 1914-18 War was the first major conflict in which Britain had engaged since the process of industrialisation had transformed the British economy. In 1914, for the first time, British national survival was entirely dependent on continuous imports of food, raw materials and manufactured goods — imports which could only be brought in by sea. This dependence on seaborne trade was so great that inability to defend it against attack would have brought defeat. Similarly, for reasons demonstrated above, inability to organise that trade efficiently would have produced the same result.

From the point of view of the efficient organisation of transport facilities in a modern war, the structure of the British import system in 1914 was not encouraging. There were no established bodies dealing with the transport system as a whole, and the traditions of the separate industries involved were extremely hostile to any interference with their absolute independence to regulate their own affairs as they saw fit. Furthermore, the degree to which the various individual constituents of the import system — the ships, the ports, the inland transport networks — were interdependent, was not appreciated. Indeed, certain of these facilities were accustomed to regard each other as offering competitive services — the railways, for example, competing with coastal shipping in certain cases, and, more generally, with the canals. The habit of looking at the import system as an integrated whole was thus lacking, indeed there was no appreciation that the system actually constituted such a whole. Tradition asserted attitudes both of mutual competition and lack of coordination between the individual transport facilities, and also of general hostility to external regulation by the state.

This attitude towards the transport system was essentially a reflection of the ruling philosophy of laissez-faire in economic matters, which had guided Britain's rise to her position as foremost among the world's economies. In 1914 there seemed no need to revise this philosophy simply because the country was at war. There had

British Transport History, 1870-1970 (Newton Abbot, 1974), 117-144 and the same author's *British Transport since 1914* (Newton Abbot, 1975), 15-29.

never been a prolonged conflict between highly industrialised nations, and there was no previous experience to suggest the folly of attempting to conduct such a war without an entirely unusual degree of state interference in the organisation and objectives of the economy as a whole.[8] The history of the First World War therefore provides a clear example of the effect of modern wartime conditions on the ability of the merchant marine to do its job.

If it is possible for a complex industry to be described in a single phrase, the shipping industry in 1914 was characterised by the concept of the traditional freedom of the shipowner to employ his tonnage in whatever trade and to whatever purpose he wished. In so far as this freedom was curtailed it was through the operations of commercially controlled regulating bodies, such as the system of liner conferences, but the state had no part in this. So far as the state was concerned, the owner could use the ship as he pleased, providing he conformed to the regulations concerning the vessel and her crew. The accepted view in 1914 was that the industry was self-regulating — that the importance of the demand for a particular commodity could be measured by its ability to pay for its transport, and that, in the constant competition for transport of the capitalist market place, those commodities which would not receive transport, (because of their inability to pay for it and still sell at an economic price), would be those least required by the nation. In such circumstances there was not only no need for the state to concern itself in the direction of ships to cargo, but such intervention would have unbalanced the system had it occurred.

As a result, the government in 1914 anticipated no need to concern itself with the commercial employment of shipping. Its activities in the shipping sector were confined to the provision of tonnage to meet the needs of the Navy and for the transportation and supply of British military forces overseas. As regards the importation of commodities into this country the situation was to remain as in peacetime, and market considerations were to be allowed to determine the import programme of this country. As the Home Secretary remarked in August 1914; 'Our desire has been not to interfere with ordinary trade at all, but to leave the traders to conduct their own business.'[9]

The most immediate result of the government's refusal to involve itself with the regulation of the merchant marine was a rise in freight rates. Actual figures as to the extent of this rise differ. Sir Arthur

[8]Tawney, 1-7.
[9]*Ibid.*, 5.

Salter suggests that by July 1915 time charter rates were as much as 230 per cent higher than in December 1914, and that by 1917 they had reached 800 per cent higher.[10] Whatever the exact figures, the magnitude of the increase is never disputed.[11] The price of goods in the United Kingdom reflected these increases, and gave rise at the time to widespread allegations of profiteering.[12] Certainly the shipowners were not loath to take advantage of so favourable a situation. Some idea of the sort of profits they were making may be obtained from the following figures. Profits from tramp shipping in 1916 were £11 million, compared with £3.8 million in 1914. The respective figures for liner company dividends were £5.3 million and £2.6 million.[13]

Perhaps understandably, this was the aspect of the problem which caught the public eye, and which attracted the attention of the government. As Salter says, 'it is not an exaggeration to say that the whole structure of economic controls developed throughout the war was a response to the necessity of curbing inflationary price and cost rises.'[14] This, however, reflected a fundamentally superficial view of the problem. There were, naturally, aspects of the rise in freight rates which could be explained in terms of inflation consequent upon wartime conditions. War brought certain extra costs which the shipowner had to meet to run his ships. The increased danger of the loss of the vessel involved him in higher insurance costs, while it also became necessary to pay his crew more for facing the unusual dangers involved in a wartime voyage. Furthermore, the increased demands of the state for men and fuel for its wartime activities involved rising costs for the shipowner through increased competition for limited supplies. (Thus, it may be noted, despite its protestations, the state found itself involuntarily interfering with the normal operations of the shipping industry to inflationary effect).

While such factors were appreciated at the time, it was considered,

[10] J.A. Salter, *Allied Shipping Control* (Oxford 1921), 45, 69.

[11] Sturmey, 52. Dyos & Aldcroft, 299, 303; Fayle, *Shipping Industry,* 104-7, and Tables 27-35, 438-45.

[12] Fayle, *Shipping Industry,* 176-184; Salter, 109-110. See also articles in the shipping magazine *Fairplay,* e.g., 12 October 1939, 19 October 1939, 7 March 1940, 11 April 1940. The very fact that such emphasis was placed on rebutting charges of profiteering in the earlier war is indicative of the strength of feeling it aroused, and, perhaps, of the owners' appreciation that their conduct required justification. It is also significant that, in the first month of war in 1939 the average increase in the valuation of steamers was 20 per cent, and that this was adduced as evidence that *no* profiteering was occurring. The reader may draw his own conclusions from this. *Ibid,.* 19 October 1939.

[13] Sturmey, 50.

[14] Salter, 109; Fayle, *Shipping Industry,* 131.

rightly, that they could not in themselves explain such a dramatic rise in the cost of sea transport. The popular explanation of this divergence was profiteering — the artificial inflation of rates beyond their 'natural' level by shipowners, in order to line their own pockets. While it would be naive to suggest that this did not occur, it seems certain that the major part of the rise in rates was attributable to the development of a scarcity of shipping. This scarcity became more pronounced as the war progressed. That is to say that there were no longer sufficient ships engaged in trading to Britain to bring in all the imports she needed and was able to purchase. Commodities requiring carriage competed for the limited shipping capacity available by offering more remunerative rates for transport. Shipowners found themselves in the fortunate position of being purveyors of a commodity in exceedingly short supply and found that shippers needed little encouragement to offer higher rates. Profiteering was rather forced upon the shipowners than engineered by them, although, naturally, they did not resent this situation.

This scarcity of shipping developed for a number of reasons. The first lies in the government's activities on behalf of the sea transport needs of the defence services. It was the accepted policy to provide for the transport requirements of the fighting services by the requisition of existing merchant ships. It is true that the government could have hired tonnage on the open market to meet these requirements, but ships engaged on military and naval support duties were frequently exposed to front line dangers, and experience had shown that owners were unwilling to charter for such services, no matter how generous the rates offered. Alternatively, the government could have built suitable ships itself, as it already did with the specialised Royal Fleet Auxiliaries. But to increase the number of such vessels in peacetime would mean some lying idle, since the shipping lobbies would not have allowed their employment on commercial services. Building after war had begun would be too slow and would involve an unacceptable diversion from warship construction.

The government had a variety of requisitioning powers at its disposal. In this case it was usual for the state to take over the management of the ship and to pay the owner a rate of hire. This rate became known as the 'Blue Book rate'.[15] In the event of loss, compensation was payable at an agreed rate. This type of charter was used to provide the Navy with Armed Merchant Cruisers, Auxiliary Patrol and minesweeping vessels, and hundreds of ships for the miscellaneous duties for which it would have been uneconomic to

---

[15] Sturmey, 49.

provide specialist vessels in peacetime. Such vessels also undertook the transport and supply of British expeditionary forces and overseas garrisons and bases. In the present context, this policy is important because it substantially reduced the amount of mercantile tonnage available for the carriage of essential imports to this country. The amount of tonnage requisitioned for these purposes varied from time to time during the war. In 1916, according to one estimate, it amounted to some 4.5 million tons gross, with another 3 millions employed providing for the Colonies and Allies. This compared with a total tonnage under the British flag in 1914 of around 19.2 millions. of which 12 millions were regularly employed in importing to this country.[16] Thus requisition for naval and military purposes alone took nearly one quarter of Britain's total tonnage in 1916.

The other primary factor contributing to the development of the shipping shortage was the effect of war itself on the shipping market. The regularisation of the shipping industry consequent upon the introduction of steam propulsion, and the practice of making 'forward engagements' for the carriage of cargo, had made the industry dependent on the ability to predict the employment of its vessels many months in advance. But, in wartime, this carefully constructed system was thrown into confusion. In the first place, the closure of markets in enemy countries to British shipping forced a realignment of many trading connections. Furthermore, in the First World War, the imports so lost could only be replaced by drawing from countries further away, involving longer voyages, and a corresponding reduction in the total amount of imports which could be transported in a given period. The simple fact of the declaration of war thus reduced the amount of imports British shipping could deliver. Additionally, owners no longer retained complete control over the movements of their shipping, since the Admiralty's responsibility for the defence of merchantmen frequently involved alterations of route and delays. The system of evasive routes designed to avoid dangerous areas or known enemy forces, involved less direct voyages and, when it was introduced, convoy also prevented the most efficient utilization of shipping, by preventing ships from sailing as soon as they had completed loading. Estimates of the effect of such naval countermeasures on overall voyage times during the 1914-18 War vary. Figures for the North Atlantic run suggest increases of from 10 to 25 per cent.[17] Although every effort was made to keep the owner informed of the date of arrival of his ship, it was not always possible to give warning sufficiently in advance for him to make the necessary arrangements for the

[16]W.P. Elderton, *Shipping Problems, 1916-1921,* (London, 1928), 7 and 8.

[17]See Ch. 2 below.

subsequent voyage with complete confidence. Such delays were multiplied with the development of port congestion, which, after 1915, ensured that even if the owner could accurately predict the time at which the ship would arrive at a port, he had no hope of predicting how long it would take to unload and clear.[18] Similar factors had affected shipping in previous wars, but in the days of sail it had been impossible to estimate times of arrival accurately in the first place, and so the industry was initially organised on less precise lines.

The effect of these accumulating delays was two-fold. In the first instance there were the simple inefficiencies produced by the consequent disruption— cargoes kept waiting for shipment, port facilities clogged with unremoved goods and so on. All this involved extra costs for the shipowner, which he could only meet by raising rates. Secondly, delays reduced the number of voyages which could be made in a given time, and thus reduced the amount of cargo which could be carried. Delays thus reduced the overall carrying capacity of the British merchant fleet.

Since the term will be used again, a definition of carrying capacity will be useful. The carrying capacity of a dry-cargo fleet may be defined as 'the amount of commodities, measured in whatever was the most appropriate way, which the existing fleet could carry in a given period of time, in response to the needs in the various areas which it had to serve.'[19] Any increase in overall voyage times, such as that which followed the closure of certain European markets to British shipping in 1914, or that which resulted from the necessity to defend merchant ships against attack by the enemy, produced an automatic reduction in the carrying capacity of the fleet as a whole. Thus the mere outbreak of war reduced the carrying capacity of the British fleet, and rendered it less capable of carrying out its function of supplying the country.

The term 'carrying capacity' is in fact central to the issues with which this book deals, and the problem of the war organisation of merchant shipping can be more closely defined as the problem of ensuring that the carrying capacity of the merchant fleet was sufficient to meet the requirements of the nation at war. In this connection it should be noted that all transport systems can be regarded in terms of carrying capacity, and that restrictions in the carrying capacity of other forms of transport could have a direct effect on the capacity of the merchant marine.

[18]C.E. Fayle, *Seaborne Trade*, I (London, 1920), 405.

[19]C.B.A. Behrens, *Merchant Shipping and the Demands of War* (London, 1955), 18.

The case of the ports was the most notable example of this in the First World War. As with the ships, the overall capacity of Britain's ports was reduced simply because of the outbreak of war. Certain ports, notably Harwich and Southampton, were taken over by the military and forbidden to commercial shipping.[20] These measures threw a strain on the other ports which had to deal with cargoes normally bound for the closed ports. Any such measure of diversion of shipping may increase delays by producing confusion and inefficiency, but its major effect is felt at the ports to which the traffic is diverted. The problem was not solely one of the ports becoming blocked with the extra traffic: most ports are not utilised to the full extent in peacetime.

The real problem was with the nature of the cargoes themselves. Just as there were specialised ships to deal with certain types of cargo, ports required specialised handling equipment if certain cargoes, especially the bulk cargoes such as grain and iron ore, were to be unloaded in the shortest possible time. Not all ports possessed such facilities, and what facilities they did possess could become over-crowded with an influx of traffic which was normally unloaded elsewhere. It was these specialised facilities, rather than the simple number of berths available, which formed the critical limit in port capacity. A further problem was caused by the nature of wartime imports. War produced an unusual demand for certain types of manu-factured goods — munitions, road transport, guns and so on. Most of these commodities were unusually heavy, and British ports, rarely having to deal with such weighty objects in peace, were ill-provided with suitable heavy lift cranes to unload such cargoes. The effects of this factor, although present in the First World War, were felt most strongly during the Second World War, when tanks and aeroplanes formed a substantial proportion of war imports. (In passing it may also be noted that such cargoes reduced the carrying capacity of the ships as well, since they were much more difficult to stow than the normal, regularly shaped, crated imports of manufactured goods, so reducing the productivity of each voyage.)

As regards the ports, however, any reduction in the speed with which vessels could be unloaded was likely to result in congestion as further vessels arrived to make use of the facilities. Inefficient handling facilities, or the congestion of a limited number of handling facilities, resulted in delays. And just as the ports were affected by the arrival of unusual commodities in unusual quantities, so were the inland transport facilities responsible for removing commodities once

[20]Fayle, *Shipping Industry*, 41.

they had been landed at the ports. These facilities also suffered from a lack of specialised equipment, and were ill-prepared to accept the strain of unusually heavy imports at certain ports. In many cases, inland transport facilities simply did not possess the capacity to remove the goods unloaded at the ports. As a result, unloaded cargoes tended to pile up on the quays, hampering the handling of the next cargo, and leading to increased congestion. A major factor in increasing the difficulties of the ports and inland transport systems in wartime was that, with the introduction of convoy, a large number of ships arrived at the port simultaneously, placing an unusually heavy strain on all the facilities.

The net result of the operation of all these factors was to cause congestion in the ports. Ships could not be dealt with as they arrived. Berths with the correct handling facilities were not available, or were choked with cargoes which had not yet been removed inland. Congestion was serious enough in itself, but it proved very difficult to overcome once it had occurred, since its removal required raising the port's capacity at a time when that capacity was already overstretched. Furthermore congestion was a self-perpetuating problem. Congestion gave birth to more congestion by delaying the efficient processing of incoming ships and cargoes.[21]

The delays to shipping resulting from the effects of congestion in the ports and in the inland distribution network produced, in both world wars, an extremely serious and prolonged reduction in the carrying capacity of the merchant marine.

To return to the narrative of events during the First World War, the effect of the growing shortage of shipping produced by congestion in the ports and the other causes considered above, was to reduce the number of voyages the average ship could make in the year. In order to maintain his profits, the shipowner was forced to increase rates, and in order to obtain shipment, cargo owners were prepared to offer higher rates. Both causes contributed to the inflation of rates.

Inflation of rates was doubly disadvantageous to the nation at war. On the simplest level it meant that prices rose generally at a time when retrenchment and the tightening of belts was the watchword. Secondly, it actively hindered the national war effort by operating as a system of indiscriminate rationing. In the absence of state control, market considerations governed the allocation of cargoes to ships. Market considerations were determined by the financial value of the goods to be transported. The more valuable a commodity, the greater the

---

[21]For the situation in the First World War, see Fayle, *Shipping Industry,* 151-3. For the general theory of port congestion, Behrens, 12ff.

freight rate it could support to ensure shipment and thus a rise in freight rates tended to exclude the less highly priced commodities from shipment. There was, however, no guarantee that high price was synonymous with utility to the national war effort. Indeed, in many cases, it is apparent that luxuries were imported at the expense of necessities as a result of the policy of allowing market forces to determine the allocation of cargoes to ships.[22] Had this occurred in peacetime, and had the necessities still been able to afford remunerative freight rates for the shipowner, then extra tonnage would have come into the trade, either from other trades or by new construction. But in wartime, even though the essential war supplies could afford the cost of shipment, the shipowners naturally chose to import the more valuable cargo which could offer them a higher rate, and the overall shortage of shipping prevented the less valuable cargoes from obtaining shipment at all. Such a situation could not long be allowed to continue.

Two solutions to this problem present themselves — the government could subsidise essential war imports to enable them to outbid luxuries, or it could directly control the allocation of cargoes to ships. The former had the great disadvantage of encouraging the rise in freight rates generally, and thus it was that the government came to adopt the latter, despite the conflict with its declared policy of non-intervention. The technique it adopted was to control the ships themselves through requisitioning.

The requisitioning of tonnage to ensure the importation of essential commodities had begun as early as February 1915, with falling imports of sugar. Some 80 per cent of Britain's pre-war sugar had come from Germany and Austria, and difficulty was being experienced in obtaining shipping to make the longer voyage to the West Indies which war necessitated. The next problem arose in the North Atlantic wheat trade, in November 1915, and the Requisitioning (Carriage of Foodstuffs) Committee was established to provide the necessary shipping. Similar problems led to the introduction of requisitioning for other trades. The essential characteristic of this policy was, however, that the incidence of requisitioning for commercial services was extended arbitrarily as shortages developed in the particular trades.[23]

By January 1916 the state policy of non-intervention in the commercial direction of merchant ships stood in tatters, and there can be little doubt that it should have been abandoned entirely at this

[22]Salter, 17-19.

[23]See both Salter and Fayle for accounts of the extension of requisitioning.

point, if not before. At the time, however, the government still clung to the idea that, even if intervention had to be tolerated, the areas affected should be restricted as far as possible. It was not appreciated that partial state intervention brought about a situation which was worse than either no intervention at all, or total state direction of the allocation of cargoes to ships. By reducing the amount of tonnage available on the open market, partial state intervention encouraged the rise in freights. Thus although it might force rates down in the trades to which it was applied, it tended to increase prices outside those trades. It made it more difficult for essential supplies to obtain shipment unless tonnage was requisitioned, for while the cost of such shipment was increasing, the number of unrequisitioned ships available was declining. Intervention in one area thus tended to produce a crisis in another, leading to more requisitioning, a smaller body of tonnage available on the open market, and an increasingly circular process.

Although this account of the events of the 1914-18 War is primarily intended to demonstrate the effect of a large scale war on the shipping industry, rather than to be a comprehensive account of the state's relationship to the economy in those years, it may be appropriate at this point to glance at the wider scene, and set shipping within a context. The policy of non-intervention which proved so malignant in the shipping field was applied across the economy as a whole, and, as with shipping, the demands of war rapidly forced its modification. The state found that conventional market economics were unable to ensure the supply of essential war materials. The War Office led the way when, in October 1914, it began to purchase meat itself to ensure supplies. In the following year it introduced control over jute, to ensure supplies of sandbags. Other examples could be multiplied, especially with regard to food supplies. Sugar itself, as well as the ships to transport it, had been controlled from the very outbreak, and reserves of other foods were built up by state purchases. Later still, intensive recruitment for the armed services began to leave key industries short of manpower, and the state was forced to intervene to control the use of manpower resources, and, at times, labour relations and remuneration.

The classic example of this process is, of course, the munitions industry, where a special ministry was established following the shell shortage of 1915. But, for our purposes, the narrative of these developments is less important than their effect on the economy as a whole. In a manner identical to the experience of shipping, the extension of state control in other areas ultimately undermined the ability of commercial bodies to regulate the economy satisfactorily.

The distorting effect of state intervention, and the very size of the demands of war, finally rendered it impossible to operate the economy with even a semblance of efficiency, without the most extensive state control. As one commentator has noted: 'By the end of 1916 it had become abundantly clear that the free price mechanism had failed to serve the country at war.'[24]

By the time such factors came to be realised, and the question of the proper structures through which state control should be exercised was considered, general dissatisfaction with the higher direction of the war was also concentrating attention on structural matters. Although Asquith's Coalition Government of May 1915, with its Dardanelles Committee, and the later War Committee, had at last abandoned the attempt to run the war through a conventional Cabinet, his unwillingness to entirely replace the peacetime convention of a departmental Cabinet resulted in the persistence of inefficiency. All major decisions were discussed twice — by the Committee, and by the Cabinet, most of whose members possessed insufficient detailed information to make their opinions apposite. Despite this they could block proposals, and the main characteristic of government at this time was its inability to achieve anything original. If the precedent of the Ministry of Munitions were to be followed, and the state were to organise its increased intervention in economic affairs through the creation of new ministerial departments, the situation could only have deteriorated, since the addition of yet more ministers to the Cabinet could only have decreased its efficiency and increased confusion. Thus it was perhaps fortunate that the administrative arrangements of higher government were revised at the very time that the problems of the war economy had become pressing.

Lloyd George's adoption, in December 1916, of the small War Cabinet, with sole responsibility for the higher direction of the war, composed of ministers untrammelled by departmental responsibilities, (and the consequent relegation of departmental ministers to a level approaching that of junior ministers in peace, with no power to criticise War Cabinet decisions), was thus timely. On the one hand, it enabled the adoption of a large number of departmental controls to administer the state's increasing activity in economic affairs, (including shipping, there were to be, ultimately, eleven new departments[25]), while on the other, it prevented this vast accession of

[24] S. Pollard, *The Development of the British Economy 1914-1950* (London, 1962). 46.

[25] These were the Ministries of Labour, Shipping, Food, Air, National Service, Pensions, Information, Health, Reconstruction, Munitions, and Blockade. H. Daalder, *Cabinet Reform in Britain, 1914-1963* (London, 1964), 48.

ministerial talent from swamping the decision-making process, since ministerial rank no longer entitled the holder to a role in that process. A further vital advantage of the adoption of the War Cabinet system was that it allowed the new ministers to be chosen without regard to political experience. Therefore, they were largely drawn from industry — Maclay (Shipping) was a shipowner, Devonport (Food) was a wholesale manager, Neville Chamberlain came to National Service from Birmingham, and there were Geddes, Northcliffe, and, at Information, Beaverbrook.[26] Such appointments not only provided government with a wealth of practical experience it could have obtained in no other way, but they smoothed the introduction of state control by reducing commercial distrust of the state's competence. It would be no exaggeration to say that most of the success of state intervention in 1917-18 derived from the enlistment of industrial leadership and cooperation, of which these appointments were the most striking example.

There would be little point in undertaking a narrative of the extension of state control over industry in 1917-18. Shipping may again serve as an example, both of the machinery of extension, and of the degree to which it could only have been achieved by a growing realisation by all parties concerned, including the shipowners, that such control was now essential if defeat was to be avoided. The shipowners were brought to this realisation as the incidence of requisitioning was extended. The policy of introducing requisitioning as the shortages manifested themselves was both haphazard and arbitrary. In the case of requisitioning for military needs it was recognised that the incidence of requisitioning should be as evenly distributed across the shipping community as possible, as requisitioned ships were tied to the rate at which they were taken up, no matter how much market rates should rise during the period of requisition. In the case of requisitioning for imports however, there was no time even to attempt to equalise the incidence of requisitioning from shipowner to shipowner. It thus transpired that several owners found themselves with a majority of their ships requisitioned and tied to Blue Book rates, while others found themselves virtually untroubled by state intervention and able to take full advantage of the rising open market rates. Not only were the owners of requisitioned ships unable to take advantage of rising market rates, but in some circumstances costs rose so much during the war that the Blue Book rates assessed in 1915 were actually unremunerative by 1918. Even after adjustment to take account of this, Blue Book rates were some 200 to 300 per cent

[26]*Ibid.*, 47.

below market rates in 1918.[27] While this differential was bad enough, the inequitable incidence of requisitioning for commercial purposes was a source of great dissatisfaction to all shipowners. Thus, in response to the arbitrary, unpredictable and uncoordinated administration of requisitioning by the state, most shipowners renounced their pre-war policy, and became advocates of thorough-going, coordinated state intervention in the affairs of their industry.[28]

This finally arrived in 1917. In December of the previous year shipping had been given a Ministry of its own under the Shipping Controller appointed in the previous month. The incidence of requisitioning was also extended. By February 1917 most tramps had been requisitioned, albeit piecemeal. In that month however, the full effects of the German declaration of unrestricted submarine warfare began to be apparent, and as a result it was decided to requisition the liner trades as well. It was to this process that the term 'Universal Requisition', used to describe the innovations of February 1917, applied. Liners posed a special problem with regard to requisitioning, since they operated regular services between stated ports at which the companies maintained a local organisation of representatives. A special process was therefore devised to safeguard this local organisation and to take account of it in awarding rates.[29] This system was successful enough to form the basis of the schemes produced for the next conflict and will be more fully described later.

In 1917 however, it was evident that requisitioning of shipping itself was not the complete answer to the twin problems of high rates and the shipping shortage. The experience of the Requisitioning (Carriage of Foodstuffs) Committee had shown that if the benefits of a more efficient organisation of shipping were to be felt in financial

[27]Dyos and Aldcroft, 303; Sturmey, 52. Fayle, *Shipping Industry*, Table 40, 450-4, contains details of Blue Book rates.

[28]Fayle, *Shipping Industry*, 202-3; A.J.P. Taylor, *English History 1914-1945* (Oxford, 1965), 99.

[29]Salter, 72. An interesting sidelight on the extent to which the state depended on the cooperation of commercial authorities in operating its schemes is provided by the history of liner requisitioning. The terms of the actual requisitioning letter were tested in a case brought by the China Mutual Steam Navigation Company, and were found to be *ultra vires*, since they requisitioned the owners' services, as well as their profit. However, the owners waived their legal rights in the national interest. Earlier in the war, doubts had been expressed about the legality of the Admiralty requisitioning ships merely to avoid having to pay high freight rates. This case was never tested in court. Both affairs, however, pay tribute to the patriotism of a class of persons frequently maligned for their conduct in the war, and underline the degree to which the state depended on the cooperation of industrialists in exercising control over the economy at a time when governmental economic expertise was notable only for its absence. Both cases are noted in MT.40/17, T.02337, Memos. on the Liner Requisition Scheme, 1937, and the former is considered in Fayle, *Seaborne Trade*, 1, 72, and the same author's *Shipping Industry*, 236-8.

terms, as well as in terms of the imports actually received, then the price of the commodity itself would have to be controlled. Furthermore, as 1917 progressed, it became apparent that there were no longer enough ships trading to Britain to bring in all the essential requirements for the war effort. It was no longer a case of excluding luxuries, but of adjudicating between competing necessities. A system of priority among conflicting demands for tonnage was required. The network of control of commodities which had been haphazardly developing since the outbreak of war was therefore systematised and extended.[30]

At the same time an attempt was made to establish a structure for allocating cargoes to shipping in the Tonnage Priority Committee.[31] This proved to be ineffective, and the Ministry of Shipping found itself increasingly responsible for such decisions. This was perhaps inevitable, since the Ministry had final responsibility for the allocation of ships to cargoes, but it was an unsatisfactory situation since the Ministry did not possess the expertise to undertake what was in fact the definition of a national import programme. Its attempts to do so were inevitably arbitrary, and resulted in much understandable discontent in the departments whose supplies were refused transport.[32]

The solution to this problem of adjudication between conflicting demands for shipping space was found in the creation of a representative and authoritative body at the highest level. A Committee of the War Cabinet chaired by Lord Milner was established towards the end of 1917 with full authority, under the War Cabinet, to allocate shipping space among claimant departments in such a way as to fulfil the strategic and economic policies determined by the War Cabinet. A similar Committee was established under Smuts to determine production priorities, while Sir Leo Chiozza Money chaired a new Import Restrictions Committee.[33]

This arrangement had taken over three years of war to achieve. By early 1918 the pre-war policy of non-intervention had been entirely superseded by a structure of departments created to control every aspect of the movement of imports from their source to the consumer. This system, despite its haphazard creation survived without significant alteration until the Armistice.

Wartime experience had exposed the fallacy of the attempt to conduct a full-scale modern war without the most extensive state

---

[30]To the point, for example, where in 1918 the government bought and sold 85 per cent. of the food consumed in Britain. Olson, 95.

[31]Fayle, *Shipping Industry,* 212-3. Salter, 75.

[32]Elderton, 10-14, 38-45; Fayle, *Seaborne Trade,* III, 67. Hancock and Gowing, 30.

[33]Fayle, *Shipping Industry,* 288; Hancock and Gowing, 37.

intervention in the direction of the economy. From the point of view of national policy — the maximisation of the war effort — it had become clear that 'supply and demand prices cannot be trusted in time of war to perform their customary function of allocating productive resources, determining production priorities, and distributing the final products among purchasers. All these processes must be governed by explicit government decision and administrative direction.'[34]

The authorities which Britain had developed to discharge these functions established a reputation as, perhaps, the most effective area of Britain's response to wartime pressure on her economic structure. If, in C.E. Fayle's words, British shipping accomplished an 'extraordinary achievement' during the war years, that achievement would not have been possible without the development of a satisfactory administrative structure to regulate all the multitudinous aspects of the problem of the import system. As Fayle noted: 'There is indeed, no lesson which stands out more prominently in the economic history of the war than the fundamental unity of the whole complex system of purchase, finance, transport and distribution which connects the consumer with the producer.'[35] By 1918, the British administrative system had both recognised this fact and come to terms with it to produce an outstandingly successful solution to the problems which the import system had faced under the twin threats of unrestricted submarine warfare and laissez-faire economic theory.

If the extension of state control over industry as a whole had proceeded falteringly and intermittently during the war years, it did not take so long to dismantle the apparatus of control once peace had arrived. The Ministry of Shipping and its associated bodies proved among the more long lasting of the wartime structures, since the shortage of shipping continued into the years of peace and the appropriate structures were retained to deal with it. Nonetheless, the Ministry was wound up in April 1921.[36]

This hasty return to something approaching normality was a natural reaction to the years of war, and this is not the place to consider its merits or demerits in the post-war world.[37] It does,

[34]Hancock and Gowing, 48.

[35]Fayle, *Shipping Industry*, 401.

[36]Taylor, 177 n.1.

[37]Several attempts at such a consideration have been made: on the general level, see, Tawney, op. cit., R. Lowe, 'The Erosion of State Intervention in Britain, 1917-1924', *Economic History Review*, 2nd ser, XXXI, (1978), and S. Armitage, *The Politics of Decontrol of Industry: Britain and the United States*, (London, 1969). For the decontrol of transport specifically, see D.H. Aldcroft, 'The Decontrol of Shipping and Railways after the First World War', *Studies in British Transport History, 1870-1970*, and the same author's *British Transport since 1914*, 15-29.

however, raise the question of the extent to which the lessons of the recent war had been identified and its experience assimilated. This question is central to the present enquiry, since the experience of the two 'world wars' of this century was so similar, as far as shipping was concerned, and since the achievements of the First War thus provide a minimum yardstick for excellence which it might reasonably be expected that preparations for the Second should excel. In the area under consideration, there were two groups of interested parties whose attitudes to the experience of the First World War merit consideration. These were the bureaucrats concerned with developing plans to deal with similar problems in a future conflict, and the ship-owners and commercial interests generally, which constituted the peacetime operators of those facilities which were the object of the bureaucratic plans. Although this study is explicitly concerned with an examination of the bureaucratic side of this dichotomy, some consideration must be given to the attitudes of the commercial bodies concerned with the industry. The traditional independence of the shipowners has been noted, as has the extent to which the state's activities during the 1914-18 War depended on their cooperation. As long as the democratic capitalist organisation of the state persisted, the necessity for such a partnership would remain, and, in the inter-war years, it was not possible for the outlook of the industry to be discounted in the planning process.[38]

As the remainder of this study will demonstrate, there can be little doubt that the bureaucracy had absorbed some, at least, of its experience in the First War. Regrettably, it is not so easy to say the same of the shipowners. In the immediate aftermath of the conflict it was, perhaps, natural that the shipowners should have joined in the general cry of 'back to 1914'. The concensus of opinion was neatly summarised by a 1918 report on shipping after the war, which described state control as 'alien to the British genius', and tending 'to paralyse individual effort'.[39] Nonetheless, such sentiments might be expected after a war which had seen an unprecedented extension of state interference in the untrammelled right of the shipowner to conduct his own business as he saw fit, and it is equally predictable that such views continued to represent the opinion of the commercial world throughout the ensuing fifteen years of peace.

[38]This was not simply a question of the advantages of mutual cooperation, for the shipping lobbies were extremely powerful in their own right. Walter Long, then First Lord of the Admiralty, noted in Cabinet in 1919 that 'there was no vested interest in the House of Commons so powerful as the shipping interest'. CAB 23/9, War Cabinet 534, 19 February 1919.

[39]Report of the Departmental Committee appointed . . . to consider the position of the Shipping and Shipbuilding Industries after the War. 1918. (Cmnd. 9092).

There was, however, one exception to this undisturbed progression. This occurred in the mid-1930s, when, under the influence of foreign competition, the poor economic performance of British shipping gave rise to a campaign for state intervention in the affairs of the industry in peacetime. The campaign envisaged, however, that such intervention should be restricted to financial support for the industry, and should not involve any interference in the actual direction of the ships themselves.[40] These objectives reflected the analysis that the crisis in British shipping resulted from the unfair competition of foreign fleets, which were able to undercut their British competitors because of subsidies received from their governments. Whatever the rights or wrongs of this analysis, it is clear that no fundamental reorientation of shipowners' attitudes to the state can be discerned in the subsidy campaigns of the 1930s. In 1935, at the height of the campaign, the President of the U.K. Chamber of Shipping declared that 'No good for shipping is ever achieved by the initiative of Governments'. Illustrations, he continued, abounded, 'to show the damage which Governments do when they profess to be able to manage shipping with views born of imagination, better than shipowners themselves with views born of experience'.[41]

Thus far, of course, the international situation had not deteriorated to the point at which it might have prompted shipowners to give serious consideration to the nature of the relationship between their industry and the state in wartime. This point may be said to have arrived with the Abyssinian crisis of 1935, and subsequent events served to keep the problem in the forefront during the years leading up to war. Yet it is evident that the shipowners' attitudes towards state control remained unchanged in these years, despite the evident danger of war. In September 1937, the editor of *Fairplay* wrote: 'Government assistance is occasionally, of course, very welcome. As a body, however, British shipowners have always striven to keep the Government as far as possible out of the business. Their desire, moreover, is to adhere to that practice.'[42] Four months later he continued: 'Many British owners of ripe experience are, of course, opposed in principle to Government interference of any kind.'[43] Ironically, at much the same time he was lobbying for the appointment of a Minister of Shipping, but only for peacetime.[44]

[40]For this, see Sturmey, Chapter IV.

[41]Speech by Mr. L.C. Harris, on his election as President of the U.K. Chamber of Shipping, quoted in *Fairplay*, 7 March 1935.

[42]*Ibid*., 23 September 1937.

[43]*Ibid*., 13 January 1938.

[44]*Ibid*., 28 April 1938.

Examples of this attitude could be multiplied almost indefinitely. It is, however, clearly important to note that such opinions continued to be expressed after war had actually arrived. Thus, at the Annual Meeting of the U.K. Chamber of Shipping in 1940, the new President, in reviewing the recently announced plans for the requisition of ships, noted that,

> No one has a higher regard for the Civil Service than I, and particularly for the ability of those Civil Servants in responsible positions in the Ministry of Shipping, with many of whom we have worked in close harmony at the Board of Trade in the past, but experience shows that Government departments by their very nature, their traditions and their methods of procedure, are incapable of running any business as efficiently or economically as the men trained in the hard school of business itself. That is particularly true of such an intricate and highly specialised business as shipping, where years of practical experience and the power of prompt decision are essential.[45]

Manifestly, shipowners' attitudes to state intervention, even well into the Second World War, remained similar to those of their predecessors in 1914, which, it could be argued, were anachronistic even then. The traditional independence of the shipowner was a strong component in these views, but cannot, in itself, entirely explain the ease with which the experience of the First World War was disregarded. As we shall see, it was possible to argue that the experience of the First War was unique, and that the measures necessary then would not be appropriate to a future conflict,[46] but it does seem as though the war had simply made no impact at all on the attitudes of shipowners. As soon as it was over they hastened in pursuit of the *ignis fatuus* of a return to 1914, and concurrently re-adopted pre-war attitudes as if the conflict had never occurred.

As Professor Tawney has remarked,[47] the multiplication of controls during the war years on an improvised basis in response to individual crises as they arose, discouraged the development of a doctrine of state intervention, and made it easier to regard the wartime experience as unique to the conditions which had given rise to it. Had the crisis during the 1914-18 War been less acute, the owners would certainly have opposed the introduction of the measures of control

---

[45]*Ibid.*, 7 March 1940. Speech by Sir Philip Haldin.

[46]See below, 68, 108.

[47]Tawney, 7.

which they then accepted.[48] There was, in fact, no psychological conversion on their part to the desirability of state intervention, and this attitude was reflected in their stance in later years. That they had been forced to accept intervention on one occasion did not imply a conversion to it in principle, nor would they feel obliged to argue for it in other circumstances, no matter how similar they appeared to those of 1916-18.

Notwithstanding these general comments, it must be stressed that the owners were always ready to cooperate with the state in devising arrangements by which it could administer its intention to intervene to control the industry in wartime. There was, no doubt, some flavour of thereby reducing, or at least modifying, the worst excesses of the state, in this readiness to advise and cooperate. And there were, of course, clashes of opinion, and occasionally mutual ill-will developed. Generally, however, both parties succeeded in putting the national advantage above their private concerns, and the record of cooperation between shipowners and the bureaucrats in the inter-war years is a surprisingly good one, as will become apparent as the narrative proceeds. On the other hand, it remains clear that the initiative in calling such discussions rested with the bureaucrats, rather than with the owners, at least as far as the discussion of wartime intervention was concerned. Although the owners were prepared to cooperate with, and to exercise some critical control over, bureaucratic intentions, their philosophical position remained that such intervention was at best unnecessary, and frequently actually harmful.[49]

This was a view which the owners were clearly not loath to express, and which they were in a strong position to canvass, both through the shipping lobby, trade circles, and through the close contacts which those civil servants responsible for planning for a future conflict deemed it necessary to maintain with members of the industry. Furthermore, it was an attitude to which the bureaucracy was not unsympathetic, representing as it did, the economic orthodoxy of nearly a century — never the sort of tradition to be lightly dismissed by a bureaucracy, especially one which shared with the shipowners a common cultural and intellectual heritage. Such attitudes clearly had an effect in determining the nature of plans produced for this area in

[48] Some owners continued to manifest strong opposition to government intervention even after 1916, as the reports of the Liverpool Steam Ship Owners' Association testify. It is clear that the shipowners' conversion to the necessity of state control in 1916 was at best grudging. Fayle, *Shipping Industry,* 202-3.

[49] Shipowners, of course, were by no means alone among industrialists in holding this view. See, for example, the attitude of the Federation of British Industry regarding rearmament, discussed in R.P. Shay, *British Rearmament in the Thirties,* (Princeton, N.J. 1977), 95-8.

the period between the wars, and thus contributed to the recurrence of problems similar to those of 1916-18 in the later conflict.

Both the major wars of this century thus saw the British struggling with crises of varying severity in their import system, crises which reflected inefficient management as well as the results of direct enemy attack. The effect of these cumulative factors was extremely severe. Indeed, traditional historiography has suggested that the crisis in the import system threatened British national survival in both wars. This view has subsequently been questioned, at least so far as the First World War is concerned, but this controversy is not important here.[50] Some attempt must, however, be made to assess the contribution of the inefficient management of the import system to these crises — to attempt to differentiate between the effect of enemy action and of organisational confusion in order to reach an appreciation of the seriousness of the problems which form the subject of this book.[51]

That a serious shortage of shipping would have occurred in both wars without the success of the German attack on British trade is certain. The effects of the closure of European markets, of the military requirements for merchant shipping, of the unusual import requirements of war, and of the closure of some British ports to merchantmen, would have produced a shipping shortage had not a single ship been sunk by the Germans. The problem is not to assert the likelihood of such a shortage, but to assess its extent.

Statistics concerning the overall effect of the crises in reducing British imports are common, but those which differentiate between the various factors involved are rare. Quantification of the effects of inefficient management of the ships themselves seems to have been impossible in the conditions of the day, and the only figures which exist refer, in the case of both wars, to the effects of congestion in the ports in restricting the normal flow of imports. This is, perhaps, only to

[50]See Olson, 86-101, 110-113. Olson concludes his lengthy and convincing discussion of the British foodstuffs situation in the First World War by suggesting that 'there is no merit . . . in the common claim that "the war on commerce in 1917 brought Great Britain within measurable distance of defeat" '. (*ibid.*, 113.) Whether true or not, this was not apparent at the time.

[51]There is, of course, no simple approach to this sort of calculation. It is not possible, for example, to relate the reduction in annual import figures vis à vis peacetime levels, to either the number of ships lost to enemy action, or to estimates of the amount of cargo lost in them, the difference representing the losses due to other factors. Such calculations take no account of the cargoes the ship could have carried on subsequent voyages had it not been sunk, nor of the effects of the various other factors reducing carrying capacity on the ship before its loss. There is no direct relationship between the individual ship and its carrying capacity, the latter depending on the nature of the cargo, and above all, on the frequency of voyage, which is in turn affected by the route on which the ship is employed, and the speed with which it can be 'turned-round' in port. For further discussion of this problem, see, Behrens, 18-20, 466; Olson, 130.

be expected, since port congestion produced tangible evidence in a restricted area, as the goods piled up on the quays, while delays and inefficient utilisation of the ships were both intangible factors, and spread across the entire merchant marine, and thus the globe itself.

C.E. Fayle has concluded that during the first two years of the First World War, port congestion was the most important single factor in reducing the carrying capacity of the British fleet.[52] It is certainly clear that, in these years, losses of imports due to port difficulties considerably exceeded those due to enemy action in sinking British merchant ships. Even during the climax of the unrestricted submarine campaign in the early months of 1917, the Shipping Controller estimated that losses due to port delays closely approached those due to enemy action.[53] Yet by this time, the Port and Transit Executive Committee had been active for over a year and had achieved a universally recognised improvement in the conditions at the ports.[54] If, despite these improvements in port capacity, congestion could cause such serious losses in 1917, it seems clear that, in the earlier years of the war, when losses due to enemy action were much smaller,[55] the diminution in carrying capacity attributable to port congestion alone must have considerably exceeded that due to enemy action.[56]

Given the fact that port delays represented only a proportion of the losses due to inefficiencies in the management of the import system, and given the general level of figures recorded above, it is difficult to avoid the conclusion that losses resulting from the crisis in the import

[52]Fayle, *Shipping Industry,* 115, 135.

[53]The respective figures were, losses due to the U-boats at an annual rate of five million tons of imports, while losses due to port delays accounted for between four and five million tons per annum. (Quoted in Fayle, *Seaborne Trade,* III, 70.) Taken as a percentage of pre-war figures, (a total import programme in 1913 of 54.5 m.t.) the 1917 figures represent an annual reduction of 9.2 per cent due to the U-boats, and of between 7.3 and 9.2 per cent due to port problems. Such percentages, however, underestimate the real effect of these factors, since the level of losses in 1917 occurred in a situation in which the level of imports was already reduced below peacetime levels by the effect of two years of war. Compared with the 1916 import figures, (44.3 m.t.), the losses due to U-boat action represent an 11.3 per cent reduction; those due to port delays between 9 and 11.3 per cent. (Figures of import totals from Fayle, *Seaborne Trade,* III, Appendix C, Table VIII, 477).

[54]Fayle, *Shipping Industry,* 171-2.

[55]Annual figures for British shipping lost were as follows: (tons gross)
1914: 241,201
1915: 855,721
1916: 1,237,634
1917: 3,729,785
1918: 1,694, 749
Fayle, *Seaborne Trade,* III. Appendix C, Table 1(a), 465.

[56]As the official historians concluded. See above, p. 6, n. 14.

system must, for the war in general, at least have equalled those due to enemy action, and probably have exceeded them. This is a startling, but apparently inescapable, conclusion. It was not until the very end of the war that the British managed to get a grip on the problems of the import system. Until that time it seems certain that the combination of the shipping shortage, and the port and inland distribution delays, resulted in a greater loss of importing capacity than did German efforts to sink British merchantmen.

The data available for the Second World War show a curious similarity to that for the earlier conflict. At the peak of the crisis in the import system in 1941, it was estimated that delays due to port congestion were causing a reduction of at least 10 per cent per annum in total imports, a figure in volume terms in 1941 of at least three million tons.[57] This is, on the face of it, a crushing condemnation of the performance of the bureaucracy in devising plans to counter these problems before the war, but in mitigation it should be pointed out that in this conflict the position of shipping was markedly worse than in the First World War for a number of reasons. Primarily, there was a thorough-going imposition of naval control from the very beginning of the war, both through the introduction of a convoy system, and through the necessity, after the Germans had captured the French Channel coast and airfields, to divert all ocean-going shipping from ports on the east coast of this country to avoid the dangers of air attack. This threw a great strain on the ports on the west coast and led to remarkable congestion in some areas. Against this must be set the rather more efficient arrangements devised to control shipping, but there is little doubt that, just as the ships themselves were more vulnerable in the Second World War, so the import system had to face less favourable conditions than in the previous war.

This, however, does not affect the seriousness of the crisis as it developed in the early months of 1941. With port delays alone accounting for a 10 per cent loss in importing capacity, the other problems of the import system and the high level of losses due to enemy action had clearly produced a situation at least as serious as that of 1917: 'in the winter of 1940-1, the United Kingdom was losing once again as large a volume of imports because of port delays as it was losing because of cargoes sunk.'[58] In fact, having started the war

[57]Behrens, 128.

[58]Hancock and Gowing, 125; Behrens, (110-11) notes that 'of the total amount by which British imports in the second year of war fell short of the rate of importation before France fell, something of the order of only 15 per cent, it seems, can be attributed to the net losses (that is to ships lost and not replaced) in the twelve months from the beginning of September 1940 to the end of August 1941.'

with a smaller merchant fleet than in 1914, and with a higher level of import requirements to sustain, the situation in 1941 was markedly worse than in the earlier war.[59] The 1940-1 figure of 31.5 million tons imported into Britain was already lower than the worst figures experienced during the previous war.[60] Later in the war, the figure of 26-27 million tons was regarded as the irreducible annual minimum figure for imports.[61] With Britain losing ships faster than they could be built, there was no prospect of increasing the merchant fleet itself in 1941-2, and, therefore, no hope of increasing imports beyond the 1940-1 figure of 31.5 million tons. This figure therefore provides a datum from which to project the next year's performance. It is evident that, had the problems of the management of the import system not been brought under control by the end of 1941, and even had the total effect of all restrictions amounted only to a level comparable to that achieved by port congestion alone the previous year, then the level of British imports in 1941-2 would have dropped to a point close to the absolute minimum.

It seems likely that, had the overall level of the reduction in British imports attributable to commercial inefficiencies remained as serious as in 1941, it would, in succeeding years, have in itself reduced the total import programmes to a point perilously close to that at which Britain's ability to continue the war would have been in doubt. Fortunately, the crisis was solved by measures introduced during the winter of 1940-1, and although Britain's import figures were reduced steadily throughout the war, this was the result of a conscious decision to give priority to military operations in the shipping budget, and did not reflect insoluble problems in the British import system. On occasion, ships were diverted from military services to relieve pressure on the British import system. In 1942, however, before the United States' shipbuilding effort had got into its stride, there were no ships to be spared to boost the import programme. Had the inefficiencies in the import system not been overcome, and had all other conditions in 1942 remained as they were, it seems probable that

[59]The relevant figures are:
  British Registered Merchant Shipping:
  1911: 11,699,000 tons net.
  1938: 10,702,000 tons net.
  Volume of net imports (1938 = 100)
  1913: 81
  1938: 100
Mitchell and Deane, chs. VIII and XI. See below, Chapter 3, 69, for a fuller discussion of this question.

[60]This was the 1918 figure of 35.1 million tons, Fayle, *Seaborne Trade*, III, Appendix C, Table VIII, 477.

[61]Behrens, 363-5.

British ability to continue the war could have been seriously jeopardised by the effects of inefficient management of the import system.

In both of the major wars of this century, therefore, crises arose in the management of the British import system which reached extremely serious proportions. In the First World War, such losses probably cost Britain more imports than the U-boat campaigns, while in the second war the situation was scarcely less serious. In both wars, the problem of the import system was but one of a series of factors contributing to the general crisis, but it was a factor of the highest importance. Moreover, the restriction of importing capacity so caused was largely an unnecessary loss, and a loss which, on occasion, threatened not only to restrict Britain's ability to develop her full war potential, but even to question her ability to survive the conflict successfully.

The development of such a serious situation in the First World War is perhaps understandable, since no previous experience of the problems of conducting a modern war on such a scale existed. Its recurrence in the Second World War despite the experience of the First, is perhaps surprising. To explain how this occurred it is necessary to consider the detailed history of attempts to plan for the import system in the inter-war years.

2

THE ADMIRALTY AND MERCHANT SHIPPING IN WARTIME

The operation of a merchant fleet in wartime is constrained by two major factors. On the one hand there are the normal commercial factors determining the distribution and employment of vessels. Although considerations of national priority largely replaced the achievement of profit as the commercial objective of seaborne trade in wartime, this involved no substantial alteration in the nature of that trade as such. In wartime, however, the freedom of merchantmen to proceed on their concerns solely in response to considerations of commercial advantage is severely restricted by the problem of ensuring their security against attack by the enemy. If the necessity for centralised control of the allocation of merchant ships to cargoes requiring transport was a new factor in the twentieth century, the necessity for organising ships to withstand enemy attack was as old as trade itself. This was, of course, the responsibility of the Royal Navy.

The Admiralty sought to discharge this responsibility with a twofold policy. The primary function of the main fleet was seen as providing the essential precondition for the safety of merchantmen by the threat it posed to the enemy's naval forces.[1] Similarly, the lighter forces at the Admiralty's disposal could be deployed to provide direct protection to merchant shipping by escorting it. This aspect of the policy therefore involved the use of the armed forces at the Admiralty's disposal in the protection of shipping. The other side of the policy lay in attempts to increase the security of merchant ships by direct involvement in the details of their equipment and operation. This latter policy itself consisted, in principle, of two components. The first involved providing merchantmen with equipment — principally, but not entirely, guns, — with which to defend themselves, and the second involved organising their activities, within the framework imposed by mercantile requirements, to ensure that ships spent as little time as possible in areas where they would be exposed to enemy attack. To administer these policies, the Admiralty created the Naval Control Service Organisation, which in many respects may be regarded as the administrative interface between the shipping industry

---

[1]CAB.4/25, C.I.D.1276-B. 'Interim Report of Sub-Committee on Food Supply in Time of War', 11 November 1936. Annex I, 'Trade Defence and Food Supply', Memo. by C.I.D. Joint Planning Sub-Committee, 2 July 1936, para. 47.

and the constraints of war, as embodied in the Admiralty requirements.

The relationship between the Admiralty and the shipping community was fundamentally different from that which the latter enjoyed with the various civil ministries concerned with shipping in wartime. The shipping industry and the civil ministries such as the Ministry of Shipping, were all concerned with commercial problems: their activities were directed towards achieving the maximum performance from the ships as carriers of trade, even if they occasionally differed over the means. On the other hand, the Admiralty was not concerned with the commercial aspect of the ship, but with the safety of the vessel itself. For the Ministries of War Transport, Food, Supply etc., ships were a means to an end, the transport of cargo to Britain, and were to be organised solely with regard to their efficiency as cargo carriers. In this respect, therefore, the Ministries occupied a position analogous to that of the owners in peacetime. The Admiralty's concern, however, stopped specifically at the vessel itself, and in many respects this responsibility conflicted with the dictates of pure commercial efficiency.

At the simplest level the Admiralty sought to provide merchant ships with a whole range of equipment to increase their security in wartime. There were guns, ammunition, personnel to fire them and stiffening to strengthen the ship against the shock of firing; paravanes and degaussing gear to protect against mines; extra wireless and signalling equipment; extra ropes and nautical gear to enable ships to sail in close company at night and in bad weather; new internal communications and damage control equipment, to say nothing of a host of regulations to be studied by the masters.[2] All this equipment and personnel involved carrying extra unproductive weight, reduced the space available for cargo, and so in turn reduced the commercial efficiency of the ship. Additionally, the Admiralty needed some control over the routes by which the ships actually sailed. There were minefields to be by-passed, ports were sometimes blocked by enemy activity, and there were always areas in which enemy warships had been reported, or which were within range of his aircraft, which would have to be avoided so far as possible. All these factors involved alterations in the normal commercial routes between ports, and since these routes were invariably the shortest practicable, involved longer voyages, with a corresponding reduction in the carrying capacity of the ships involved. There was thus a delicate compromise to be achieved between the commercial needs of the nation's trade and the

[2]For a brief summary of such equipment, see the 'Interim Report of the Shipping Defence Advisory Committee', 31 July 1937, in ADM.116/3978.

military objective of preserving merchantmen from damage by the enemy. As the opening paragraph of the Naval Control Service Manual for 1923 put it, the objective of the organisation was to achieve 'adequate protection coupled with a minimum of trade dislocation'.[3]

Thus, while organisations such as the Ministry of Shipping controlled the allocation of ships to cargoes and decided the quantity of any particular commodity which it would be possible to import in each year, the Admiralty was responsible for directing the actual voyage of the ship to and from the ports designated by the other authorities. The naval authorities in the various areas were empowered to decide the routes upon which merchantmen could sail, the times at which they could sail, and, if necessary, to postpone sailings altogether if unusual dangers threatened. But while the sailings of merchantmen were controlled and directed by the naval authorities entirely in the light of the military considerations obtaining at the time, this was always subject to the overriding consideration that ships must sail, and must sail as frequently as possible, however great the dangers. There was no point in safeguarding ships if they were not to be used. The task of the Naval Control Service was therefore, by its equipment programmes and routing organisation, to make the sailings of merchantmen as safe as possible. There were few occasions during the war when the dangers to merchantmen were held to be too great to allow them to sail, and those occasions generally involved the discovery of a new minefield off the port concerned, which had not yet been swept. In such cases a short delay might be acceptable — it was generally only a few hours. Longer delays were seldom accepted, and the axiom that the ships must be kept running was so central to the whole theory of the Admiralty's policy for the protection of shipping, that they never found it necessary to state it in any of the instructions to the Control Service. The Admiralty's arrangements concerning merchantmen were reported to the Shipping (Diversion) Room, where they were co-ordinated into the centralised direction of shipping in the manner to be described.[4]

The arrangements through which the Admiralty administered this control over the voyages of merchantmen were almost infinitely flexible, as indeed they had to be, bearing in mind the diversity of the ships and their masters, and the geographical extent of British trade.

Clearly, in dealing with a world wide trade such as Britain's, the

[3]ADM.116/3127, M.0796/23, July 1923.
[4]See below, Chapter 3.

severity of attack to be expected in the various areas of the globe would differ. Some areas would be beyond the range of the enemy's forces and would therefore be entirely secure. In such cases the imposition of full wartime control would be unnecessary and inefficient. But nowhere could be entirely secure from the depredations of, say, a disguised raider which had slipped through the patrols, and the rapid imposition of a full war organisation in an area which had previously been regarded as entirely secure might be required if losses were to be avoided. The Admiralty had developed a policy of sufficient flexibility to meet these disparate needs.

In essence it proposed the introduction of statutory control by the Admiralty over the movements of all British merchantmen at the earliest possible moment. Authority for this control would be provided by the Royal Prerogative and the Defence of the Realm Act. Having established the principle of control, the Admiralty could then apply it to a greater or lesser degree as local conditions required. Staffs would be set up throughout the globe so that control could be tightened in any particular area without delay. The basic structure of control would be provided by the system of 'evasive routing'. This involved informing merchantmen about to sail of the position of enemy forces close to their intended route and, where necessary, providing them with a special 'evasive route' intended to avoid such dangers. These measures would be combined with a system of trade defence patrols in those areas where geographical restrictions reduced the value of evasive routes. Only in areas where this structure was expected to prove inadequate would a greater measure of control, convoy, be instituted. The most important reason for the Admiralty's unwillingness to introduce convoys generally lay in the disruption of the normal operations of merchant shipping which they inevitably caused. The overriding consideration was to 'place all British shipping under control at the earliest possible moment', even though it was anticipated that control would be purely nominal in many areas.[5]

In the mid-1920s these arrangements were clarified by the introduction of a scale of three degrees of control to be exercised according to the severity of attack anticipated or experienced. The First Degree would be purely nominal, and would be exercised where voyages were expected to proceed without interference. No routing instructions would be issued: all a merchant ship would require would be permission to sail. The Second Degree would be applied when interference was considered possible, and would involve the giving

[5] ADM.116/3127, op. cit. (The quotation is from CAB.5/4, C.I.D.131-C, 'Empire Naval Policy and Co-operation', February 1921, Chapter VI, para. 10).

and following of an 'evasive route'. Such routes would be laid down by the local Naval Control Service Staff at the port of departure. The Third Degree of control applied when enemy interference was considered likely. In general it would involve convoys for vessels slower than 15 knots, faster ships proceeding independently on their evasive routes. The decision as to the degree of control appropriate to each area would be taken in the Admiralty, and local authorities informed accordingly.[6]

To ensure that a sudden deployment of enemy forces into an area previously unaffected did not catch the organisation unprepared, each staff would be capable of administering the tightest degree of control. In the event of war, a Naval Control Service Staff would be established at every port in which the peacetime Naval Intelligence Service maintained a Reporting Officer. Five scales for such staffs were established, according to the amount of traffic using the port in question. These staffs would be responsible for the local application of Admiralty control over merchantmen, in response to instructions from London. Apart from the fundamental instruction of the degree of control to be applied, the Admiralty did not intend to concern itself in the detailed operation of the organisation. Local Commanders-in-Chief were to be entirely responsible for the protection of shipping within the area of their commands, and any necessary co-ordination in the passing of a ship from the area of one Naval Control Service Staff to that of another would be the responsibility of the regional bodies concerned.

The Naval Control Service Staffs would be wartime appointments and some delay would occur before they arrived at their respective ports. At this time there would naturally be some confusion within the shipping industry, and it was felt that in these conditions the task of routing could be adequately carried out by the existing Naval Intelligence Service; specifically the Reporting Officers. Such officers would commence routing at once. In most cases, their work would be confined to pointing out to the masters concerned the possible dangers on their intended route. On the arrival of the Naval Control Service Staff, the Reporting Officer would surrender his responsibilities to them.

Naval Control Service Staffs were given detailed instructions concerning ten separate functions:

(a)   Supervision of the movements of merchant ships when not in convoy.

[6]ADM.116/3128, 'Naval Control Service Operational Policy, Vol. II', M.02091/25, December 1926, Chapter I.

(b)   Issue of routing instructions to vessels sailing independently.

(c)   Issue of routing instructions to vessels sailing in convoy to guard against the possibility of their dropping out of convoy, or of the convoy dispersing.

(d)   Operation of the system of approach routes to major ports, and of diversions due to local conditions.

(e)   Arrangements for the assembly of convoys.

(f)   Arrangements for the bunkering and victualling of ships until their assembly in convoy.

(g)   Berthing of ships arriving in port to ensure the most convenient assembly in convoy.

(h)   Dealing with arriving or passing convoys.

(i)   Issuing sailing instructions to convoys.

(j)   Interviewing masters and confirming that ships were properly equipped.

Except in cases where the staff was unusually small, each staff would divide itself into routing and convoy sections.[7]

At the time this edition of the Naval Control Service Manual was prepared, the Admiralty expected to be able to provide adequate protection on most of the trade routes without the introduction of a convoy system. The basic assumption leading to this assessment appears to have been a belief that unrestricted submarine warfare against merchant vessels would not be practised in a future war, and that belligerents would observe the laws of war relating to such matters. Definitions of such laws, such as those produced at the Washington and London Conferences of 1922 and 1930, made such demands on the attacker as to virtually prohibit submarines from attacking merchant ships — which was the real intention anyway.[8] But these resolutions contained no incentive to induce nations to apply such proposals, and it seems difficult today to understand the Admiralty's belief that other nations would observe rules so favourable to this country. Nonetheless, even as late as 1936, the Admiralty continued to consider the possibility of the introduction of unrestricted submarine warfare in any future conflict as remote.[9]

[7]*Ibid.*, Chapters II and V.

[8]See, for example, the London Naval Treaty of 1930, Part IV, Article 22.

[9]CAB.4/25; C.I.D.1276-B, Annex 1, 2 July 1936, para. 20.

The Admiralty's attitude to submarines conditioned its attitude towards convoys. This is not the place to review the arguments concerning convoy. It must be stressed, that despite what has been said above, it was always the Admiralty's intention throughout the inter-war period that convoy should be introduced in wartime if circumstances required it. As an Admiralty appreciation for the Imperial Cabinet of 1921 put it, convoys were 'the most effectual system of direct trade protection'.[10] On the other hand, the Admiralty recognised the disadvantages which convoys involved — they anticipated a reduction in the carrying capacity of the merchant fleet of 12 to 20 per cent, compared with peacetime, if convoys had to be introduced.[11] But they also realised that if the situation was serious enough to require a convoy system, no reduction in carrying capacity might be involved, compared with other methods of trade protection.[12] The Admiralty's main objection to convoy rested on its profligacy of escorts,[13] but this cannot detain us here.

Nonetheless they still recognised that, if the worst came to the worst, the introduction of convoys could not be avoided. The refusal to adopt convoy as an automatic response to the outbreak of war stemmed, therefore, from the hope that it might not be militarily necessary in the conditions of the day. There was no objection to convoys on grounds of principle, as in the First World War, — that lesson, at least, had been learned. Their introduction would be considered in terms of their expediency in the conditions of the day.

In 1921 this policy was embodied in the vague expression that convoys would be introduced only in areas where the Admiralty believed merchant ships would be exposed to great danger of enemy attack. With the 1927 Naval Control Service Manual, this formula had crystallised into their introduction in areas where the 'Third Degree' of risk was anticipated.[14] In real terms this policy never changed, and the Admiralty remained determined to be ready to meet unrestricted warfare, even while they denied its likelihood. In 1936 they noted that:

> While the conclusion reached is that it is doubtful whether an enemy would, in fact, adopt unrestricted warfare against our shipping, the safety of our trade in war is such a vital matter

[10]CAB.5/4, C.I.D. 131-C, February 1921, Chapter II, para. 18.

[11]ADM.116/3128, December 1926, Chapter V.

[12]CAB.5/4, C.I.D. 131-C, Chapter VI, para. 8.

[13]*Ibid.*, Chapter II, Part (ii).

[14]Above, 44, n.5 and 45, n.6.

that in preparing our measures of defence it is only prudent to assume that such attacks may develop, even at the commencement of a war, and our preparations should provide against such a contingency as far as possible.[15]

At this time, the Admiralty was especially concerned with evaluating the efficiency of convoys as a means of protection against air attack. This reflected strong opposition from the Air Ministry to any commitment of air forces to naval co-operation duties. The Air Staff had criticised convoys on the grounds that they provided a concentrated target for the aircraft, and, it is hard to escape concluding, because it was easier to justify demands for air support for convoys than for individual ships.[16] As a result of such pressure, the joint staffs concluded in 1936 that, in the event of sustained attack on a convoy from the air, it might be necessary to break the convoy and 'force upon the aircraft the necessity of identifying each ship before carrying out an attack'.[17] This assumed that the attacking aircraft would comply with the laws of war.

Fortunately, such counsels did not shake the Admiralty's confidence in convoys as a means of countering unrestricted attacks from both air and sea. In November 1937 the Joint Planning Committee and the Chiefs of Staff Committee reviewed the question.[18] Having discounted the effectiveness of action by submarines and aircraft within the accepted principles of international law, the report considered problems posed by unrestricted attack. Regarding the danger from aircraft, the report estimated the possibilities for dispersion afforded by the waters around this country to be insignificant, and, therefore, that the advantage of the combined gunfire of the convoy and escort should not be sacrificed. Furthermore, there was always the possibility of fighter cover for convoys near to the coast, and careful routing should permit convoys to pass through exceptionally dangerous waters under cover of darkness. The report concluded: 'We therefore base our plans on the adoption of the convoy system if unrestricted attacks develop.'[19] This policy remained unchanged throughout the period. It still contained the proviso regarding unrestricted attacks, which confirms the suggestion that the Admiralty hoped to be able to avoid the introduction of a convoy system. In this respect it is surely significant that, in Captain Roskill's

[15]CAB.4/25, C.I.D.1276-B, Annex I, 2 July 1936, para. 20.

[16]*Ibid*., para. 83.

[17]*Ibid*., para. 87.

[18]CAB.4/26, C.I.D.1368-B. 'The Protection of Seaborne Trade', 26 November 1937.

[19]*Ibid*., para. 15.

words, 'not one exercise in the protection of a slow mercantile convoy against submarine or air attack took place between 1919 and 1939.'[20]Nor were the Admiralty alone in this hope, for there was a strong body of opinion among the shipowners which was suspicious of the utility of convoy.[21] However by 1939 the Admiralty was administratively prepared for the introduction of a convoy system. Most importantly, they were also prepared to run convoys immediately war broke out. This had not always been the case.

Despite having expressed the view that 'in a future war it is safe to assume that no breathing space will be allowed by the enemy and our Mercantile Marine will be subjected to the full vigour of attack on the declaration of hostilities',[22] during the greater part of the period, the Admiralty professed itself unable to introduce convoys until at least six weeks after the outbreak of war. The major reason was said to be the inability of the Naval Control Service Staffs, who had to be sent out from England, to become operational before that date.[23] Another factor was the length of time which would be required to equip the Armed Merchant Cruisers which were to provide the 'ocean escorts' of the convoys. These assumptions were reviewed in 1938.

In February the Director of Plans, then Tom Phillips, produced an appreciation on 'Convoy at the Outset of a War with Germany'.[24] This paper distinguished five conditions which would have to be met if a convoy system was to operate satisfactorily. Two were administrative: the augmentation of the staff of the Trade Section in London, and the establishment of Naval Control Service Staffs at the relevant ports throughout the world. As regards the first, nucleus staff would be earmarked in peacetime, so there was no excuse for delay at the Admiralty end. Similarly, most of the Naval Control Service Staff personnel had already been appointed and arrangements were being made to fly out those who were not already at their stations on the outbreak of war. This organisation could therefore be ready within a few days of the outbreak. Should delays in this process occur, it was felt that the combination of local Commanders-in-Chief and the peacetime Staff Officers (Intelligence) would be capable of handling the convoy system as an expedient.

The other three factors were material — the provision of ocean

[20]S.W. Roskill, *Naval Policy between the Wars,* I (London, 1968), 536.

[21]See, for example, the editorial comment in *Fairplay,* 10 February 1938.

[22]CAB.5/4, C.I.D.131-C, February 1921, Chapter VI, para. 7.

[23]ADM.1/9501, 'Convoy at the Outset of a War with Germany'. Memo. by D.O.P., 19 February 1938, para. 4.

[24]*Ibid.*

escorts, and of anti-submarine and anti-aircraft escorts, and the provision of special equipment necessary to enable merchantmen to sail safely in convoy. It was accepted that there would be deficiencies to some degree in each of these areas. However, since the entire convoy system could not be brought into operation at once (on many routes it would take time to accumulate sufficient ships to make a convoy worthwhile) it was felt that such deficiencies should not prevent the introduction of convoys. With some forethought a rotation system could be established to ensure that sufficient vessels were available to allocate an escort to each convoy. It was felt that the advantages of introducing convoys would outweigh the danger that a full escort could not be provided for each one in the early days of the war.

The situation regarding the provision of special equipment for merchantmen could not be improved. Such equipment — principally special lights, fog buoys, signalling apparatus, zig-zag clocks, and provision for direct communication between the bridge and engine rooms (which appears to have been lacking in many cases), could not be provided in haste, and ships would have to do without it. It was not anticipated that this would cause any great difficulties.[25]

This memorandum was approved by the Board[26] and a letter sent to the various Commanders-in-Chief accordingly, stating the Admiralty's intention that 'we should be ready to institute convoy in the Atlantic and Home Waters either comprehensively or on certain selected routes, according to our information as to enemy dispositions and intentions, immediately on the outbreak of a war with Germany'.[27]

During the interwar period the Admiralty produced a series of detailed proposals for the administration of the convoy system.[28] Naturally, these proposals changed with alterations in the international situation and in the identity of the enemies Britain expected to face. All sought to maintain a degree of flexibility to combat unforeseen circumstances. All, furthermore, were based on the same fundamental assumptions. Firstly, that convoys would only be introduced as a response to unrestricted submarine warfare. Secondly, and as a consequence of the first assumption, that the introduction of convoys could be confined to certain restricted geographical areas formed by

[25]*Ibid.*

[26]*Ibid.*, Minute by D.O.P. 17 May 1938.

[27]*Ibid.*, Draft of 26 May 1938, by S.H. Phillips.

[28]Examples may found in CAB.5/4 , C.I.D.131-C; CAB.4/25, C.I.D.1276-B and CAB.4/26, C.I.D.1368-B.

the limits of the operational range of the enemy's submarines. It thus became possible to begin to construct an organisation for the convoy system based broadly on that of the First World War.

In a war with a European enemy, given the performance of the average submarine of the 1930s, persistent attacks need only be expected in the vicinity of the British Isles — the Western Approaches — and perhaps the Mediterranean. This appreciation enabled the basic organisational pattern to be established. Ships would sail from Britain in escorted convoys until they reached the limit of 'the Danger Zone', as it was termed. There they would separate and proceed independently, while the escort picked up an incoming convoy. All ships homeward bound to Britain of a type suitable for convoy would have to call at a convoy assembly port on their homeward voyage, and join a convoy. This convoy would be escorted by an ocean escort, partly to protect it from surface raiders, and partly to ensure navigational accuracy, until it reached that point in the Western Approaches at which the radius of action and availability of anti-submarine escorts enabled it to be picked up. From this point it would proceed under close escort until it broke up, ships sailing to their destinations within the coastal convoy network.

The most critical statistic for the convoy system was, therefore, the number of ocean-going vessels arriving daily at British ports. In 1936 the figure was approximately twenty-four. The twin necessities of providing protection for this vital import trade, and ensuring that ships were diverted as little as possible from their normal routes in order to join convoys, gave the number of convoys that would be required. In 1936 it was estimated that three homeward-bound and three outward bound convoys would have to be at sea at any given moment in the Western Approaches. Each convoy would contain from fourteen to thirty ships. Additionally, there would be the coastal convoys — four at sea at any time in the North Sea, plus a Scandinavian convoy, and any Gibraltar and Mediterranean convoys necessary. By this time it had been decided to divide convoys into fast and slow, the division being 12 knots. Slow convoys would make 8 knots.[29]

This basic organisation remained unaltered and was validated by war experience. By 1938, however, it was obvious that adequate escorts could not be provided for all these convoys, and the Admiralty was forced to consider the possibility of tailoring the convoy network

[29]CAB.4/25, C.I.D. 1276-B, Annex I, 2 July 1936, Appendix I, 'The Control of Merchant Shipping', paras. 11-20.

in the light of escort availability.[30] By the time of Munich the proposed seven coastal convoys had been reduced to five, and two of these would not begin to run until forty-two days after the outbreak of war, with escorts released from covering the laying of the Dover barrage.[31] The same study refers to an ocean convoy network sailing from three overseas ports, Halifax, Nova Scotia, Kingston, and Sierra Leone, at six day intervals, each convoy containing thirty to forty ships. No regular Gibraltar convoys would be run. Outward sailings would be timed to fit this pattern.

By and large this was the pattern with which Britain started the war. Despite all the organisational effort devoted to starting convoys immediately war broke out, the ocean convoy system did not get really into its stride until mid September 1939. This reflected escort shortages, the fact that Germany did not commence unrestricted submarine warfare until the close of September,[32] and the availability of shipping. The first regular mercantile convoys (as distinct from sporadic convoys for especially important vessels) ran between the Thames and the Firth of Forth on 6 September 1939. Outward bound ocean convoys started from Liverpool and the Thames on 7 September, including a Gibraltar convoy, with ocean escort only. The corresponding homeward convoys from Halifax, Kingston and Freetown, Sierra Leone began in the middle of the month. Gibraltar homeward convoys started on 26 September. Norwegian convoys began in November. This network sufficed until mid 1940 when a thorough coastal system had to be introduced, and opportunity was taken to modify the ocean system slightly.[33] The value of the convoy system in itself, despite the serious weakness in escorts at the start of the Second World War, is shown by the statistics of losses: up to the end of 1939, 5,750 ships had sailed in convoys, and only four were lost when in convoy. As the official historian says,

> In spite of the chronic shortage of escort vessels the success of the system was immediately proved; it paid tribute not only to the careful planning by the Admiralty but to the work of the Naval Control Service Staffs at home and abroad and to the willing co-operation of the owners and masters of the merchant ships themselves.[34]

[30]CAB.4/26, C.I.D. 1368-B, Appendix II, 26 November 1937.

[31]ADM.1/10207, 'Convoy scheme in the event of war with Germany, Italy being hostile', 28 September 1938.

[32]Roskill, *War at Sea,* I, 103.

[33]*Ibid.,* 94 and 598 (Appendix J).

[34]*Ibid.,* 94.

The Admiralty's responsibility for the safety of merchant shipping in wartime was not confined to measures designed to avoid enemy attack. The Board also sought to provide merchantmen with various types of equipment to increase their ability to withstand such attack should it occur. The major items in such equipment were, of course, guns and the men to operate them, and the provision of such weapons was termed the defensive equipment of merchant ships — DEMS. The fitting of armament to merchant ships for defensive purposes was a procedure long recognised in international law, and in no way altered the status of the merchantman as a non-combatant.[35]

In 1914, as in so many areas affecting the safety of our seaborne trade, matters were not well advanced — only thirty-nine ships carried guns, and even they carried no ammunition. By the end of the war the situation was transformed. In 1919 some 2,000 vessels of over 3,500 t. were armed permanently, and some 2,300 more were able to ship guns when they required them. Some 4,354 guns were controlled by the DEMS organisation.[36] There was clear statistical proof that armed merchantmen were much more likely to escape attacks carried out within the restrictions of international law than were unarmed vessels.[37] Even with the introduction of unrestricted submarine warfare, it was felt that the threat posed to the submarine by DEMS was important — this time in preventing the submarine from making a surface attack, and forcing it to use torpedoes of which it carried few, so reducing the number of attacks it could make.[38] As the First Lord put it in 1937, 'experience in the late war proved beyond dispute that defensive armament in merchant ships is of the utmost value against attack by lightly armed surface vessels and submarines'.[39]

After the war a sub-committee of the Admiralty Reconstruction Committee considered future policy regarding DEMS.[40] Pressure from commercial sources forced the removal of the guns mounted during the war in order to be able to use the space and weight so saved

[35] See CAB.4/30, C.I.D. 1574-B, 'Defensive Arming of Merchant Ships in Peacetime', Memo. by First Lord (Stanhope), 18 July 1939.

[36] ADM.I/8549/248, 'Report of Sub-Committee of Admiralty Reconstruction Committee on DEMS', 9 January 1919. Also ADM.116/3978, 'Interim Report of Shipping Defence Advisory Committee', 31 July 1937.

[37] ADM.116/3976, Adm. Memo. to Treasury Inter Services Committee on DEMS, 26 June 1937.

[38] CAB.4/28, C.I.D. 1466-B, Memo. by First Lord (Duff Cooper) 21 July 1938.

[39] CAB.24/271, C.P.215(37), Memo. on 'Stiffening of Merchant Ships', 22 September 1937.

[40] ADM.1/8549/248, 9 January 1919.

for earning revenue. The 'stiffening' (special structural strengthening to enable the merchant vessel to withstand the stress of firing) could not be removed. These policies were approved by the Board in January 1919.[41]

Notwithstanding these events, the sub-committee on DEMS recommended the maintenance of the right and capability to arm merchant ships at short notice, irrespective of the situation regarding international agreements on the status of non-combatants at sea. Accordingly it suggested that the policy should be to make 'provision for the future by ensuring that all new merchant vessels should be so constructed as to be rendered capable of being defensively armed should occasion arise'.[42] That is, vessels were to be 'stiffened' while under construction. The Cabinet approved this policy,[43] but opposition from shipowners forced its abandonment. In November 1919 the Cabinet noted that 'the provision of stiffening in merchant vessels generally should not now be made obligatory'.[44] In the 1920s and 1930s government policy was to encourage the stiffening of ordinary ships, but the owners were expected to pay for it themselves. Between 1922 and 1937 only two ships, both tankers, were provided with stiffening.[45]

Consideration of the problem revived in 1937. The Admiralty and the Board of Trade established a Committee, with commercial representation, known as the Shipping Defence Advisory Committee to consider problems of trade defence. One of its sub-committees — 'D' — was concerned with DEMS. The committee noted the failure of the stiffening programme and suggested that all new construction, and selected existing tonnage, should be stiffened at government expense.[46] Simultaneously the Admiralty urged an identical policy on the Treasury through the Treasury Inter Services Committee.[47]

The Treasury remained adamant, and in September 1937 the First Lord took the matter to the Cabinet, with a practically verbatim transcription of Sub-Committee 'D''s proposals.[48] He urged haste on the grounds that we dare not leave stiffening until the outbreak of

[41]*Ibid.*, Board of 30 January 1919.

[42]CAB.24/92, C.P. 82, 28 May 1919.

[43]*Ibid.*

[44]CAB.24/92, C.P.39, 31 October 1919 and CAB.6(19), 12 November 1919.

[45]ADM.116/3978. Report of Sub-Committee on DEMS, 31 July 1937.

[46]*Ibid.*

[47]ADM.116/3976, 26 June 1937. For this Committee, see Shay, 101.

[48]CAB.24/271, C.P.215(37), 22 September 1937.

war because we should not be able to interrupt trade to the extent necessary to fit all ships rapidly, and because the labour and materials would then be urgently required elsewhere.

The Treasury continued to oppose the Admiralty's plans, on the grounds that the owners should make some financial contribution to the scheme, since their ships derived increased security from stiffening, and the loss in carrying capacity was estimated at a mere 5 tons per vessel.[49] In the event, the Cabinet agreed to accept liability for stiffening selected vessels already built or under construction, but that the owners should be approached through the S.D.A.C. concerning future construction.[50] Discussions with the owners took place, and in January 1938 they agreed to accept the cost of stiffening ships at present building as well as for any future construction.[51] This result went far to justify the Treasury's attitude during the negotiations of the previous Autumn, but precious months had been lost.

It was also early in 1938 that the Admiralty began to give serious consideration to the allocation of guns to ships. This was an extremely complicated subject, and little more than a general summary can be attempted here. The S.D.A.C. had estimated that some 4,000 guns were available for DEMS. However, all these were low angle weapons, and it was by now apparent that guns mounted in merchantmen were more likely to be used against aircraft than against ships. In 1938 the Plans Division estimated that 4,473 guns and mountings existed, and that around 4,500 ships would need a weapon.[52] But the intention to mount two guns in every ship larger than 1,600 t. gross[53] meant that a considerable shortfall of guns versus requirements existed.

The Admiralty spent the next eighteen months attempting to decide a policy for dealing with the numerical shortfall and the simultaneous shortage of anti-aircraft weapons.[54] A major problem was that weapons suitable for DEMS were interchangeable with those

[49] This figure is from ADM.116/3978, 31 July 1937.

[50] CAB.23/89, CAB.35(37), 29 September 1937, and CAB.36(37), 6 October 1937. On the approach to the S.D.A.C. see ADM.116/3976, PD.06445/37, 8 October 1937.

[51] CAB.24/274, C.P.3(38). 'Stiffening of Merchant Ships for Defensive Armament', 6 January 1938.

[52] ADM.I/9663, 'Provision of DEMS'. Memo. of 7 March 1938.

[53] ADM.I/9662, 'Stiffening for DEMS'. Memo. of 19 February 1938.

[54] For these details see ADM.I/9101, 'Control and Operation of the Fishing Fleet in War', 1937-9; ADM.I/9663; CAB.21/1236, D.P.R.320, 'Additional Needs of the Navy', 3 July 1939; CAB.4/30, C.I.D.1557-B, 'Protection of Merchant Shipping against Air Attack', June 1939.

required for naval auxiliaries and, occasionally, smaller warships. The assessment of priority among such conflicting demands was complicated. Another difficulty concerned the policy of converting old low-angle mountings to permit high-angle fire. This was cheaper than building new guns and mountings, but was a source of much confusion since some mountings were not suitable for such conversion. The stock of long-range guns for DEMS ultimately included six combinations of guns and mountings — three based on the 12 pdr., two on the 4 in., and the 3 in. anti-aircraft gun. The problem was therefore complex.

It took the Admiralty until July 1939 to produce concrete proposals to the C.I.D. regarding this confusion.[55] These involved an expenditure of £1,350,000 to convert and construct weapons to overcome the deficit, and were approved in August.[56] Fortunately the Admiralty had been steadily converting the old 12 pdr. guns to high-angle mountings throughout this period. Thus the outbreak of war found the Admiralty better prepared for the provision of high-angle guns for merchantmen than its proposals to the C.I.D. might suggest. The position regarding close range anti-aircraft guns for DEMS was, however, in Stanhope's words, 'most unsatisfactory'.[57] The Admiralty had hoped to install the British 2 pdr. pompom, but the guns were too complicated and were not available in large numbers. The Swiss Oerlikon gun was adopted as a replacement, but until August 1939, only 500 had been ordered because of Treasury opposition. In that month another 2,000 were ordered, but these would take at least fifteen months to deliver. Even the initial 500 would not be available until June 1940.[58]

The current atmosphere of financial caution undoubtedly constrained Admiralty plans for providing guns for DEMS. But it must be noted that the British armaments industry did not possess the capacity to make additional guns in 1938 and 1939 — every available resource was already employed.[59] Hence the Admiralty's policy of juggling

[55] CAB.21/1236, D.P.R. 320, 3 July 1939.

[56] CAB.2/9, Minutes of Meeting No. 371, 1 August 1939.

[57] CAB.4/30, C.I.D.1557-B, 18 July 1939, para. 44.

[58] CAB.21/1236 and CAB.2/9, C.I.D. 371st Meeting. The actual achievement in wartime somewhat exceeded these estimates. By March 1941 2,943 British ships had been fitted with low-angle guns, 1,693 had been fitted with long range anti-aircraft guns and 3,434 had been fitted with close range anti-aircraft guns (few of these were Oerlikons, most of which seem to have gone to warships). Roskill, *War at Sea*, I, Appendix B., 574.

[59] ADM.1/9101. Minute by Chief Superintendent of Armament Supply, 23 November 1938.

figures for conversions and allocations was less prodigal than it might seem. Nonetheless, it does appear that this process took an excessively long time. Every month was vital at this stage and the Admiralty appears to have dragged its heels in producing its proposals.

The situation regarding stiffening was more satisfactory, although this derived in large part from commercial pressure. It will be recalled that the government had accepted liability for the cost of stiffening selected existing ships. The Admiralty conducted the process of selection, considering only ships trading to the United Kingdom. No ship smaller than 1,600 t. gross or older than 13 years was accepted. It was estimated some 1,100 ships fell into these classifications.[60] With the darkening international scene, the Admiralty found that owners were quick to take advantage of the scheme. Submissions of ships were especially heavy during the Austrian and Czech crises, and the Admiralty accepted every suitable ship. In doing so, on both occasions, it exceeded the financial allocation for such alterations. On both occasions the Treasury granted extra finance and the scheme thus accelerated beyond the original estimates under commercial pressure. By January 1939, 430 ships had been stiffened.[61]

Even so, the scheme only applied to selected tonnage. In May 1939 pressure developed for its extension, with a letter from the United Kingdom Chamber of Shipping, which viewed 'with the gravest concern the prospect that, even after the outbreak of war there must elapse a considerable period of time before even those vessels which have been stiffened can be armed, and that the majority of vessels will not even have been stiffened'.[62] In fact, some 2,000 vessels over 1,000 t. gross would remain to be stiffened after the completion of the programme in progress. The Admiralty used this pressure to support its own case for the extension of stiffening, and in July proposed to stiffen 2,500 vessels (in all) by 1941.[63] This was approved by the C.I.D. on 1 August.[64] Once again the Admiralty may be accused of dragging its feet, although Ismay suggested that the Treasury had hitherto refused to allow them to touch vessels smaller than 2,000 t. gross.[65] Whatever the exact situation there can be little doubt that financial stringency prevented a more energetic policy in

[60]ADM.116/3976, MFO.198/38, Memo. by Plans Division, 9 May 1938.

[61]*Ibid.,* ADM. Memo. No.311, 10 January 1939.

[62]CAB.21/1236,Letter from Mr. Cleminson, General Manager, 17 May 1939.

[63]*Ibid.,* D.P.R.326, 22 July 1939.

[64]CAB.2/9, 371st Meeting.

[65]CAB.21/1236, Ismay to Chatfield, 25 May 1939.

this area. It was perhaps fortunate that pressure for the acceleration and extension of the scheme developed from commercial sources.

Thus by the time war broke out the Admiralty had received approval for its entire programme both for stiffening the ships, and for providing the guns and mountings for them. A substantial proportion of these programmes would be achieved by early 1940. This, however, prompts consideration of the effectiveness of the protection merchant ships would obtain from the mounting of guns. The Admiralty arguments in favour of the policy had been based on experience of the First World War, but this provided no guide as to considerations of anti-aircraft defence, which by 1939 were predominant in the minds of those concerned. The effect of anti-aircraft fire, even from warships, was in constant dispute between the Admiralty and the Air Ministry in this period. In the absence of practical experience there was no way of adjudicating between their divergent views. A sub-committee of the C.I.D. on Bombing and Anti-Aircraft Gunfire Experiments was established, and reported in January 1939. Its conclusions did not seem to support the Admiralty view that guns would be as effective against aircraft as they were against submarines, by deterring them 'from coming to effective bomb or machine gun range'.[66]

The Committee concluded that:

> The broad results to date are that two hits on every aircraft carrier and one on every cruiser may be expected for every aircraft hit, and that destroyers are virtually defenceless from air attack ... In particular it is clear that such attack will be most dangerous when directed on lightly armoured vessels rather than on [those] heavily armoured and well gunned ... It is difficult for us to avoid the conclusion that the problem of the protection of merchant shipping from air attack is at present unsolved. Improvised methods of arming merchant ships with obsolete equipment are absolutely valueless.[67]

These conclusions were particularly striking since the experiments had been conducted with aircraft flying at only 130 m.p.h.

A report exclusively concerned with merchant shipping followed, penned jointly by the First Lord and the Secretary of State for Air. They considered that low level attacks, or shallow dive bombing were the most likely tactics to be adopted, and recommended that 'the

[66]CAB.4/28, C.I.D.1466-B, 21 July 1938.

[67]CAB.4/29, C.I.D.1518-B, 'Third Interim Report, Sub-Committee on Bombing and Anti-Aircraft Gunfire Experiments', 30 January 1939, paras. 14 and 15.

merchant ships should be so armed that they can usefully supplement the fire of the escort when in convoy, and be able to deter the enemy from taking 'sitting shots' at them when not in convoy'. They were

> strongly of the opinion that, if for no other reason than that of morale, it is essential that merchant ships should be capable of hitting back under all conditions and regardless of any other steps taken for their defence against air attack . . . While, therefore, we are not unmindful of the conclusions drawn by the Sub-Committee on Bombing and Anti-Aircraft Gunfire as to the effect to be expected from these weapons, the Admiralty consider that they must be fitted.[68]

In fact the Admiralty were much more anxious to get some anti-aircraft armament fitted than the Air Ministry, however ineffective it might actually be. In July Stanhope suggested that the 12 pdrs. would only 'provide an effective defence against medium level bombing attacks, and will, in addition, serve the purpose of defence against submarines'. No mention of low level attacks or dive bombing here. In a letter to Simon later in July, Kingsley Wood noted the Air Staff view that the guns could only have 'a moral effect'. They considered that dual purpose guns should be fitted but that 'the provision of special long range anti-aircraft guns in merchant ships should take a low order of priority'.[69] As regards the effectiveness of close range weapons (the Oerlikons) no one was prepared to make any assessment since the guns had not been tried in this country.[70] Although it could not be admitted at the time, the general tenor of these documents suggests that anti-aircraft guns were provided in merchantmen for three reasons — because they were available, because of their morale effect, and because it was unthinkable that no attempt should be made to defend each individual ship against aircraft attack. Little concrete success was expected of them, and indeed the restrictions on their use were substantial, to ensure that shells did not fall onto friendly vessels, and that friendly aircraft were not attacked in error.[71]

The Admiralty faced one further problem with DEMS: that of when the guns should actually be mounted. Traditional Admiralty policy was to delay the decision until after the outbreak of war had enabled the enemy's tactics to be established. It was thus hoped to

[68] CAB.4/30, C.I.D.1557-B, 18 July 1939, paras. 15, 36 and 39.

[69] CAB.21/1236, Stanhope to Simon, 20 July 1939, Kingsley Wood to Simon, 25 July.

[70] *Ibid.*, Stanhope, 20 July.

[71] *Ibid.*, PD.07348/38, 10 January 1938, which quotes from 'Masters and Officers Handbook', Article 53, 'Conditions under which fire may be opened.'

deny him any pretext for illegal action or an easy means of recognising British ships.[72] In 1938 the First Lord proposed a modification of this policy. He pointed out that the enemy could introduce unrestricted warfare by a single signal, whereas the process of arming merchant-men (if trade were not to be disrupted) would take from six to twelve months. During this period the protection afforded to merchantmen would be correspondingly inadequate, and might lead to serious losses. He thought the enemy would be unlikely to introduce unrestricted warfare immediately on the outbreak of war, and concluded: 'I am therefore inclined to think that the risk of not arming in peace can be accepted; but I am convinced it is essential that arming should be put in hand immediately upon the outbreak of war.'[73] The following proposal was approved by the Cabinet on 27 July 1938:

(a) Recognised policy should be to commence the defensive arming of merchant ships immediately upon the outbreak of war.

(b) That the instructions to Masters of ships with an armament should be to the effect that they should use their guns to resist any attack or attempt at capture by an enemy warship, submarine or aircraft, whether made in accordance with the rules of war or not, as long as there appears to be a reasonable chance of escape.[74]

This policy remained unaltered until July 1939, when the matter was raised again following intelligence reports in March and April that the Germans were maintaining up to twelve submarines in mid Atlantic at any moment, in areas from which they could rapidly deploy to threaten our trade in the South Atlantic and Mediterranean. As a result of the distances involved the Admiralty could not undertake to attempt action against these boats. As the First Lord said, 'at the present moment our only countermeasure against submarine attack in the Mediterranean and South Atlantic is evasive routing of our merchant ships, which is an entirely defensive measure'. Owing to lack of facilities most of the ships on the South American routes would have to return home to receive their defensive armament, and in view of the delay involved, the First Lord continued: 'In order, therefore, to provide an additional (and in the opinion of the Naval Staff, essential) protection to our trade during the first few months of war, it is now proposed that the defensive armament should be mounted in peacetime in ships normally employed on certain routes.'

[72]CAB.4/25, C.I.D.1276-B, Appendix I to Annex I, 2 July 1936, para. 4.
[73]CAB.4/28, C.I.D.1466-B, 21 July 1938, para. 6.
[74]CAB.23/94, CAB.35(38), 27 July 1938.

He noted that there could be no objection in international law to this procedure, but that certain port authorities might refuse access on safety grounds to ships carrying ammunition. 'It is considered therefore, that the object at which we should aim is that ships should not only carry their guns mounted in position, but also the necessary ammunition; but that, if it is found by experience that the carrying of ammunition has to be given up they should nevertheless still carry the guns.'

The provision of ammunition was a comparatively simple matter. At first the measure was to be restricted to vessels trading with South America and whaling vessels operating in the South Atlantic and Antarctic.[75] The C.I.D. assented to this proposal on 1 August.[76]

The carrying of guns in peacetime involved a certain dislocation of the commercial operations of the ships concerned, and raises the question of the shipowners' attitude to DEMS as a whole. In the main the Admiralty enjoyed an easier relationship with the shipowners than did the Board of Trade. The shipowners' attitude was, for most of the period, to cooperate with any request made by the Admiralty, so long as they were not required to pay for it. If the period was not an easy one, financially, for the Admiralty, it must be remembered that shipowners also had their problems in the 1920s and 30s. Once the urgent necessity of adopting the Admiralty's recommendations became clear to the owners — say, after the Anschluss — then they proved ready to take whatever measures were required, even at their own cost.

In the official records their major forum lay in the Shipping Defence Advisory Committee. The S.D.A.C. consisted of representatives of the Admiralty, the Board of Trade, the Shipping Federation, the Shipowners, Lloyds' and the War Risks Clubs,[77] but largely confined its investigations to matters which concerned the Admiralty — it did not consider problems related to the commercial organisation of the merchant marine. Through its various sub-committees it made recommendations concerning a wide spectrum of topics: the means whereby the Admiralty was to maintain information concerning the whereabouts of ships, and how confidential advice was to be communicated to them at sea; the issue of confidential books and instructions regarding the painting of ships in wartime, use of radio, showing of lights, sailing instructions, and so on. Also the

[75] CAB.4/30, C.I.D.1574-B, 18 July 1939.

[76] CAB.2/9, 371st Meeting, 1 August 1939.

[77] CAB.4/26, C.I.D.1323-B, 'Review of Imperial Defence', Naval Appendix, 24 March 1937, para. 11.

training of merchant navy personnel in war duties, the issue of equipment to facilitate sailing in convoy and to increase protection against mines (paravanes and degaussing), and, of course, DEMS. But none of the recommendations made were in themselves such as would not have been arrived at without the Committee. Its main importance really lay in providing concrete evidence of the desire of the Admiralty to take account of the views of the owners, and in providing a forum where owners were able to make their views known, and felt that attention was being given to them.

The owners were as anxious as the Admiralty that all practicable steps should be taken to render their vessels as secure as possible from the moment war broke out, but their regard for this objective was qualified by commercial considerations. Sir Norman Hill summarised these arguments in a memorandum produced after the first meeting of the S.D.A.C.[78] He urged that the defence of individual ships should not be allowed to obscure the fact that ships were only a means to an end — the import of cargoes into the United Kingdom. If their primary purpose was to be efficient cargo carriers, it was essential, both in peace and war, that measures taken for their defence should not impede their ability to carry out this function. Loading them with unnecessary equipment would both reduce their cargo capacity, and, in peace, place them at a disadvantage vis à vis neutrals. Similarly, their status as non-combatants should not be impaired. If they were denied, say through mounting guns, the status of trading vessels, their commercial operations in both peace and war would be greatly impeded. As we have seen concerning the question of mounting guns in peacetime, the Admiralty were fully conscious of these considerations and tailored their proposals accordingly.

The Admiralty's willingness to take account of the owners' views undoubtedly contributed to the successful relationship between the two. Clearly the Admiralty felt close sympathy for the owners, especially where the problem of financial expenditure arose, as in the question of stiffening ships to accept guns. In the 1930s the shipowners were even more cost conscious than usual, and as early as 1936, the editor of *Fairplay* wrote that, with questions of defence becoming apposite once more, 'it would be of something more than academic interest to know how the financial end of the problem would be tackled in order to make it meet the material'.[79] As we have seen the Admiralty supported the owners' contention that the cost of modifying their ships to accept defensive armament should be borne by the

[78] ADM.116/3978, Letter of 25 May 1937.
[79] *Fairplay*, 5 March 1936.

Treasury since the ships were a national asset. There is no doubt that common opposition to the financial restrictions of the government greatly strengthened the existing bond between these two groups of seamen.

A final factor promoting good relations was the Admiralty's evident respect for the independence of the owners. Their policy was to confine their interference with shipping to the absolute minimum. In terms of the commercial organisation of merchant ships, Admiralty control was a necessary but unwelcome restriction. The natural resentment of owners at interference with the normal commercial routine of sailings and at the necessity to carry guns, ammunition and gun crews was only allayed by the fact that the ships stood a much better chance of surviving as a result of these measures. Since the Admiralty at no point attempted to dictate to the majority of owners where their ships should ply or what cargo they should carry, their relationship proved much smoother in war than that which the Ministry of Shipping enjoyed with the same body of individuals.

The Admiralty's activities in the shipping sector were in principle identical to those undertaken in the First World War, and were justified by reference to that conflict. Useful though this argument was in obtaining shipowners' consent, it raises the question of the effectiveness of the Admiralty's policies in the conditions of 1939. Were they simply superbly prepared to fight the 1914-18 war again in 1939, or did the measures taken have true relevance to the time?

Regarding the Naval Control Service Organisation, there can be little doubt that the Admiralty's proposals were entirely adequate. The basic conditions of the attack on trade had not changed in the twenty years since 1919, developments in weapons technology having merely extended the areas of the globe in which attack would have to be expected. In this respect the Admiralty's organisation was faultless — it was worldwide, and capable of exercising exactly the appropriate grade of control demanded by the situation without internal re-arrangement. Undoubtedly, the principle of applying control throughout the globe, and relaxing it in suitable areas was correct, and the 'flexible response' so achieved was one of the most successful and beneficial aspects of the organisation as a whole.

But while the organisation can justly be described as entirely successful, the policies for which it was responsible were less effective. In some cases their only justification appears to be that they were better than doing nothing at all, which was the only alternative. This was particularly the case regarding the problems of anti-aircraft defence. It will be remembered that considerable doubts had been raised concerning the effectiveness of convoy against aircraft attack. In wartime the traditional principle of convoy, concentrating the defence at the vital point, was found to hold good against aircraft as well as submarines, despite the fact that the Admiralty's assessment of the value of the anti-aircraft gun both on warships and merchantmen, proved to be optimistic. The alternative, leaving the ships to fight it out individually, proved unacceptable. Convoy enabled the concentration of the fire of escorts and merchantmen, whereas independent ships would have been easily swamped. The assumption which appeared to guide consideration of such problems before the war, that each ship would only be attacked by one aircraft at a time, did not hold true, and was a further argument for a combination of defensive fire. The other view expressed before the war that independent sailing, by forcing enemy aircraft to identify each ship they attacked as hostile, would somehow impede them,[80] proved of little substance in a war where the trade of Britain's enemies vanished from the high seas and neutrals were a short-lived phenomenon.

Furthermore, convoy enabled merchantmen to employ their anti-aircraft weapons in the most effective way, in barrage fire. There is no doubt that the Admiralty had considerably over-estimated the effectiveness of the individual anti-aircraft gun, particularly against dive bombing and torpedo attack. In the absence of radar-controlled prediction and proximity fuzes, aiming individual guns against individual aircraft was not as effective as simply throwing up a heavy barrage and allowing the aircraft to fly into it. It rapidly became obvious that the safety of individual merchantmen from air attack was unlikely to be guaranteed by the provision of one long range and one close range gun per ship. Indeed, the services were well aware of this before the war. However, when combined in convoy the barrage effect of such weapons was not inconsiderable and provided a justification for the policy of DEMS, which until then had appeared to be very much a case of adopting a traditional policy because the equipment was there and no one could think of anything better to do with it. Thus, paradoxically, although the introduction of the convoy system deprived the DEMS policy of one justification, for the guns were unlikely to find a use in the low angle role except in unusual circumstances, it justified the considerable expenditure on anti-aircraft guns and mountings, which, in the pre-war period had seemed almost a gesture of hopelessness. What had appeared to be mainly a morale-boosting exercise, and a particularly expensive one at that, thus became, almost in contradiction to the intentions of the Admiralty, the cornerstone of the only effective policy for providing

[80] CAB.4/25, C.I.D.1276-B, 2 July 1936.

merchantmen with anti-aircraft protection. Even had the equipment necessary to provide individual ships with anti-aircraft security through their own efforts been available, and technically it was not, it could never have been mounted in merchantmen. It and its crew would have taken up too much weight and space, and it would have been far too sophisticated to be maintained in an efficient condition on the resources afforded by the normal cargo ship. Only by grouping merchantmen together could the maximum performance be obtained from admittedly inferior weapons and, at least early in the war, inferior training. Almost by chance then, the pre-war policy regarding DEMS turned out to be the most economical method of providing merchantmen with effective anti-aircraft defence, and, combined with the convoy system, represents the unexpected success story of the Admiralty's efforts in this sphere. [81]

Regarding the question of the general introduction of a convoy system, little remains to be said. The Admiralty were prepared to introduce convoy should it prove necessary, and did in fact do so. Their reluctance had been based on doubts as to the ability of the Royal Navy to provide adequate escort for convoys, and these doubts were, to some extent, justified. As the body responsible for the naval defence of the Empire, the Admiralty must bear the blame for these inadequacies, but they were prepared to introduce the convoy system, and did establish an organisation which proved capable of administering it satisfactorily. This achievement was a vital precondition for the success of any convoy system, no matter how many escorts were available, and it should not be overlooked.

Much the same can be said regarding the provision of anti-aircraft guns for merchantmen. The Admiralty could clearly have taken measures much earlier to clarify the situation regarding the availability of guns, and to make adequate provision to overcome any shortages. Manufacturing capacity could then have been provided and guns stockpiled. They could not, of course, have been fitted generally pre-war, because of commercial considerations. Nor is it likely that the stiffening programme could have begun much earlier, since the owners would not have appreciated the necessity for taking their vessels out of service to have stiffening fitted, or for carrying the weight around, before the international situation became serious. Nor would the Treasury have accepted the necessity to pay for it. Further-

[81] There are no statistics readily available which show the proportion of successful to unsuccessful attacks for either submarines or aircraft, or for aircraft attacking convoys or independent ships. For a general discussion on similar lines see Roskill, *War at Sea*, III, Part II, 402, 3. Appendix ZZ contains details of the ships lost to submarine and air attack, but gives no indication as to how far the imbalance reflects a greater exposure to attack by submarine.

more, at the time, no one could have foreseen that German aircraft would be established along the French Channel coast in mid 1940. That fact alone gave the provision of anti-aircraft guns for merchantmen an urgency not apparent before the war. Nonetheless, the overall performance of the Admiralty must be considered disappointing in this respect.

Alongside the conspicuous activities regarding convoys and guns, there existed the wider range of the activities of the Naval Control Service. The provision of special equipment of all descriptions and uses and of instructions for all eventualities was at least as important in the overall objective of keeping British shipping running with the highest degree of safety practicable. The effect of such routine and unexciting measures, as, for example, providing up to date charts showing wrecks, minefields and new lighting and buoying arrangements is apt to be overlooked.

It is common to decry the performance of the Admiralty in the period before the war with regard to the defence of merchant shipping. The failure to provide enough escorts, and the general failure to equip the Navy against the threat of the aircraft, are frequently cited arguments. While it is true that in many of these areas, and not least those concerned with providing escorts for merchantmen, the Admiralty did concentrate too much on the traditional role of the battle fleets, such criticism cannot reasonably be made of the measures they proposed for the organisation and equipment of the merchantmen themselves. They introduced convoy shortly after the outbreak of war, and while they may be accused of dragging their heels over the provision of anti-aircraft guns for merchantmen, it must be remembered that they were constrained by manufacturing capacity as well as financial stringency.

But if the degree to which the Admiralty successfully foresaw the problems in these areas appears surprising, it is only necessary to recall that, except for the aircraft problem, the experience of the 1914-18 War showed them the way. With the clear lessons of the former conflict before them, it would have been surprising, indeed negligent, of them not to have made such satisfactory preparations.

3

THE CONTROL OF SHIPPING

While the necessity for the Admiralty to exercise control over merchant ships in wartime was clear in 1914, we have seen that the necessity for the state to involve itself in the commercial direction of the ships was only realised during the war. After the Armistice the main question was naturally that of determining which parts of the wartime structure should be maintained in peace. It was not until 1921 that it proved possible to consider the shape of the peacetime relationship between state and shipping industry. On 8 March of that year, the Cabinet decided

> That one Government Department should be appointed, not only to liquidate all war work but also to be charged in the future to look after all Government shipping work and the general interests of mercantile shipping in time of peace (having ever before it war possibilities) and that such Department should be affiliated to the Board of Trade.[1]

As a result of this decision, the Ministry of Shipping was disbanded in April, and the Board of Trade set up the Mercantile Marine Department.

The new department had two responsibilities. Firstly, to complete the run-down of the wartime structures, and to constitute those sections whose retention in peacetime was thought desirable. Secondly, it was to define the nature and extent of the relationship between the state and the shipping industry in any future war.

The early history of the M.M.D. was troubled. The Admiralty found it had lost control over the provision of merchant ships for its own use in wartime, and would not rest until it had regained this control. This was eventually achieved by making the Director of Sea Transport of the M.M.D. responsible to the Admiralty for those sections of his work concerning the Navy — a unique division of responsibilities.[2] In return, the M.M.D. obtained the use of the R.N. Transport Service and its worldwide staff, at no expense to itself.[3]

In discharging its responsibility to plan for future conflicts, the M.M.D. had to consider two sets of factors. The first was the

[1]CAB.23/24, CAB.12(21).

[2]ADM.I/8646/204, Memo. by the Secretary to the Admiralty, (Oswin Murray), 24 January 1924. ADM.I/8673/235, Memo. by Hipwood, 9 July 1924.

[3]MT.40/2, Memo. by Faulkner, 19 May 1924.

experience of shipping control in the First World War, which provided a clear indication of the problems to be faced and of possible solutions to them. This has already been described. The second was any directions which might be issued from higher government concerning the nature and scope of the plans themselves.

The First World War had provided the M.M.D. with a substantial amount of information concerning the detailed operation of the various schemes available for the control of shipping. What it did not do, however, was to indicate the relative effectiveness of individual schemes in the various circumstances which might arise in a future war. In the 1914-18 war, control had been improvised as crises developed in various sectors of the import system. There had been no policy or predetermined plan. It was thus not clear that a similar degree of control would be needed in a future war, even one of similar magnitude to that of 1914-18. It might be that the consistent application of a less thorough form of control would serve as effectively.

What was, however, apparent, was that some degree of control would be necessary. But this intention to maintain 'a wider control on all industry in wartime', as one official of the M.M.D. put it,[4] was limited by the principle of the Defence Regulations that the liberty of the individual should be restricted only to the minimum degree consistent with the achievement of national security.[5] This then provided the second of the factors the Department had to consider — the declared intention of government that the state would intervene in the affairs of the shipping industry in wartime, but that this intervention should be restricted so far as possible to the absolute minimum. The definition of that minimum was left to the M.M.D., and to the other departments of the bureaucracy concerned with such questions. The legitimacy of this decision will be examined later.[6]

The first problem facing the M.M.D. in planning for the next war was therefore the definition of the degree of control over shipping which would be necessary in the situation expected to occur in such a war. Would chartering by the government combined with a licensing scheme be sufficient, or would circumstances demand requisition? Any attempt to answer such questions was necessarily dependent on a number of factors which could only be accurately assessed when war actually arrived. The identity of the belligerents, and the purposes for

[4]MT.40/17. T.02337, Memo. by Mr. Glennie, 20 May 1937, para. 3.

[5]MT.59/1233, C & SS 108, Memo. by Board of Trade Solicitor, 28 October 1937.

[6]See below, Chapter 8.

which it became necessary to employ shipping were such factors. All, however, were subordinate to one central criterion — the adequacy of the mercantile marine to perform the services demanded of it. If the surplus of available tonnage over import requirements was large, then the allocation of cargoes to ships could proceed on normal commercial lines, for there would be sufficient capacity to ensure the importation of all essential commodities. Correspondingly, centralised control of the employment of shipping became more necessary as the surplus of available tonnage decreased. In 1936, when the darkening international situation induced the M.M.D. to consider war plans, it therefore began with an enquiry into the capacity of the British mercantile marine in relation to the import requirements of this country in a future war.

British shipping had suffered heavily during the depression of the early 1930s. In 1936 Britain herself (excluding the Commonwealth tonnage) possessed less tonnage than in 1914 — 17.3 m.t. gross compared with 19.26 m.t. gross.[7] Furthermore, the composition of the British fleet had altered significantly. British tanker tonnage had increased by nearly 200 per cent compared with 1914, to 2.7 million tons gross. Thus the overall reduction in the amount of British dry-cargo tonnage suitable for serving the United Kingdom import programme was a startling 18 per cent compared with 1914.[8] In view of the difficulties experienced in the First World War, there was obviously grave cause for concern.

The investigation fell into two sections. The first, the calculation of the import capacity of the mercantile marine, was the natural concern of the M.M.D. The second, that of the assessment of the import requirements of this country, lay outside its sphere of competence, and it turned to other departments for guidance. It should be noted that at this stage no attempt was made to cut down the figures of import requirements, since the object of the enquiry was to assess the capacity of the mercantile marine vis à vis the ideal import programme. The ideal was obviously a situation in which all needs could be supplied. By chance, the M.M.D. found that an estimate of the wartime import demands of the British economy had already been made.

As part of the Distribution of Imports enquiry into the state of British ports,[9] the Board of Trade had produced a memo. on the

[7] Sturmey, 36, 61.
[8] Behrens, 3.
[9] See below, Chapter 6.

'reduction in volume of trade to be achieved by the banning of non-essential imports and the corresponding increase in the importation of war material' for the first year of war.[10] This memorandum, which considered the effect of a war with France, dealt only in the most general terms, but it was the only estimate available to the M.M.D., and had to be accepted, despite its inadequacies. Basing its figures on statistics for the years 1927-28-29, the memo. estimated that war would make little overall difference to the volume of imports required by the United Kingdom. Although 4.8 per cent of total imports could be saved by the banning of non-essential manufactured goods, it was estimated that increased import of war materials would be equivalent to 7.6 per cent of the peacetime total. This would give an overall increase of 2.8 per cent over peacetime levels.

These figures were entirely arbitrary. The reduction in non-essentials was calculated by halving the peacetime figure for the import of manufactured goods, while the increase in import of war materials was assessed by adding 25 per cent to the peacetime figures for such commodities as metals, leather, timber, etc. No justification for such arbitrary assessments was ever produced. The memorandum concluded by suggesting that the expected increase in import requirements could be accommodated by closer stowage of cargo in ships.

In 1938 the M.M.D. dispensed with this latter suggestion, and compared these estimates with its own calculation of the carrying capacity of the mercantile marine. The Department had begun this estimate with the fundamental assumption that 'there would be control of British cargo tonnage from the outset', by licensing or requisitioning.[11] It then calculated the annual carrying capacity of the deep-sea tonnage under the British flag. These figures were accurate. The actual tonnage in use was surveyed on four occasions in 1936-7 and an average was calculated. An estimate of the annual carrying capacity of each ship was obtained from the M.M.D.'s own records. These estimates were then added together to produce a figure for the total annual carrying capacity for the British deep sea dry cargo fleet. This figure was estimated to be 72.1 million tons (measurement).

This was then compared with the estimate of import requirements. However, this had itself been reviewed in 1936 by the C.I.D. Sub-Committee on Food Supply in Time of War. Through a misunderstanding of terms, the conclusion of this enquiry appeared to the M.M.D. to suggest that wartime food imports could be cut by 25 per

[10]CAB.16/114, D.I.C. Paper No. 16, 19 July 1934.
[11]MT.40/9, T.02252, Draft of Memo., August 1937, para. 3.

cent below peacetime levels,[12] resulting in a total for UK imports in the first year of war of 65.8 million tons measurement. The M.M.D. then estimated the extent to which the defence services' requirements for ships would reduce the capacity of the mercantile marine. The largest allocation of shipping for such purposes yet envisaged was 4.5 million tons measurement. Thus the total demands on the British fleet in wartime were estimated at 65.8 + 4.5 m.t.m., a total of 70.3 m.t.m., while the estimated carrying capacity of that fleet in the first year of war was 72.1 m.t.m. A surplus of 2 million tons was thus expected. As the official historian put it, 'it was Mr. Micawber's idea of happiness'.[13]

To be fair, the Department did note that an enquiry conducted on such a level of statistical generalisation could not be considered conclusive. After the statistical discussion, the memo. reviewed a number of what it called favourable and unfavourable factors, the effect of which could only be estimated in the most general terms. The Department noted four unfavourable factors (those tending to reduce the carrying capacity of the merchant fleet). There was the possibility that the defence services would require more tonnage than had been estimated. The Department considered this unlikely during the first year of war.

Secondly, the Department noted that no allowance had been made for losses of ships as a result of enemy action. Advice from the services suggested that improvements in anti-submarine technology would severely restrict losses from this cause. On the other hand, no one was prepared to estimate the effect of air attack on merchant ships. So the M.M.D. adopted the average loss of dry cargo tonnage per annum during the 1914-18 war — 1,940,000 tons gross — as the maximum figure for the first year of the projected war. It suggested that this could be offset by a combination of factors. Our shipyards were expected to produce 1,000,000 tons gross during the first year of war, while ships captured from the enemy, or retained instead of being scrapped, were expected to balance the remainder of our losses.

The third unfavourable factor involved the delays consequent upon Admiralty measures for the defence of merchant ships. Evasive routes were by definition longer than commercial routes, while ships would have to wait considerable periods for convoys to assemble, and then to proceed at lower speeds than normal in peacetime. Such factors could not be quantified even in general terms. The Department suggested that war would reduce the length of the average voyage by

[12]See below. Chapter 4.
[13]Behrens. 37.

reducing the number of ports of call, and by enabling better co-ordination of ships and cargo. It was concluded that this reduction would balance out the effect of wartime delays.

The final factor concerned the statistic that in 1918 some 23 per cent of Britain's tonnage was employed in the service of her Allies. Since most of this figure had been devoted to Italy and the United States of America, neither of which were potential allies in a future conflict, the Department assumed that no comparable diversion of tonnage need be expected.

Each part of this system of judicious correlation can be shown to be unsatisfactory.[14] Here it is only necessary to record the conclusion which the M.M.D. reached at the end of its enquiry. While noting the uncertain nature of the comparisons described above, and while aware that all hinged on the arbitrary and unsatisfactory figure of the 25 per cent reduction in the United Kingdom's food imports postulated by the Sub-Committee on Food Supply (since if this did not occur, the surplus of tonnage would be instantaneously converted into a deficit), the Department nonetheless firmly concluded 'that British shipping is adequate for the first year of war'.

Even the Department itself showed signs of disquiet with this statement, since the calculated surplus of shipping over requirements was less than 2.5 per cent. But it noted that the memo. had entirely excluded neutral tonnage from its calculations. There was far more neutral tonnage than could be employed in the neutral countries' own trades, and the Department theorised that it would have to be employed somewhere in any future war.[15] The Department regarded the availability of neutral tonnage as a 'long stop' in case its estimates concerning the British marine proved optimistic, and this contributed to the confidence with which it asserted the adequacy of British tonnage alone. The memo. containing the results of these calculations was presented to the C.I.D. as part of a more general enquiry into the Mercantile Marine, in November 1938.[16] It was approved by the Committee later in the same month.[17] The conclusions of the memo. thus became accepted policy, and affected all the arrangements subsequently made.

Efforts to determine the structure of the organisations which

[14] See below, Chapter 4.

[15] MT.40/9. T.02252, Briefs for the President of the Board of Trade for the debate on the Mercantile Marine in July 1938. 7 July, (by Hynard).

[16] CAB.4/29, C.I.D.1481-B, 3 November 1938.

[17] At the 339th Meeting, 24 November 1938, conclusion (b). The Committee noted: 'that the shipping position may be regarded as adequate . . .' CAB.2/8, Minutes.

would actually control the commercial employment of ships had not waited on the conclusion of the enquiry into the adequacy of the merchant fleet. The problem of devising a licensing scheme for British ships had been raised in the M.M.D. as early as 1930,[18] but until 1937 such investigations remained intermittent. In that year prolonged discussion of potential schemes got under way.

A useful summary note of the methods used in the First World War for the control of the commercial activities of ships had been produced by the Board of Trade in 1931.[19] This identified five methods of controlling British ships: forms of chartering or requisitioning for ships for duty with the fighting fleet; a scheme for tramps employed on commercial services; a Liner Requisition Scheme; a space requisition scheme, and the Ship Licensing Scheme. The M.M.D.'s attitude to such schemes was conditioned by the principle that state interference should be kept to a minimum. In the Department's view, 'the provision of tonnage will function most efficiently if left to market forces'.[20] Since chartering implied the least degree of governmental interference with the industry the Department's proposals for this field will be considered first.

Cargo liners would be chartered by direct approach to the shipowners' agents, but this was not expected to occur on a large scale. In the case of tramps, whose management organisations were less readily accessible, state chartering work was to be arranged through commercial brokers. Suitable arrangements were agreed with Messrs. Lamberts, and, for colliers, Messrs. Mathwins.[21]

Although these firms agreed that their objective during the chartering negotiations should be to obtain the lowest rate possible, chartering on the open market possessed the major disadvantage that the government would have to pay rates broadly comparable to open market prices. Furthermore, shipowners could force rates up by refusing to take urgent cargoes at the rates offered. Thus it was intended to employ chartering only if there was a world surplus of tonnage, and rates were low. If these conditions did not apply, the first step would be to introduce a ship licensing scheme.

Despite the initiative of 1930, proposals for a licensing scheme

---

[18]MT.59/1043, T.01555/21, Minute from Hynard to Alcorn, 31 December 1930.

[19]MT.40/6, T.01922, Memo. of 14 May 1931.

[20]MT.59/1069, extract from T.02644, containing, Memo. on 'The Provision of Tonnage for the Sea Conveyance of Commodities', Board of Trade, 7 July 1938.

[21]MT.40/15, T.02379, Minute by Hynard, 21 August 1937. Minute of Meeting with Lamberts, 29 October 1937.

were not produced until early 1938. They began by suggesting that,

> In any future war on a major scale it may be taken for granted that the
> experience of the Great War will be repeated, and that the number of
> ships employed on Government service under requisition will sooner
> or later be so large as to leave an insufficient volume of free tonnage
> available to lift the full normal imports of the country.[22]

Hence freight rates would rise, as shippers outbid each other for the
limited space available. All the problems of the allocation of essential
cargoes to shipping experienced in the First World War would then
follow.[23]

Such a situation, the memo. argued, could be alleviated by the
introduction of a ship licensing scheme. A committee of government
officials and commercial representatives, known as the Ship Licensing
Committee would be established to 'control the employment of all
British ships not under requisition by means of the issue of licences,
without which the ships could not obtain bunkers or clear from port'.[24]
Shipowners would continue to arrange voyages for their vessels as in
peacetime, but each voyage would require the approval of the
government, signified by the grant of a licence by the Ship Licensing
Committee. The Licensing Committee could enforce conditions
concerning the employment of the ship. In particular, it could limit
freight rates by refusing to licence a voyage where the rate was
considered too high, and could attempt to break high rates in any
particular trade by forcing large numbers of ships into it. By granting
or refusing licences, the Committee could ensure that essential
imports received shipment, and could prevent the import of luxuries.

Although the Committee could, by granting licences for certain
services only, force shipping into those trades, the scheme as a whole
was not intended as a measure of direction. It was hoped that owners
would identify the essential trades and that patriotism would induce
them to seek service in them, in which case the Committee's activities
would be restricted to approving applications for licences. The
constitution of the Licensing Committee, and of its administrative
structure, had been agreed by November 1938.[25]

[22]MT.59/1043, T.02215/ST20, draft of November 1938.

[23]The apparent inconsistency between this analysis and the conclusion of the enquiry
into the adequacy of British shipping in wartime was presumably resolved by reference
to the latter's specific restriction to the first year of war only, a narrower field of
reference than that considered in the licensing scheme.

[24]MT.59/1043, T02215/ST20.

[25]*Ibid.*

The experience of the First World War was a major factor in the ease with which the details of the Licensing Scheme were devised. The same is true of the organisation for requisitioning. The state had long possessed requisitioning powers, enabling it to control any piece of private property in wartime when a supreme national interest was involved. The property could then be operated, by the state, in the national interest. Each tramp steamer could be requisitioned individually by the Requisitioning Branch of the wartime Ministry of Shipping.[26] The owner was paid a rate of hire for the use of his ship, but no longer possessed any control over its activities. As in the First World War, rates would be assessed by an Official Committee on the basis of standardised calculations, with an Arbitration Tribunal to adjudicate in the event of disagreement between the owner and the Committee.[27] Finally, the state accepted the War Risk Insurance of requisitioned ships, and in the event of loss paid the owner a mutually agreed sum in compensation.[28] The structure of the Requisitioning Branch was complete by January, and the principles of the financial arrangements agreed by July 1939.[29]

The requisitioning of cargo liners, however, proved a more difficult undertaking. The problem lay in the organisations which served the Liner Companies as agents at each port of call. If each liner were requisitioned individually and employed as circumstances dictated, this network of agents would become useless. The liner companies would be involved in heavy financial liabilities if they sought to maintain it, but if they dismantled it, local contacts and traditional trade would be lost to neutrals, perhaps irrecoverably.

The existence of these organisations could be reconciled with requisitioning in two ways. In the first — 'space' requisitioning — the state merely requisitioned part of the liner's cargo space for its own use, leaving the rest of the ship's capacity to be filled by normal commercial processes. The requisitioning powers enabled rates to be fixed at reasonable levels by the government, while the free space enabled the owner to cover the administrative costs of his local organisations.[30] Space requisition, however, had one serious dis-

[26]MT.59/481, R.25, 'Organisation of Requisitioning Branch', 28 January 1939.

[27]MT.59/483, R.42, Meeting of Committee, 21 July 1939.

[28]MT.9/2977, M.8311/38. 'War Risks under Clauses in Government Charter Parties', September 1935. Also MT.59/495, AT/RB.327, 'War Risks Insurance, Requisitioned Ships', May 1940.

[29]MT.59/481 and 59/483.

[30]MT.40/17, T.02481, Memo. by Glennie on 'The Liner Requisition Scheme'. (undated).

advantage. By forcing uncontrolled goods to compete for a smaller amount of unrequisitioned space, it forced rates up. This was contrary to the general policy of the state in wartime, and the 1914-18 War had seen the construction of a more complicated scheme to control liners without destroying their local organisations. This was known as the Liner Requisition Scheme, and was adopted practically unaltered in the plans made before the Second World War.

Under this scheme both the ships and the local organisations were requisitioned, on a trade basis. Ships would continue to run under their owners' or charterers' direction. But they would be run, financially, on government account, at Blue Book rates and conditions of service, (i.e. at rates decided by the organisation also responsible for tramp rates described above). These rates would include remuneration for the management services and local organisations of the liner companies. Each trade or liner conference would establish a small Executive Committee to liaise with the Ministry of Shipping. This Committee would control the allocation of tonnage to cargoes within its trade, in the light of national requirements assessed by the Ministry. The Ministry could modify the programmes produced by the trade committees as it felt the national interest required. It could also transfer vessels from their normal trade to other employment if necessary. Thus, while the companies' administrative structures were maintained, the necessary central control was assured.[31] Furthermore, the state became the beneficiary of the companies' expertise in allocating ships to cargo. As the Requisitioning Letter to the companies put it, the government 'confidently rely on the willing co-operation of the Company in managing the ships so requisitioned and look to the Company to conduct business with as much zeal and care as if its interests alone were still involved'.[32]

The only disadvantage of the scheme lay in the complexity of the financial arrangements involved in calculating the rates for individual ships. The basic principle was that the gross earnings of the ships were paid to the government, less the Blue Book rate of hire, the permanent overhead charges of the companies' administration and any other incidental out-of-pocket expenses. Proposals for the whole scheme were produced in 1938, and a small committee was established in 1939, with representatives of the owners, to consider the details. The accounting procedures involved were simultaneously re-considered by the Finance Branch of the M.M.D. The Committee only met twice

[31]*Ibid.*

[32]MT.59/222, AT/GEN. 70, Requisitioning Letter, 30 January 1940.

before the outbreak of war, and so matters were little more advanced at that date.[33]

This structure of individual controls was backed by the development of a central authority, to be known in war as the Ministry of Shipping. The Ministry was organised on the basis of a number of Directorates, each responsible for one aspect of the problem of the control of ships. Among the more important Directorates, there were the Directorates of Merchant Shipbuilding and Repairs; of Sea Transport; of Shipping Controls; of Requisitioning and Shipping Intelligence; of Ship Management and of Commercial Services. There were also a number of Committees, such as that for ship licensing. This structure closely approximated that which had been developed for the Ministry of Shipping in the 1914-18 War, and requires little further comment. Its outline had been devised and provisional staff appointed by June 1938.[34]

It was, of course, by no means essential that imports to Britain should be brought in in British ships, and another of the functions of the Ministry of Shipping in wartime would be to obtain neutral shipping to trade with this country. However, considerations other than those of the import programme alone were involved in the shipping authorities' attempts to influence the employment of neutrals, since a further objective of British policy was to prevent the enemy receiving assistance from neutral shipping. This endeavour fell within the responsibility of those departments of government concerned with the 'blockade' — more properly, the exercise of economic pressure on an enemy — and their activities regarding neutral tonnage required co-ordination with those of the Ministry of Shipping.

Attempts to influence the employment of neutral ships fell into two major categories — those by which normal commercial processes of chartering were employed to secure tonnage for British use, and those relying on pressure brought to bear on neutral shipowners and their governments, i.e. those involving a measure of compulsion by Britain. The organisation for chartering neutral tonnage on the open market was similar to that for chartering British ships. Its broad outlines were determined by a series of memoranda within the M.M.D in March and April 1938.[35] A Neutral Chartering Section of

[33]MT.40/17, T.02481, Letter by J.L. Blake, (Member of Committee), 10 August 1939.

[34]MT.40/178, T.02271, 31 May 1938, and MT.59/481, R.25. Office Memo. on Organisation, 30 October 1939.

[35]MT.40/18, T.02529, memos. by Dorrell, 25 March 1938; Hynard, 8 April 1938; Foley, 13 April 1938; and Wills, 16 June 1938, (approval of designate staff, M.O.E.W.). MT.59/1069, T.02609, Minute by Keenlyside, 24 October 1938.

the Directorate of Ship Management, Ministry of Shipping, would be established to control chartering. Charters would be arranged by a Government Broker, as with British ships. In this case a joint organisation was to be formed by Messrs. Furness Withy and Lamberts.[36] This organisation would arrange charters on the open market in response to requirements determined by the Directorate of Commercial Services, Ministry of Shipping.

However, in many cases the chartering of neutral vessels could be facilitated by exerting various forms of pressure on neutral owners or their governments. In such cases it would obviously be unwise to leave policy in the hands of the Ministry of Shipping because of the wider issues involved. In these cases, the same executive organisation would apply a policy determined by a Neutral Tonnage Policy Committee, which would be responsible for considering all problems involved in the application of economic pressure to the chartering of neutrals. This committee would be part of the Ministry of Economic Warfare, and would consist of representatives of that Ministry, the Admiralty, the Ministry of Shipping, the Foreign Office and the Dominions, Colonial, Indian and Burma Offices.[37]

British policy towards the chartering of neutrals in the early stages of war reflected overconfidence in the ability of the British Mercantile Marine to transport the import requirements of this country, combined with an unrealistic assessment of the extent to which neutrals would be ready to charter their ships to Britain. It was expected that the outbreak of war would be followed by a slump in the international shipping markets caused by uncertainty as to the effects of war. In these circumstances the British expected to be able to charter large blocs of neutral tonnage for extended service at cheap rates. Such hopes were encouraged by pre-war negotiations with Norwegian tanker owners anxious to charter their ships to Britain before war broke out. The Norwegians, however, were mainly motivated by a desire to avoid German reprisals which might be provoked by chartering to Britain during wartime.[38]

Despite this optimism, extensive investigations had taken place into the various forms of pressure which might be applied, should the necessity arise. Such weapons ranged in severity from direct compulsion to mere encouragement to avoid the delays and diversions of the blockade system. The most widely known form of pressure was

---

[36]MT.59/1069, T.02609. Memo. by Hynard, 13 February 1939.

[37]MT.40/18, T.02529, Minute by Hynard, 8 April 1938.

[38]For the course of these negotiations, see MT.40/27, T.02785.

also one of the most direct, and is conveniently termed 'Bunker Control'. This system had developed, like most of the methods of pressurising neutrals, out of attempts to induce neutrals to come into British ports for the examination of their cargoes as part of the blockade system. During the 1914-18 War, when most merchant ships were coal-fired, and Britain provided most of the coal for them, the British found it possible to exercise a remarkable degree of control over the movements and employment of neutrals. Should a neutral refuse to comply with British instructions, she could be virtually immobilised by the refusal of coal. Consequently, in general, neutral owners chose to employ their ships on approved services, even if the freight rates were lower.[39]

The organisation developed to administer this system proved so successful that it was not thought possible to improve it in the 1920s.[40] A small committee of the Admiralty and Board of Trade was established to monitor the situation regarding supplies of bunker fuel at ports throughout the world and to tabulate its results for rapid reference.[41] This Committee, the Standing Committee on Bunker Control, continued to function into the 1930s. There was some concern during the 1930s as to whether the increasing use of oil fuel for merchantmen would reduce the effectiveness of the control Britain would be able to exercise in a future war, since Britain controlled relatively few supplies of oil fuel.[42] However, investigation showed that almost as many neutral ships burned coal in 1939 as in 1914, and there was no reason why Britain's ability to influence these ships would be restricted. She would also be able to exert some pressure on the oil burners, which now formed some 40 per cent of the total.[43]

These investigations revived interest in the organisation of bunker control as a whole, and the structure was revised and modernised. Control was intended to serve three objectives: to control the supply of fuel to ensure that British ships suffered no shortage; to control the

[39]CAB.47/2, A.T.B.6, 'Bunker Control in the Great War.' Trade Division Memo., 24 November 1924.

[40]Ibid.

[41]CAB.4/14, C.I.D.658-B, 'Advisory Committee on Trading and Blockade, 2nd Annual Report', 9 December 1925. MT.40/174, and CAB.47/3, A.T.B.54.

[42]MT.40/18, T.02529, Memo. by Dorrell, 25 March 1938. MT.59/2254, Memo. on 'The Bunker Control Committee', 4 October 1939.

[43]The actual figures were:
  Neutral tonnage (total) 1914: 6.0 m.t., all coal burning,
  Neutral tonnage   "   1938: 9.6 m.t., 5.3 m.t. coal burning.
                                    4.3 m.t. oil burning.
MT.40/18, T.02529, Memo. by Dorrell, also MT.40/177, T.01864, pt.1, B.O.T. Memo., January 1939.

supply of tonnage to ensure that we could charter sufficient neutrals to meet our needs, and to exert pressure on the enemy. As such its objectives cut across normal departmental boundaries, and a new structure was therefore developed. Two inter-departmental committees were created. The first, to be set up during the precautionary period, was the Bunker Supplies Advisory Committee. This continued the work of the Standing Committee, and was also responsible for maintaining supplies to bunker stations under wartime conditions.[44] It consisted of representatives of the Admiralty, Board of Trade, Mines Department and commercial bunkering firms, and was to be responsible to the Director of Shipping Controls, Ministry of Shipping.[45]

Responsibility for the allocation of bunkers to the ships themselves was to lie with a separate committee, the Bunker Control Committee. This would consist of representatives of all the major ministries, including the Foreign Office. It would also be responsible to the Ministry of Shipping, but would apply policy established in the Ministry of Economic Warfare regarding the severity of pressure to be exerted.

Applications for bunkers would be made through local Customs authorities. Initially it was intended to establish broad classes of ships and voyages for which bunkers would be supplied, and only doubtful cases would be referred to the Committee for decision. As the situation clarified itself, these classes would be superseded by White and Black Lists. Owners who did not comply with British wishes would be placed on the Black List and their vessels denied bunkers. Owners would be invited to place themselves on the White List by a suitable undertaking, so putting the psychological onus of exposing himself to countermeasures firmly on the neutral owner. The Ministry of Shipping was to be responsible for monitoring the actual performance of neutrals.[46]

The full rigours of this policy were not applied immediately on the outbreak of war, nor could they be, since they depended to some extent on the compilation of information concerning the activities of neutral vessels. Furthermore, as an appreciation made early in the war pointed out, we could no longer hope to do more than inconvenience a vessel by placing her on the Black List.[47] Nonetheless there was a

[44]MT.40/175, T.01789, pt.1.

[45]Ibid.

[46]M.T.40/177, T.01864, January 1940; M.T.59/2255, 29 January 1940.

[47]M.T.59/2554, 4 October 1939.

deliberate policy, up to the end of January 1940, not to apply pressure to neutrals so as not to prejudice them against engaging in British service on commercial terms.[48] Generally, all ordinary facilities of trade were made available to neutrals.[49] From that date, however, the principles of the White and Black Lists were applied, and bunkers refused accordingly.[50]

Bunker Control was only one of several forms of direct pressure which could be applied to neutrals to force them into service to the British cause. Britain also controlled a substantial proportion of the world's repair facilities and victualling supplies, and judicious manipulation of these resources was a useful reinforcement to bunker pressure itself. Most important of all however, was Britain's preeminence as a financial and insurance centre for the world's shipping. Several of the smaller neutral states, such as Greece, possessed no national facilities for war risks insurance, and Britain could make her extension of such insurance dependent on the performance of suitable services. In many cases British charter parties for neutral ships took over the cost of war risk insurance, and this was a substantial inducement to charter to Britain.[51] Refusal to provide insurance or financial facilities was another more direct method of capitalising on Britain's advantageous position in this field.

Britain could also exert pressure directly on the neutral governments concerned. Alongside direct diplomatic or military pressure, there were more subtle activities, such as the rationing of supplies to neutral states. Viewed overall, the ultimate objectives of Britain's exercise of economic pressure at sea may be described as an attempt, not only to prohibit the maritime trade of her enemies, but also to exercise control over the activities of as much of the remaining maritime trade of the world as was practicable. While the executive details of such an endeavour could be left to the departments concerned, the questions of policy raised were beyond their competence. Fortunately, the experience of the First World War had demonstrated the far-reaching implications of the exercise of such pressure, and also the interdependence of the individual aspects of it. Consequently, departmental planning in the inter-war years proceeded on the assumption that the definition of policy for the area would be the responsibility of some higher authority, and that the

[48]M.T.59/2255, Memo. by Mr. Weston (Ministry of Shipping), on a 'Comprehensive Scheme for Bunker Control', 29 January 1940.

[49]M.T.59/2260, 'Record of decisions on Bunker Control' to 1 November 1939.

[50]M.T.59/2255.

[51]M.T.59/1069, T. 02609, Meeting of 27 September 1938, at Board of Trade.

correct objectives of departmental planning lay in the construction of executive bodies to administer that policy.

The nature of this higher authority was subject to discussion during most of this period. Initially, in the 1920s, it was to be a Ministry of Blockade, located in the Foreign Office, while in 1938 it eventually emerged as a Ministry of Economic Warfare.[52] Only once, however, was its existence seriously challenged when, in 1937, the Board of Trade suggested that an Advisory Committee might adequately fulfil the same function.[53] A Sub-Committee of the C.I.D. Advisory Committee on Trade Questions rejected this suggestion in January 1938, and the organisation of the Ministry of Economic Warfare was rapidly finalised in the succeeding months, designate staff being appointed in June of that year.[54]

The Ministry of Economic Warfare was to form part of the Foreign Office. It would possess no executive power, but was to decide policy across the field of economic warfare, and to coordinate the activities of the individual departments concerned, including particularly the Bunker Control and insurance activities of the Board of Trade.[55] The crucial fact, however, lay in the intention to control and coordinate the activities of all departments concerned through a single Ministry, possessed of a centralised intelligence and statistical section. The establishment of such a body was no guarantee of the adoption of effective policies, although the experience of the First World War was a pretty sure guide in this case, but at least it ensured that efforts were not vitiated by uncoordinated and contradictory planning by the departments.

The thorough-going adoption of the policy of centralised control in the Ministry of Economic Warfare was sharply at variance with the philosophy which ruled in other areas of planning. The general attitude to state intervention was to restrict it to the minimum. The dichotomy between these two views on the problem of organisation for war contained within one bureaucracy should not be made too much of. The problems of economic pressure at sea were a special case. The exercise of such pressure required machinery specifically erected for the purpose by the state in wartime - there was no call for bunker pressure in peace. Furthermore, as a corollary, there were no

[52]CAB.47/2, ATB.31, 29 April 1926. CAB.47/6, ATB.163, 19 January 1938.

[53]CAB.47/5, ATB.150, Note by Board of Trade, 8 June 1937.

[54]CAB.47/6, ATB.163; CAB.47/6, ATB.172, 17 June 1938.

[55]CAB,4/27, C.I.D.1403-B, 'Organisation of Ministry of Economic Warfare'. Note by Chairman of Advisory Committee on Trade Questions, 21 February 1938.

peacetime organisations concerned with such questions which could be employed to administer wartime measures. The exercise of economic pressure at sea in wartime was exclusively a bureaucratic concern — no commercial bodies were concerned in the organisation or administration as such; there were no commercial interests to be respected or reconciled. This made it easier to introduce the sort of centralised bureaucratic control which other areas of state intervention in maritime economic affairs so sadly lacked.

The organisation thus constituted swung smoothly into existence in the first days of war. The Ministry of Economic Warfare was created with the other wartime Ministries hard on the heels of the constitution of the War Cabinet.[56]

For the sake of a comprehensive treatment of neutral shipping, it has been necessary to anticipate the arrival of war. It is now time to return to consider the last minute preparations concerning British vessels.

Although the experience of the First World War was of considerable assistance in determining the details of schemes for the control of British shipping, it was less helpful in deciding which of them would be appropriate at the start of any future war. It was never doubted that some form of control would be necessary, but the decision between licensing and requisitioning was less easy. The matter was, effectively, decided in May 1937, in an important memo. entitled 'A General Note on Control of Shipping' by Mr. Glennie of the M.M.D.[57]

Glennie noted that almost the only thing which could be stated with certainty about a future war was that 'its dimensions cannot be foreseen'. He considered that:

> The necessity of having a "cut and dried" scheme for the complete control of shipping is therefore a matter of necessity, though it will not be possible to decide whether it is required to be put into operation, in whole or in part, until the conditions of the emergency are apparent.

The principle of flexibility so stated runs throughout the memo., and indeed lies at the basis of all planning in this field.

As regards the decision between licensing and requisitioning, Glennie's memo. stated that 'whichever method is adopted would seem to depend largely upon the extent to which tonnage is available on the various trade routes, and the extent to which the seas are

[56]Taylor, 556.

[57]MT.40/17, T.02337, 20 May 1937.

rendered safe for shipping'. He noted that requisition would in any case be necessary to meet service requirements, and that 'in a war of maximum effort', 'universal' requisition had much to recommend it. In present circumstances, however, since the extent of the future war was not clear, 'it may be considered desirable to proceed slowly and operate various methods of control'. In effect this implied restricting control to a licensing scheme on the outbreak of war. Such a scheme involved no serious disruption of the normal operations of the industry. Depending on the day to day assessments of the Licensing Committee, it could be applied flexibly, both as to its severity and as to the proportion of British trade over which control was to be exercised. Furthermore, in the inevitably confused situation at the beginning of a war, licensing had one great advantage over requisitioning. This was that it left much of the initiative for the arrangement of voyages with the shipowner. As Sir Arthur Salter was to put it later, at the start of a war, the defects in the state's knowledge of the services to which it is important to apply shipping

> constitute the ground for leaving a fringe of undirected tonnage or utilising a system which gives an opportunity for the shipowner to utilise his special knowledge of particular trades and to test relative need through the ordinary competitive system, while allowing us to give priority, so far as we judge necessary, to demands about which we have sufficient knowledge.[58]

One further factor which encouraged the M.M.D. to proceed cautiously with the introduction of control of shipping was the attitude of the shipowners themselves to such schemes. It must be stressed that none of the schemes described could have functioned without the cooperation of the owners. Most of the Committees and Directorates of the Ministry of Shipping relied on co-opted members of the industry to provide advice and practical experience of the ways of shipping and of what was possible and what was not. Government chartering plans involved the use of commercial brokers, the licensing scheme depended for the arrangement of voyages on normal commercial processes. Even requisition itself, at least requisition of liners, depended on the owners' cooperation, since in the famous test case of 1917 the owners had proved the Liner Requisition Scheme to be *ultra vires,* since the requisition of the services of the owners and their staffs was beyond the powers of the Ministry. The owners, however, having proved their case, waived their legal rights and put their services at the disposal of the state. Shipowners' cooperation was therefore critical.

---

[58]MT.59/489, AT/RB.136, Memo. on 'General Policy as to Requisitioning and Licensing', 28 November 1939, para. 2.

In January 1937 the M.M.D. had submitted its calculations on the adequacy of the marine to various owners for their comments. The replies contained more than the Department expected. The general burden of these letters, which continued for three clear months, was that in view of the experience of the last war, the state should leave the industry to its own devices in wartime. Shipping would operate most efficiently if state interference was kept to a minimum.[59]

These arguments, and the general assessment in 1939 that 'in general it may be stated [that while it was impossible to quantify all the demands on tonnage] it is anticipated that there will be sufficient available to meet all essential needs',[60] ensured that a licensing scheme alone was introduced on the outbreak of war. On 3 September 1939, the Director of Sea Transport, W.G. Hynard, noted the intention to introduce a licensing scheme from 11 September.[61] At the outset licences would be granted almost automatically. Only when information as to the nation's requirements had been collected, would a greater measure of direction enter into the Committee's decisions. To preserve the liner services' local organisations licences would be issued on a general basis to the liner companies, and not for individual ships or voyages.

Thus Britain entered the Second World War.

[59]MT.40/9, T.02252, Correspondence January-April 1937. See also Chapter 1 above for shipowners' attitudes.

[60]MT.40/6, T.01922, 'Memo. for Dominions on Shipping Controls', 21 March 1939.

[61]MT.59/1046, AT/SL.28, Letter to Griffiths.

4

THE EMPLOYMENT OF SHIPPING IN WARTIME

The war was six weeks old when the Ministry of Shipping was established. It took over control of the commercial employment of British shipping and inherited the plans produced by the Mercantile Marine Department before the war : in Sir Arthur Salter's words 'the general rule with which the Marine Department started us, that requisitioning should be applied to Admiralty and Army needs but not for "commercial" cargoes, these being dealt with by the licensing system'.[1]

The only criterion for the effectiveness of pre-war planning is the success of its policies under the test of war. Judged by these standards, the M.M.D's performance is open to criticism. The efficiency of the Licensing Scheme came under question by November 1939, by which time circumstances had already forced the requisitioning of 31 ships for commercial service. By 9 December, with the recent introduction of requisitioning for the Northern Range Cereals Programme, some 650,000 t. deadweight of shipping was under requisition for commercial services. On that date, the Director General of the Ministry of Shipping ordered the preparation of schemes for 'universal' requisition. In the following week another 400,000 t. dwt. was taken up for the cereals programme, and on 18 December the Minister accepted proposals for the requisition of all tonnage employed on commercial services. This decision was announced on 4 January 1940. By 14 March some 4,661,655 t.dwt. of shipping operating on commercial services was under requisition, and by 25 June (the fall of France) some 90 per cent of all British ships had been taken up.[2]

Thus within four months of the outbreak of war, the basic policy established by the M.M.D. had been abandoned. The reason was quite simple — the licensing system did not ensure the most efficient allocation of shipping to Britain's wartime import requirements. To provide against this failure, the Ministry was forced to resort to the requisitioning of ships.

The failure of the licensing scheme may be described in terms of

[1]MT.59/489, AT/RB.136, Memo. of 28 November 1939, para. 4.v.

[2]The statistics come from MT.59/489, AT/RB.136, Minute by P.F. Rodgers on 'The History of Requisitioning', 15 March 1940. For June 1940, see Behrens, 54 n.i. The advance of policy towards requisition is described in MT.59/211, AT/GEN.10.

two major obsessions of pre-war planning: the necessity for reducing the intervention of the state to a minimum, and the necessity for securing equality of sacrifice, so that no one should benefit from a national emergency. The fundamental principle of the licensing scheme was that the state played no role in arranging voyages, it merely signified its approval or disapproval of charters arranged in the normal way by the relevant commercial bodies. The successful operation of this system therefore depended on the readiness of owners to undertake voyages in the national interest — which could then be approved by the Ship Licensing Committee. In the words of the official historian, this forced on owners

> a burden of moral responsibility larger than they should have been required to shoulder, forcing individual firms to decide whether, or how far, the national interest required them to sacrifice their ships in trades for which they had not been designed, or to expose their crews' lives in dangerous voyages, when there were plenty of safe and attractive alternatives...[3]

Furthermore, as early as November 1939, the government itself had become both the predominant purchaser of the essential commodities required for the national war effort and the predominant charterer of British tonnage.[4] Apart from the desire to control commodities, the major objective of this policy was to keep freight rates low. This objective did not encourage owners to arrange voyages in these trades, particularly when more remunerative — and frequently safer — employment was available on the open market. Consequently, a situation arose in which the owners could not be relied upon to engage in voyages in the national interest, and the modus operandi of the licensing scheme began to break down. As the Director-General of the Ministry of Shipping put it; 'a large number of applications are presented which the Committee find it necessary to reject. This is partly due to the fact that the freight rates fixed for Government cargoes have not been attractive.'[5] And again, 'the theory that ... owners, in general, would come forward with charters mainly for the voyages most urgently required in the national interest, was in danger of remaining a theory.'[6] The government's determination to prevent the occurrence of profiteering by shipowners as in the First World

[3]Behrens, 53.

[4]MT.59/489, AT/RB.136, Memo. on Control of Shipping, by Director-General, M.O.S., (Sir Cyril Hurcomb), 11 November 1939, para. 20.

[5]*Ibid.*, para. 15.

[6]*Ibid.* Note to Minister on 'Requisition or Control by Licence', by Sir Cyril Hurcomb, 11 December 1939, para. 4.

War, had induced it to establish control of freight rates.[7] But this control served to remove the one incentive to owners to engage in the essential trades — that under a system which operated on commercial principles, the essential trades should have been able to bear the highest rates.

To ensure the importation of essential commodities in such circumstances, the licensing scheme had to be used as a method of direction. In Salter's words; 'the owner is not only prevented from undertaking one job, he is told that he can do another (and, increasingly), that he will be refused a license for any but one job)... To that extent the system approximates more and more closely to one of requisition and specific allocation'.[8] Unfortunately, however stringently such a system was applied, it could not give the same control over the allocation of ships without loss of time as could requisitioning. The appearance of maintaining the elasticity of commerce, which the system was designed to secure, became illusory when the preferences of owners and charterers had to be drastically disregarded. Yet at the same time the system ensured that the major advantage of centralised control, the rapid and efficient allocation of ships to cargo, could not be achieved. The necessity of refusing requests for licences nullified a large amount of work by owners and charterers. Yet an indication that a licence would be granted for other employment did not eliminate the necessity of proceeding through the normal commercial processes yet again to arrange that employment. At the least, this was extremely inefficient. In general, under such conditions the licensing system increasingly exhibited every conceivable defect.

This fact was not lost on the shipowners, whose time and money was thus squandered. The Licensing Committee could not avoid giving the impression, not entirely justified, that the grant and refusal of licences was decided in an arbitrary and inefficient manner. Under the pressure of events the Committee could only allocate to service those vessels for which applications for licences were in progress. Unlike a system of requisitioning it could not always ensure that the most suitable ship was directed to the task, nor that the incidence of allocation to dangerous tasks was spread evenly across the industry. No consistent policy for the employment of shipping could be prepared. Nor, forced as it was to operate a system of flat rates, (as the Director General put it, 'a controlled rate must be a flat rate')[9] could it

[7]See *Fairplay,* 7 March 1940. Speech by Lord Essendon to the U.K. Chamber of Shipping.

[8]MT.59/489, AT/RB.136, Memo. of 28 November 1939, para. 4.

[9]*Ibid.,* Memo of 11 November, para. 22. On the rates actually introduced, see MT.59/746, C.S.81, 'Control of Freight Rates for Government Cargoes,' 1939.

prevent inequalities arising in payments. An owner of an old or inferior ship would find generous a rate which would be un-remunerative to the owner of a modern vessel. These inequalities in the incidence of the scheme, as in the First World War, induced the owners to welcome the introduction of requisitioning, despite their opposition to state intervention before the war.

The Ministry of Shipping, however, abandoned licensing for requisition because the latter enabled the more efficient use of tonnage. As the shipping and import programmes developed, the advantages of complete central control of tonnage became obvious. Allocation of ships to cargoes was more rapid — the delays involved in renegotiating charters were abolished. With the entire mercantile marine at its disposal, the Ministry could ensure that suitable ships were allocated to cargoes requiring specialised facilities. Under requisitioning, all ships were treated alike and there could be no criticism on the score of inequality — the incidence of dangerous services could be spread evenly over the industry, while all rates were assessed on comparable terms.

The key advantage of requisitioning from the state's point of view was that it enabled more accurate planning. Under licensing there was no assurance that tonnage would be submitted for use when it was required by the import programmes. Under requisitioning the Ministry did not have to wait for ships to be submitted to it. Having obtained details of the import programmes the Ministry could plan months in advance for the allocation of ships to cargoes, and, by intelligent coordination of its ships' activities, could ensure that they were used as efficiently as possible. This assurance of transportation at the opportune moment enabled the entire activity of the economy to be predicted with much greater accuracy. It enabled the limitations of the import system to be foreseen, and for shortages to be predicted. This in turn enabled the consumers of imported goods to take counter-measures and to economise rather than to engage in competitive struggles for a larger share of the finite importing capacity. Requisition of all ocean going tonnage was, in short, an essential precondition for the success of the type of planned economy which wartime conditions were forcing Britain to develop.

But this is no criticism of the M.M.D.'s decision to confine intervention to a licensing scheme in the early stages of a war. In this period Britain had not developed a system of centralised economic control, and in such circumstances a restriction of state intervention possessed certain advantages. We have seen Salter's views on the desirability of leaving some undirected tonnage to make good any inadequacies in controlled programmes resulting from the state's inexperience in the field. Additionally, the disruption and the administrative demands inherent in the introduction of requisitioning were so great that it was unwise to impose them on either industry or bureaucracy while both were in the critical early stages of adjusting to wartime conditions.[10]

The history of the war seems to support such arguments. The official historian suggests that the decision to control by licensing rather than requisition in the early months, had little effect:

> 'It seems unlikely, considering the other impediments at this time to harmonious marriages between ships and cargoes, that these hand to mouth methods, which prevailed until January 1940, when it was decided to requisition all deep-sea dry-cargo ships, significantly diminished either the total volume of British imports or even the importation of essential commodities.'[11]

This conclusion must be qualified in the light of the readiness of the shipping authorities to requisition tonnage for commercial service whenever it was apparent that the licensing scheme would be unable to supply the need. Even so, there is no evidence that wholesale requisitioning would have significantly improved the national performance in this period.

Licensing, then, became inappropriate as the general extent and competence of state intervention in the economic life of the nation increased. As the state took over ownership of the majority of essential imports, the rates offered for their carriage became unattractive by commercial standards. In order to ensure their importation the state had to resort to the direction of ships to cargoes, and once this position had been reached logic suggested that the most efficient form of direction should be employed. It is true that plans for requisitioning were by no means complete on the outbreak of war, but no suggestion was ever made that the introduction of requisition for commercial services was delayed because of this.

Simultaneously with the introduction of requisitioning for British ships, events forced a reappraisal of the policy of relying on competitive chartering in the open market for the provision of neutral ships for British services. Policy on the outbreak of war had been to exercise no unusual forms of pressure on neutrals, for fear of the friction which might result, and from confidence that market conditions would encourage neutrals to charter to Britain at cheap rates.[12]

[10]On the disruption, see Behrens, 44.

[11]*Ibid.*, 53-54.

[12]M.T.59/2254 and M.T.59/2255; M.T.40/21, T.02575, Memo. by Sir E.J. Foley, 5 May 1938; and M.T.40/28, T.02796, Memo. by Mr. Meredith, 29 August 1938.

In the event market rates rapidly rose above peacetime levels. These rising freight rates, the German policy of sinking neutral vessels in British convoys, and the British insistence on the time-charter of blocks of tonnage, nullified the hopes which had been so prevalent before the war. Without the heavy pressure from the British which they had expected,[13] neutral owners saw no reason to charter for extended periods or at cheap rates on dangerous voyages, when safer and more profitable services were available. In short, the British had under-estimated the resilience and extent of the world's trade in war conditions, and neutrals were, at this period, under no obligation or pressure to charter to Britain. It was not until mid-October 1939, with the arrival of Winston Churchill at the Admiralty, that serious consideration of British failure in this area began. At this stage, however, matters rested unchanged, with a policy of unsupported negotiations for blocks of neutral tonnage at cheap rates on time charters.[14] At the same time, the supply departments of the Ministries of Food and Supply had complicated matters by taking it upon themselves to enter the market for neutral tonnage on their own account.[15] These efforts were uncoordinated.

It was not until the new year that the seriousness of the position became apparent. Very roughly, imports in neutral hulls were running at 25 per cent of the total, compared with peacetime figures of 40 to 50 per cent.[16] Swift action followed. All chartering of neutrals was centralised in the Ministry of Shipping/Ministry of Economic Warfare organisation, and the duplication consequent upon the supply departments' unilateral chartering was brought to an end.[17] A comprehensive scheme for bunker control was introduced almost simultaneously,[18] followed by the various forms of financial and insurance pressure. Even so, it was not until the summer that the full scope of the British measures began to be felt, since until the occupation of Europe neutral facilities for bunkers, ships stores, insurance etc., continued to exist. In the summer of 1940, however, the British were able and indeed, were compelled, to put forth the full

[13] MT.40/27, T.02785, Letter from C.L. Paus (Commercial Secretary, British Embassy, Oslo) to C.C. Farrer (Dept. of Overseas Trade), 16 February 1939.

[14] MT.59/1541, F.S.R.2016, Note by Foley, 15 October 1939, WP (G) (39) 37, Memo. by Churchill, 16 October 1939, WP (G) (39) 48, Memo. by Simon (Chancellor of the Exchequer), 19 October 1939.

[15] MT.59/1707, F.O.N.4602, Memo. for Director General, Ministry of Shipping, (unsigned), 10 February 1940.

[16] Behrens, 64.

[17] MT.59/1707, F.O.N.4602.

[18] MT.59/2255, 29 January 1940.

degree of their power. A ship warrant scheme was introduced, under which a neutral vessel required a certificate or warrant to be able to use any British facilities. These warrants were only obtainable in exchange for an undertaking to abstain from trading with the enemy and to place the activities of the ship under the supervision of the Ministry of Shipping. This scheme, with the increasingly friendly cooperation of the United States, soon reproduced the conditions of the First World War under which no neutral vessel could move very far or for very long without such a warrant.[19]

In order to arrive at this position the British had found it necessary to employ every variety of pressure available to them. Applied individually and piecemeal no single source of pressure had proved sufficient to achieve the desired effect. The establishment of a Ministry of Economic Warfare with an overall control was the essential pre-requisite both of ultimate success, and of the success of the process of identifying areas of departmental responsibility within the whole.

By the time the organisation for the control of neutral shipping was approaching perfection, its importance had, paradoxically, been overtaken by events. After the summer of 1940, German occupation of their homelands had brought the most significant blocks of neutral tonnage under direct British control, and for the purpose of the rest of this chapter, it is not meaningful to make a distinction between British and neutral ships.

British ships, it will be remembered, had been brought under requisition early in 1940, in an attempt to solve the developing crisis in the import system. Requisition, however, did not prove to be the solution to this problem. The unfavourable shipping situation, which had been attributed to the inefficiencies of the Licensing Scheme, persisted and indeed deteriorated, despite the introduction of re-quisitioning. Before the war the M.M.D. had considered that the main shipping problem would be the adjustment of an adequate overall capacity to meet temporary shortages in individual commodity-trades. Now it was gradually realised that the nation was suffering from the effects of an overall shipping shortage — that there was insufficient capacity in service to transport all of the essential commodities required by the national war effort.

It is not necessary to describe the manifestations of this shortage in any detail. The figures for overall imports into the United Kingdom tell their own story. For the first year of war the demand for imports

[19]Behrens, 96.

had been assessed at 47 m.t. weight, and the capacity of British ships at 48 m.t. In the event, British ships only brought in 37 m.t.wt. in that period, although the neutral contribution fortuitously balanced the figure for total imports back up to 47 m.t.wt. In the first year of war, then, British shipping capacity was actually 10 m.t.wt. per annum less than had been estimated in peacetime.[20] The figures for September 1940 to August 1941 are even more striking. With the fall of France, Britain received a substantial increment of tonnage. Not only did the necessity of providing shipping for the French cease, but with Nazi domination of Europe, Britain was able to conclude arrangements with the European governments in exile for the use of their tonnage. It is estimated that at least 3 m.t. deadweight were thus added to the fleet under the immediate control of the Ministry of Shipping in London.[21] The Ministry estimated that this strengthened fleet could import 42 m.t. within the coming year. In fact in the second year of war the British only imported 31.5 m.t.[22]

Further elaboration of such figures would add little. The existence and importance of the shipping shortage have been adequately demonstrated. A great number of factors contributed to the development of this shortage. The closure of European ports and the Mediterranean to British shipping forced an increase in the average length of voyage, which was estimated at between 30 and 40 per cent overall.[23] Additionally there was the crisis in the ports, which is investigated in subsequent chapters. But for present purposes only the fundamental aspects of the situation need be considered.

A shipping shortage consists, essentially, in an incorrect relationship between its two major factors — the carrying capacity of the ships available, and the amount of cargoes requiring transportation. In wartime, a true shipping shortage only exists if the amount of essential commodities requiring shipment is greater than the ships' capacity. The situation in which luxuries are imported at the expense of necessities is not a true shortage, but merely a misalignment of the resources of the mercantile marine. It can be dealt with by import prohibitions as effectively as by control of ships. In 1940 and 1941, however, there was emphatically a true shortage of shipping. Since the extension of requisitioning over the entire British merchant fleet was virtually complete by the autumn of 1940, the control of the ships themselves was organised on the most efficient principles available.

[20]*Ibid.*, 36.

[21]*Ibid.*, 102 and Appendix XV, 113

[22]*Ibid.*, 111.

[23]*Ibid.*, 109.

This would seem to suggest that the origin of the crisis lay in the other aspect of the problem — with the cargoes themselves.

The plans developed in the 1930s for the control of commodities in wartime were relatively rudimentary. Even so, involving as they did control over all foods, raw materials, manufactured goods and agricultural and industrial products, they were far too complex to consider here. In the present context, attention must be confined to the arrangements made for obtaining shipment for the essential commodities which the government intended to control in wartime.

There was never any doubt within the bureaucracy that the state would have to assume control over the import of commodities essential to the war effort. The Mercantile Marine Department, in particular, was fully aware of this. Mr. Glennie's memo. on the control of shipping stated that, although

> It is not known to what extent the control of commodities will be undertaken in a future war, [it was clear that] ... no system of control of tonnage alone will enable rates to be kept at reasonable levels, so long as the commodity itself is uncontrolled ... whatever methods are adopted either to secure complete or partial control, it is essential that the plans of the Departments controlling purchase of commodities abroad must be related to the possible supply of tonnage. If this is not done, it seems inevitable that either waste of tonnage or inability to provide it will result.[24]

The M.M.D. accepted some responsibility for achieving this relation of purchases to shipping available, and its plans for wartime organisation included a Directorate of Commercial Services. This Directorate would be responsible for dealing with the shipping requirements of other government departments.

The M.M.D. envisaged two stages in dealing with such requirements. In the first, irrespective of the situation regarding the control of shipping, the departments purchasing the goods would themselves be responsible for arranging sea transport for them. These departments — in wartime the supply departments of the Ministries of Food and Supply — would, at this stage, set up individual chartering organisations and compete in the open market for shipping to carry their goods. Charters would be arranged through normal commercial processes. The Ministry of Shipping would be informed of arrangements so made, but its activities would be confined to supervision of the most general nature, (unless the Ship Licensing Committee should find reason to object to any voyage).

[24]MT.40/17, T.02337, 20 May 1937.

In the second stage, as the position in regard to the supply of tonnage deteriorated, the process of actually arranging the charter would be taken over by the Ministry of Shipping. Commercial Chartering Organisations would be established within the Directorate of Commercial Services — one for each commodity requiring shipment. The requirements of the supply departments would be fed to the Commercial Chartering Organisations by the existing departmental chartering organisation. The Directorate, or more correctly the Assistant Director of Commercial Services himself, would revise the supply departments' schedules in the light of tonnage available, and the charters would be concluded by the Commercial Chartering Organisations.[25]

Stage I of this organisation, more or less, came into effect in 1939. The exception was the refusal of the Ministry of Supply to set up its own chartering organisations. The Ministry argued with a totally uncharacteristic degree of foresight, that such bodies would come into direct competition with similar organisations set up by the Ministry of Food, and requested the Ministry of Shipping to make arrangements for providing tonnage for raw material imports. The Ministry of Shipping was forced, reluctantly, to concur, but emphasised that it too intended to work through normal commercial channels:

> In referring to our acting as your charterers, what is meant is that we instruct brokers and supervise the arrangements made for obtaining tonnage, for the movement of supplies for which you are responsible. In these cases, just as I understand you arrange for purchase through commercial channels, so we have the tonnage arranged through the ordinary chartering facilities provided by the market.[26]

This did not last long. The shipping authorities' Commercial Chartering Organisation was set up even before the Ministry of Shipping had come into existence, and from 18 September 1939, began to take over responsibility for chartering from the commodity authorities.[27] The reason for so early an abandonment of the first stage was not stated. Clearly, however, the change did little to prevent the development of the crisis in the import system.

Such a crisis cannot reasonably be ascribed to the operations of any single factor. In the case under consideration, shipping losses, the necessity for making longer voyages, and the crisis in the ports and

[25] MT.59/1069, extracts from T.02644, 'Organisation and Procedure within the M.O.S.' (undated).

[26] MT.59/753, C.S.122, Foley to Sir Arthur Robinson, 22 August 1939.

[27] *Ibid.*, Hynard to Lloyd, (F.(D.P.)D), 17 September 1939.

inland transport, all contributed to the problem. There were also inefficiencies resulting from the inexperience of the authorities involved, the Ministry of Shipping included. Nonetheless, there was one other major factor, perhaps the predominant one. This was the disorganised manner in which the Ministries controlling imported commodities approached the problems posed by wartime conditions. The two organisations involved, the Ministries of Food and Supply, controlled between them commodities which comprised some 90 per cent of Britain's peacetime import total.[28] Yet on the outbreak of war neither Ministry had produced more than rudimentary plans for a policy to control the importation of the commodities for which they were responsible.

Neither Ministry can have been unaware that the official estimates — those adopted by the M.M.D. for its enquiries into the adequacy of British shipping — did not expect the import capacity of the merchant fleet for the first year of war to exceed 85 per cent of the normal peacetime figure. Yet the Ministry of Food's initial estimate of its requirements for the first year of war envisaged no reduction of imports below peacetime totals.[29] Moreover the Ministry of Supply actually proposed to increase its total import programme beyond the peacetime average.[30] Neither Ministry showed any inclination to reduce these demands, despite preliminary warnings from the Ministry of Shipping. Indeed, it is doubtful whether either possessed an organisation capable of deciding the questions of coordination and priority involved in the production of a meaningful import programme — that is to say, one which restricted imports in the light of the tonnage available to transport them.

Of the two Ministries, that for Food was unquestionably the further advanced in the development of such an organisation on the outbreak of war, yet it had achieved only a rudimentary structure when circumstances forced its employment. The Ministry itself lacked any established criteria for food policy as a whole — for example, the government had delayed its rationing plans. In these circumstances it must have seemed wisest to plan on the basis of peacetime levels.[31] The Ministry of Supply was in an even worse position. Its import programme had to be based on the requirements of three distinct areas — war production, civilian use and export production, whose respective importance was continually changing

[28] Cmd. 6564, 'Statistics Relating to the War Effort of the United Kingdom', 1943-44.

[29] R.J. Hammond, *Food, Vol. I, The Growth of Policy*, (London 1951), 72.

[30] Hancock and Gowing, 132 n.2.

[31] Hammond, 62, 68, 113.

within the economy as a whole. The complexity of the problems it faced is some explanation of the failure of the Ministry of Supply to match even the slow progress of the Ministry of Food towards an import programme or budget.

The early days of both Ministries were inevitably confused. This partially explains their inability to make the accurate estimates of import demand requested by the Ministry of Shipping, but there were other factors at work. Among the most important of these was the institutional factor — the structure of the Ministries itself. Both were organised on commodity lines. They were subdivided vertically into a series of compartments, each concerned with a single commodity, which it would guide through all its dealings with the Ministry.[32] Thus, for example, one section of the Ministry of Food dealt with sugar in all its aspects — purchase, refining, arrangement of shipment, distribution from the port, and allocation to retailer. The weakness of such a structure lies in the coordination of the activities of these individual parts. In both Ministries, facilities for coordination were initially poor. In 1939, in the words of the official historian, the Ministry of Food consisted of a group of 'semi-independent commodity controls'.[33]

The significance of this structure was twofold. Firstly, in the situation in which each commodity control organised its own chartering of shipping — either directly, or through the submission of its requirements to the Ministry of Shipping — it frequently happened that commodity controls within the same Ministry were directly competing with each other for shipping. Secondly, the absence of a coordinating body above the executive controls hampered the creation of a clear and integrated import programme by each Ministry. The tendency was to lump the individual commodity controls' estimates together and regard the simple summation as the required amount. This gave the impression of being, indeed it actually was, an irresponsible and uncritical approach to the problem, and did not endear the estimates to the shipping authorities.

The Ministry of Shipping found its activities hampered by the inadequacies of the import programmes. In October 1939 an official of the Ministry described the position as 'impossible', and a strongly worded note was sent to both the Ministry of Food and the Ministry of Supply. Signed by the Director of Commercial Services, it read: 'You will appreciate that our difficulties here in the allocation of tonnage for the conveyance of essential foodstuffs and raw materials have been considerably enhanced by the lack of complete and precise information

[32] *Ibid.*, 54.
[33] *Ibid.*, 57.

as to the current and future requirements of your Department ...' As a result the Ministry issued a standard type of statistical return which it hoped the supply departments would use in making out their import budgets.[34]

At this stage the situation was more inconvenient than critical. Requisition had yet to be introduced, and the shipping shortage was yet to come. The problem was simply that the figures of import requirements were not being supplied in a coordinated, concise and consistent form, nor were the figures actually supplied sufficiently accurate or precise. The Ministry of Shipping was hampered in its arrangement of charters for individual commodities by its inability to coordinate them within a larger framework formed by the Ministries' demands as a whole. But, even when two or more commodity controls made simultaneous demands on the same tonnage, as could frequently occur when there was no structure for co-ordinating those demands, it was still a question of leaving whichever demand was assessed as the least pressing to be met by the redirection of tonnage from non-essential import duties.

The development of the shipping shortage altered the nature of this problem. What had been a problem of coordination became, with the shipping crisis, a problem of priority. It was no longer a question of reducing inefficiencies in the transport of essential goods, or of reducing delays in their arrival in the United Kingdom. As shipping became incapable of transporting all the essential commodities which the supply departments desired to import, it became necessary to decide which should be left behind. More accurately, this was a question of defining the size of the cut in its import quota which each essential commodity would have to accept. These cuts would be perpetual. The shipping situation was expected to get worse before it got better and commodities denied transport would, under foreseeable circumstances, never receive it. These were, therefore, far more serious calculations than those involving mere delay of the commodity. To decide which commodities should be restricted would be to affect Britain's entire wartime production. Such decisions could only be made in the light of scales of priorities: among the productive industries of the nation (which would determine the priority to be accorded to the import of each raw material); between the respective importance of each individual foodstuff in the national diet, and between the respective importance of the overall import quotas for all raw materials and all foods, within the total import programme of the

[34]MT.59/747, C.S.83, Minute by Picknett, 12 October 1939. Letter by F. Vernon Thomson, 11 October.

nation. Such decisions of priority would have to be binding once made, so that the incidence of shortages resulting from the reduction in import capacity could be predicted with accuracy and, so far as possible, related to a more general view of the activities of the economy.

The shipping shortage did not develop overnight, and the Ministry of Shipping had long predicted its arrival. It might be expected, therefore, that the departments concerned with the import of commodities would have taken steps to establish and perfect an organisation to determine priorities, at least among the commodities with which each was concerned. This, however, was not the case. This omission is both more serious and more surprising than the failure to produce import programmes at the start of the war. Both derived, ultimately, from an over-confidence in the capacity of the mercantile marine, which itself derived from the optimistic conclusions of the M.M.D's enquiry before the war. The conclusion of that enquiry was so emphatic that it could easily obscure the detail that it was based on a substantial reduction of food imports below peacetime levels, and that failure to achieve even a proportion of this reduction would transform the surplus into a deficit. As a result, in 1939, 'Whitehall as a whole ... never envisaged an immediate and continued shortage of shipping, severe enough in itself to demand the limitation of imports beyond the point dictated by lack of foreign exchange and the loss of sources of supply'.[35]

This confidence in the M.M.D.'s estimate was so firm that the Ministry of Shipping's warnings were discounted. Early shortages were ascribed to inefficient management of shipping, and, later, to the time taken to bring requisition into full effect. Furthermore, the very nature of the situation meant that the Ministry of Shipping could not be proved right until at least a year had passed. Until then, full annual figures would not be available, and any present crisis could be attributed to the incomplete operation of the relatively new structure of controls. Thus it was not until the late autumn of 1940 that the true seriousness of the situation became apparent to all the departments concerned. Until that point various anomalies and inefficiencies had persisted. For example, chartering of neutrals for the import programmes was not removed from the individual commodity control chartering organisations and centralised in the Ministry of Shipping until March 1940.[36] Even in mid 1940 the Ministry of Supply remained disorganised — it did not know the size of its stocks or its

[35] Hammond, 67.
[36] MT.59/1707, F.O.N.4602, 10 February 1940.

rates of consumption of commodities.[37] Once again the Ministry of Food was more advanced. Plans for a General Department to decide policy over a wide front were being laid, and such a Department was in fact established in November 1940,[38] but it required time to become truly effective.

If the situation concerning the coordination of demands and the determination of priorities within these two Ministries was thus rudimentary, the situation concerning determination of their overall respective proportions of the total import capacity was no less vague. An Economic Policy Committee had been set up in October 1939,[39] but in the face of the Ministry of Supply's inability to present this Committee with any rational arguments to support its demands, the Committee did little more than approve the Ministry of Food's more presentable estimates. This situation continued until the formation of the Import Executive Committee in December 1940. This Committee was the first major step to rationalised planning in this field, and was responsible for determining short-term shipping priorities as well as reviewing import programmes.[40]

This is not to suggest, however, that there had been no procedure for rationalising between the conflicting demands of the supply departments prior to the winter of 1940-1. The first stage in the establishment of such an organisation has been noted above, in the Ministry of Shipping's request for the other departments to adopt a standardised statistical return. In the following month (November 1939), an interdepartmental committee was established in the Ministry of Transport, to decide 'priority among claims on shipping space'. Although it met regularly for eighteen months, the committee made no real contribution to a solution of the overall problem, being restricted by its departmental situation.[41] In fact, even before the first Christmas of the war, the Ministry of Shipping found itself compelled to undertake the task of reducing the demands of the supply departments to conform to a realistic calculation of importing capacity.

The Ministry's ships were, at this stage, the critical factor in the import system — it was this shortage which rendered the requirements proposed by the supply departments excessive. In the absence of a body concerned to relate those requirements to available capacity at a

[37]Behrens, 106.

[38]Hammond, 57.

[39]Hancock and Gowing, 93.

[40]Behrens, 105-6, 196-7, Hammond, 163.

[41]The records of this committee are contained in MT.59/800, C.S.680.

prior stage, such a relation could only be achieved at the stage of the physical allocation of cargoes to ships, that is, at a point within the Ministry of Shipping's sphere of responsibility. However, the Ministry was not content merely to deal with this crisis on the particular level and to decide each conflict of commodities requiring shipment as it arose. Realising that to accept one essential commodity for shipment was to deny shipment to another, and that such decisions could affect the productive capacity of the economy as a whole, the Ministry felt obliged to lay down the outlines of a policy of priorities within which such decisions could be made. This enabled it to justify to the supply departments its apparently arbitrary decisions to accept or refuse shipment, and allowed preliminary steps to be taken to develop a coordinated import policy. In turn this would enable the incidence of shortages to be predicted and would allow the development of an overall policy for war production to reduce the effects of those shortages. Above all it would provide the statistical description of future imports which was critical to any attempt at centralised forward planning for the economy as a whole.[42]

The Ministry of Shipping did not suppose that this task was one for which the shipping authorities were suitable. Yet circumstances forced its hand. It began to suggest programmes for the allocation of cargoes to ships, and for the reduction of the supply departments' import quotas where these exceeded the capacity available. Some friction resulted from the reductions in allocations, but this was a minor problem. More serious in the early stages, was the sheer inability of the supply departments' rudimentary organisations to produce plans involving levels of importing lower than in peacetime. However, as the Ministry of Shipping's import quota organisation developed, so did the supply departments' organisations. By the time the whole structure of import quotas was reviewed early in 1941, these organisations were sufficiently developed and coordinated for them to be retained. Thus it was that throughout the war, the Ministry of Shipping, subsequently as a constituent of the Ministry of War Transport, was responsible for the preparation of the overall shipping budget, based on the individual import programmes it calculated for the supply departments and their individual commodity organisations. The supply departments produced estimates of their requirements, but it was the shipping authorities who adjusted those requirements in the light of the tonnage available and a scale of priorities.

The contribution of the shipping authorities in this field was thus

[42]Behrens, 47-50, 104-111, 196-8; Hancock and Gowing, 132, 265-6.

critical to the success of the economy as a whole during the war. But this success must be qualified by appreciation of the fact that the general failure to develop suitable organisations to discharge these duties is largely attributable to over-confidence in the capacity of the merchant fleet engendered by the pre-war estimates of the M.M.D. Confidence in the adequacy of shipping had lulled the supply departments into believing that the levels of expertise and involvement they would have to develop would be low. They did not perfect their organisations for the control of goods, let alone develop plans for adjusting their import demands in accordance with any consistent and rational system of priorities. Similarly, the need for a higher authority to decide between the conflicting demands of the two Ministries for shipment was overlooked.

The M.M.D.'s plans were also affected by over-confidence. The only provision made for coordination consisted in the Assistant Director of Commercial Services and his staff. This was little more than a token gesture. The Department must be severely criticised for this omission. Even had its estimates of the capacity of the merchant marine proved correct, it should have realised the urgent need for a more substantial structure of coordination. An overall adequacy does not imply that shortages in particular trades will never occur. Furthermore, even if a serious situation was not expected to recur, the experience of the First World War should have revealed the dangers inherent in even a moderate crisis in the import system. In these circumstances the M.M.D.'s failure to accept that it might be called upon to repeat the experience of the Ministry of Shipping in the 1914-18 War and decide import priorities, and to make preparations accordingly, can only be described as a refusal to accept its proper responsibilities.

In 1931, the Board of Trade had concluded

> it is important to emphasise the necessity for co-ordination between the commodity control department and the shipping control department. In the last war serious difficulties constantly arose owing to departments taking measures to purchase or control commodities which involved sea transport before the possibilities of sea transport had been investigated.[43]

The M.M.D.'s failure to establish the coordinating structures which this comment advocated was not, however, a simple error of ignorance or omission, wilful or otherwise. Believing that a shipping shortage was unlikely to occur in a future war, the Department argued that such structures would not be required. It is now necessary to

[43]MT.40/6, T.01922, Memo. on Control in Great War, 14 May 1931.

examine the process by which the Department reached this conclusion, and to identify the errors which rendered its analysis inappropriate.

The M.M.D.'s belief that a shipping shortage was unlikely to occur was based on the conclusion of its enquiry into the adequacy of the British Merchant fleet. Events were to prove this conclusion optimistic. Yet the M.M.D. was supposedly an expert bureaucratic organisation, and was intended to produce accurate answers to such problems. Where, then, did it go wrong, and must its failure be attributed entirely to its own mistakes?

To assess the adequacy of the mercantile marine was basically to make an estimate of its carrying capacity. Some of the problems of calculations of carrying capacity have been touched on before, but the M.M.D. should have been capable of overcoming such factors. If it was not, then it was incapable of carrying out its duties. However, in the calculation in question, the Department was considerably hampered by the hypothetical nature of the enquiry. The only facts which could be statistically verified throughout the whole course of the enquiry concerned the number and tonnage of the ships under the British flag. Beyond this, all was supposition. Most importantly, neither the enemy, nor the exact nature of the war, could be accurately foreseen in 1936. This made the M.M.D.'s calculations of carrying capacity very difficult. Apart from the physical restrictions of the ship herself, the carrying capacity of a vessel depends on two factors — the nature of her cargo and the length of her average round voyage. Inability to define the exact form of the future war rendered both these factors more or less unquantifiable.

The types of raw materials and manufactured articles of war which Britain would need to import would depend to a considerable extent on the nature of the war in which she was engaged. For example, in a large scale European war she might need to support an expeditionary force abroad. If so she would need more tanks and motor transport, more guns and ammunition, than if she restricted her military intervention. In such circumstances there might be a need for the import of more iron ore to make steel, or more finished steel, or more assembled tanks and transport vehicles. The demands of the services for sea transport would also increase. Correspondingly, if Britain adopted a maritime strategy and relied on the blockade and on the air force to attack the enemy, she would have less need of tanks — and perhaps more need of aircraft, either assembled, or in component form.

War cargoes, particularly assembled weapons such as tanks and aeroplanes, were more prodigal of shipping space than the normal peacetime cargoes. These articles were heavy, bulky and awkwardly shaped. They could not be stowed so efficiently in a given space as objects of more regular shape, which could be closely stacked. Another difficulty was that they were rarely imported in peacetime, so that ships and ports were inexperienced in dealing with them. Inexperience produced delays, which reduced carrying capacity. This dual ignorance — both of what quantities of such goods Britain would need to import, and of the best methods of handling them — removed all chance of assessing the effect of such factors. No basis of comparison with peacetime experience existed, and it appears that no pre-war calculations were ever made of the possible effect of war cargoes on carrying capacity. It is certain that the figures used by the M.M.D. in producing its estimate of the adequacy of the marine made no allowance whatsoever for such factors, and the Board of Trade's estimate of Britain's import requirements for the first year of war was based on the assumption that there would be no expeditionary force. Consequently it based its estimates of the increased importation of war materials solely in terms of increases in raw materials such as were already imported in peace.[44]

The identity of the enemy could also have a critical effect on carrying capacity, by forcing alterations in the average round voyage time. The 1936 estimates were based on a single enemy in Europe. This, it was calculated, would necessitate an automatic reduction in Britain's short sea trade of some 70 per cent of normal levels. The estimate noted that 'The general effect is to increase the proportion of imports which will have to be brought from distant countries, in order to make good the reduction in imports from the near countries.'[45] This involved longer voyages, a reduction in the number of round trips made each year, and thus a loss of carrying capacity. Not knowing the sorts of cargoes ships would be required to bring in, nor where it would be acceptable — say for exchange reasons — to obtain these cargoes, the M.M.D. could make no estimate of the effect on the overall capacity of the fleet of this closure of European ports. In connection with its estimate of the capacity of the tramp fleet it noted that its calculations had been based on peacetime loading areas, and continued, 'It is, however, likely that the loading areas would be substantially different since sources of supply of essential commodities would be transferred as far as possible to closer areas, to economise on the length of voyage times'.[46] Since short sea imports represented,

[44]CAB.16/114, D.I.C. 16, 19 July 1934. See above, p. 70.

[45]MT.40/9, T.02252, Memo. on Adequacy of Shipping (draft), August 1937.

[46]Ibid.

in peacetime, some 50 per cent of British trade, this adjustment of loading areas would have had to make up a shortfall, resulting solely from the closure of European ports, which might approach 30 per cent of total British imports.[47]

The M.M.D.'s readiness to make such generalisations says much concerning its appreciation of the limitations of statistics. The entire bureaucracy functioned at a level of statistical naivete surprising, even for its time. One example will suffice. This was the vexed question, thrown up by the estimate of import requirements used by the M.M.D. in its calculations, of the 25 per cent reduction in food imports supposedly sanctioned by the Sub-Committee on Food Supply in Time of War.[48] In actual fact, in considering overall import requirements for food in wartime, that Committee had stated that a long term reduction in imports of 25 per cent was likely to occur anyway, and that it could be accepted without danger.[49] This merely represented a generalised figure for the ultimate effect of war on Britain's food import requirements. The M.M.D. was mistaken in equating this with an immediate cut in food imports on the outbreak of war. Owing to the nature of the food trade, with advance contracts for many shipments, such a cut would have been impossible to enforce, even had the food authorities possessed an organisation capable of administering it. Thus imports of food in the first year of war could not be reduced anything like 25 per cent below peacetime levels, even under the most favourable circumstances. Yet this is what the M.M.D.'s calculations assumed. As has been noted, a failure to achieve this 25 per cent reduction in food imports would automatically transform the meagre surplus of the adequacy enquiry into a shipping shortage.

It should be noted that such blunders were not confined to the M.M.D. The Food (Defence Plans) Department instructed its Trade Directors to write up all its purchasing levels by 25 per cent on the outbreak of war, under the impression that this proportion represented the percentage of cargoes which it was assumed would be lost in transit to this country.[50] The level of economic expertise available to these departments clearly left much to be desired. Those commercial

---

[47]*Ibid.*

[48]See above, pp. 70-1.

[49]CAB.4/25, C.I.D.1276-B, 11 November 1936.

[50]Hammond, 67. The practice of overestimating purchasing and stock levels of food to guard against a failure of imports continued, even into the third year of war, and introduced serious distortions into the import programme generally. See *Ibid.*, 169-70. For a general comment on the statistical capabilities of the bureaucracy, see G.D.A. MacDougall, 'The Prime Minister's Statistical Section', in *Lessons of the British War Economy,* D.N. Chester, (ed.) (Cambridge, 1951), 62-63.

experts who had been employed in the First World War had returned to the industry. Indeed this is one serious criticism of the policy of employing commercial experts to run the wartime Ministries — after the war they returned to industry and their expertise was lost. The M.M.D. could have obtained the assistance of commercial experts in making its plans in the 1930s, but it did not do so, partly, no doubt, as a result of bureaucratic prejudice, but mainly through ignorance. The Department did not know enough even to realise that it did not fully understand the way in which it was using its figures. It did not realise the mistakes it was making, and thus did not see the need for outside advice.

Such advice would undoubtedly have exposed many of the fallacies in the M.M.D.'s conclusions. But it was not obtained, and so the Department soldiered on through an increasingly confusing maze of conflicting arguments. In doing so it made an increasing number of incorrect appreciations. It will be remembered that the M.M.D. had identified a number of unquantifiable factors at the end of its estimates of the adequacy of the merchant marine. These factors, it had been suggested, would balance each other out.[51] Experience, of the First World War particularly, suggested otherwise, and it seems certain that the Department placed too heavy a reliance on those factors tending to assert the adequacy of British shipping. This was particularly true in two cases. It was suggested that the effect of losses might be counterbalanced by new construction coupled with a number of less important factors. Losses were expected to average 1,940,000 tons gross per annum. Shipbuilding was expected to produce 1,000,000 t.g. of dry cargo ships per annum. This latter estimate can only be described as unrealistic. In 1912 and 1913 British yards had produced over 2,000,000 t.g. of merchant ships per annum, yet even so, in 1914-15 this production was halved, and halved again, to a mere 500,000 t.g. in 1915-16.[52] In no year between 1931 and 1938 did British yards turn out 1,000,000 t.g. of all types of merchant ships combined, yet the Department considered them capable of exceeding that figure, in dry cargo tonnage alone, in the first year of war. That is to say, they were expected to improve on their peacetime performance at a time when normal experience, with the turning over of yards to warship building, suggested that the ability to turn out merchant ships would be severely reduced.

The Department also suggested that the effect of wartime delays on the carrying capacity of the merchant fleet could be offset by more

[51] See above, pp. 71-2.
[52] Salter, 48.

efficient allocation of ships to cargo and by the cutting out of unnecessary ports of call. In itself this is a startling denunciation of the efficiency of the shipping industry in peacetime, and directly contradicted the Department's own statement that, as a general principle, the allocation of tonnage would function most efficiently if left to commercial principles. The M.M.D. estimated that a saving in voyage times of 15 per cent could be achieved under wartime conditions through shorter voyages and better coordination of ships and cargo.[53] Unfortunately, it ignored estimates of the effect of wartime delays in the First World War, which suggested that round voyage times would be increased by 20 to 25 per cent over peacetime levels.[54] Furthermore, the Department made no allowance for port congestion, or for confusion consequent upon the diversion of shipping from the east coast ports. Even had the M.M.D.'s figures for the increased efficiency of the wartime structure of control of shipping been correct, there would still have been a substantial fall in carrying capacity.

This history is remarkable. The Department seems to have entirely ignored the experience of the First World War in making these calculations, and yet, despite the substantial bias in its figures, could still only produce a surplus of some 3 per cent overall. Had the Department been better versed in statistics it would have realised that such a margin did not exceed what could be described as a reasonable margin for statistical error. It was certainly well within the margin which Ministry of War Transport statisticians allowed later in the war. Yet the M.M.D. — on the basis of an almost entirely hypothetical assessment, involving disjointed estimates, prepared at different times for different purposes and on the basis of different conditions, and containing a number of factors which it readily professed to be unable to quantify — still considered its estimates sufficiently accurate to justify the unqualified conclusion: 'British shipping is adequate for the first year of war'.

Any attempt to explain how the M.M.D. could produce so confident a conclusion must begin with the inexperience of the Department in handling such complex statistics. It obviously failed to appreciate the limitations of statistical enquiries. Even without the numerous mistakes, the Department's acceptance of the 3 per cent margin as sufficient in all circumstances is clear proof of this criticism. There is also the possibility, already mentioned, that the Department was relying on the help of neutrals in the event of its estimates proving incorrect.

[53]MT.40/9, T.02252, (draft) August 1937.

[54]Fayle, *Seaborne Trade,* estimated 25 per cent (III, 192), Elderton (31) rather less. The Admiralty suggested 12 to 20 per cent (see above, p. 47, n 11.)

And yet the experience of the First World War was there to demonstrate the dangers of the situation. Not only did the Department possess its own body of material, there were also the published works of Salter and Elderton who had served in that war, and of Fayle, the official historian. The only logical conclusion to be drawn from the evident fact that the Department was aware of the experience of the previous war, is that, in the circumstances of the day, and without the benefit of a second example before it, the conclusions apparent in 1936 were different to those apparent today. It is at least possible that the M.M.D. misread the history of the First World War. From the evidence of its balancing of factors at the end of the adequacy enquiry it appears that the M.M.D. believed the shipping shortage in the earlier conflict to have resulted mainly from three factors. Firstly, there was the simple absence of any coordinated shipping policy until 1917. Secondly, there were the losses caused by Britain's unpreparedness in the face of the German submarine campaign. Thirdly, the enormous demands of Britain's allies, and particularly the United States, for tonnage, amounting to almost one quarter of her total in 1918. Of these factors, the Department itself intended to deal with the first, while the services assured it that the submarine menace could no longer present the same danger. As regards Britain's allies, there was no prospect of their demands reaching such levels again. These factors, bolstered by the apparently conclusive result of the adequacy enquiries, seem to have convinced the M.M.D. that a shortage of shipping was not to be expected.

The consequences of this decision in delaying the formation of plans to establish full control over both ships and commodities have been noted. To be scrupulously fair to the M.M.D., however, it must be remarked that, as a result of its confidence in shipping, certain alterations were subsequently made in the assumptions which had guided its calculations. Thus, for example, the services, by December 1939, had been allowed to requisition nearly one third more tonnage than the maximum allowed under the information conveyed to the Department originally.[55] Such factors were, however, marginal.

One aspect remains to be considered in this assessment of the M.M.D.'s performance. The central failure of the plans, in administrative terms, has been shown to consist in their failure to establish a centralised control over the entire import system. This omission was encouraged by the failure to foresee the shipping shortage, but it also derived from the pre-war policy of government in this area — that state intervention should be restricted to the minimum compatible

[55]MT.59/489, AT/RB.136, 'The History of Requisitioning', 15 March 1940.

with national security. This directive induced a certain disposition against intervention in the departments concerned with the import system. The M.M.D. for the most part, accepted this bias uncritically — and in doing so echoed the views of the shipowners, who also doubted the efficiency of intervention. There were, it is true, certain doubting voices. Mr. Glennie spent a considerable amount of time urging the development of more extensive plans, but such dissent was in a minority. The Department's attitude was thus predisposed to regard problems in terms of whether or not they could be solved without the necessity for intervention, rather than in terms of the most efficient solution, whether this happened to involve intervention or not. Its approach to the problems of shipping control was therefore a negative one, it sought to restrict control to a minimum rather than to organise wartime structures on the most efficient lines. Its criteria for considering possible solutions to any problem were not those of efficiency, but those of economy.

The desire to restrict state intervention led to a failure to develop organisations for coordinating the activities of the individual departments, or even the individual controls within these departments. Thus the expression of the intention to control all industry noted by Glennie,[56] in practice implied merely the creation of individual bureaucratic authorities for the individual constituents of industry. Faced with a crisis of supply, such uncoordinated bureaucracies were likely to compete as fiercely with each other for the scarce commodity as the commercial authorities they had replaced would have done. State intervention in 1939 may have extended across the face of industry, but it was partial in the sense that it involved little machinery for coordination.

The effect of such omissions in the shipping sector has already been described. By January 1940 the state's hand stretched out effectively over the whole import system, (except in the allocation of inland transport from the ports), and yet the shipping shortage had hardly begun to develop. When that shortage did develop, the only solution was found to be an effective coordination of the allocation of cargoes to transport, in accordance with a system of priorities devised with regard to the overall objectives of the war economy. In short, the state had to abandon its attempt to restrict intervention, and take over full responsibility for the wartime economy. This is not the place to consider the objectives of government in attempting this restriction of its authority, but the effects of the policy must be made clear. Not only did it encourage the M.M.D. to accept an unnaturally restricted view

[56]MT.40/17, T.02337, 20 May 1937.

of its responsibilities, but it contributed to the seriousness of the eventual crisis in the import system, both by restricting the scope of planning and by hindering the Ministry of Shipping's attempts to instil a more responsible attitude. The state had not grasped the central lesson of the First World War, that there can be no halfway house between state intervention and no state intervention. The mere fact of state intervention (the requisition of ships for military purposes or the desire to control rates to prevent profiteering) reduced the ability of the normal commercial controls to operate. If it had not proved possible for these commercial organisations to run the import system successfully in 1914, when state intervention was at a minimum, it was unlikely that they would be successful in 1939, when the acceptable minimum of state intervention had become extended. Once the state had intervened, efficiency demanded that it take over complete control. These facts were not realised, however, and the M.M.D.'s performance must be judged against this backcloth. In Britain at that time there was a general unwillingness to face squarely the implications of taking a highly industrialised technological society into a war for national survival. Centralised planning was a necessity if the wartime economy was to be run predictably, if disruption and unexpected shortages were to be avoided, and if maximum productivity was to be achieved.

Two criteria may be adopted in an attempt to reach a final assessment of the performance of the M.M.D. in planning for the control of shipping in war. The first involves consideration of the administrative machinery which the Department devised. Did the detailed structure of controls which was established prove competent to discharge the immediate administrative tasks for which it had been created? This criterion assesses the M.M.D.'s competence to design an organisation to achieve a particular administrative objective — in short, its competence as a designer of administrative structures. The second aspect concerns the relation of those structures to the problems which they had to face in war. How well did the M.M.D. foresee the problems which would prove critical in the war years, and how successful were the organisations it created, and the policy it laid down to guide them, in meeting and overcoming those difficulties? This discussion will assess the M.M.D.'s performance in isolating the critical areas in the import system, and in identifying the correct solutions to the problems — in short, its competence as a creator of policy.

There can be no grounds for criticism of the M.M.D.'s competence as the creator of administrative structures to discharge specific tasks. Its plans for the control of shipping, viewed solely as administrative exercises, functioned smoothly and efficiently. The organisations the M.M.D. devised to control the processes of chartering, licensing and requisitioning, indeed the basic organisation and structure of the Ministry of Shipping itself, all proved successful in discharging their immediate administrative functions. The licensing system was not abandoned because of any shortcomings in its administration, but because the policy which the organisation was applying had proved inadequate in the conditions of the day. The problems in the administration of the requisition of shipping had all been correctly identified during the planning process and suitable means of tackling them had been developed. The size and complexity of the task resulted in some problems with the introduction of general requisition, but no changes in the structure of the requisitioning process or in its day to day administration proved necessary, either then, or later in the war. Nor did the basic structure of the Ministry of Shipping undergo any major modifications, despite the fact that it came to administer powers far beyond those originally envisaged by its creators in the M.M.D. The union with the Ministry of Transport which occurred during the war was a result of the need for more efficient coordination of the national transport system as a whole, and implied no reflection on the Ministry of Shipping's ability to direct ships in the most efficient manner.

However, the experience of the First World War played a large part in determining the details of these schemes, and praise of the M.M.D. must be qualified in this light. The administrative problems faced during the earlier conflict were clearly related to those with which the Department was concerned. Although the schemes had not been administered as a coherent whole in 1914-18, this detracted little from their ability to demonstrate the administrative problems posed by the introduction of control over the various sectors of the industry, and in many respects highlighted both the satisfactory and the unsatisfactory aspects of the schemes. This made the M.M.D.'s task much lighter, and in many respects the plans it produced were carbon copies of those evolved and tested in the previous war. Thus the Liner Requisition Scheme of 1917 was adopted almost verbatim in 1940, the only changes being some clarification of the accounting procedures which had proved troublesome before. The experience of 1914-18 provided the Department with a reasonably clear idea both of the administrative problems it would face in establishing control over shipping, and of reliable methods of overcoming them.

But the experience of the previous war was less of a guide with regard to the problems forming the second criterion mentioned above. However competent the individual measures introduced during the

1914-18 War, they had been devised and applied haphazardly and without relation to a coherent philosophy concerning the problems facing the import system, or the role of the state in helping to solve them. Indeed, it now appears that the authorities in the First World War had made a fairly serious miscalculation in their analysis of the malaise affecting the import system. The emphasis given by the rudimentary economics of the day to the problem of inflation of freight rates and profiteering has been noted. There is little doubt that this emphasis obscured the more fundamental problem of the shortage of shipping so far as the bureaucracy of the time was concerned, and there is evidence to support the contention that a residual over-emphasis of this financial aspect warped the M.M.D.'s attitude to the shipping problem. All the M.M.D. policy statements — even, for example, Glennie's crucial memorandum[57] — contain references to the necessity to keep freight rates down as one of the objectives of the control of shipping. The crucial fact is that this was a mistake. The proper objective of the control of shipping, the *only* proper objective, was the prevention or amelioration of a shortage of import capacity. Control of rates could have been achieved by direct financial intervention without the need for control of shipping as such. This fact was pointed out to the M.M.D. in June 1939 by a paper on the Liner Requisition Scheme prepared by Mr. Irvine Geddes, a member of the small committee established that year to consider the problem of liners.[58] But in the scramble on the outbreak of war this warning was lost to view.

The effects of this obsession with rates in restricting the availability of tonnage for the transportation of essential imports was one of the major reasons for the failure of the licensing scheme. But apart from the practical aspect, it diverted attention from the really fundamental problem of the capacity of shipping. The object of control of shipping was to maintain that capacity, so far as possible, in excess of the volume of essential commodities requiring import. Anything else was peripheral to the M.M.D.'s function and its failure to realise this represents a failure to think through to the fundamentals of its position.

But if, in some respects, the M.M.D. payed too much heed to the experience of the 1914-18 War, it was, nonetheless, aware that the circumstances of a future war would not be entirely comparable to previous experience. It was in the attempt to consider the nature of the

[57]*Ibid.*, para. 3: 'the necessity of avoiding the abnormal freights experienced in the 1914-18 war . . . '.

[58]MT.59/211, AT/GEN 10. Mr Geddes represented Messrs. Anderson, Green and Co. Ltd.

present situation of the industry that the Department made its one crucial mistake. This was the enquiry into the adequacy of British shipping. Basically because of its own inability to deal properly with statistics, the Department made a serious error. On the basis of dubious calculations, it drew over-optimistic conclusions. The point is not that the M.M.D. was itself incapable of making an accurate estimate of shipping capacity, for it is doubtful whether even the most brilliant of statisticians could have succeeded with the information the Department had at its disposal. The failure lies in its inability to see the limitations of its conclusions. Leaving aside all the lesser errors, the Department's critical mistake lay in its assumption that a 3 per cent surplus was a sufficient margin to permit it to assert that a shortage of shipping was not to be expected in a future war. Even after the most accurate of calculations, such a tiny margin would not realistically justify the assertion that a shortage was improbable, let alone unlikely. It is true that the Department was not familiar with calculations of such complexity, but the narrowness of such a margin, especially in the light of the admitted inadequacies in the calculations, should surely have given pause for thought. Simple logical consideration should have exposed the shortcomings of this conclusion. It is a striking condemnation, not only of the M.M.D., but of the whole bureaucracy concerned with the import system, including the C.I.D., which approved these calculations and their fatal conclusion, that not one official questioned the wisdom of so forthright an assertion based on such minute grounds.

From this crucial suspension of criticism all else followed. Failure to foresee a shortage of shipping brought about the failure to establish systems of coordination and priority to minimise its effects. The plans of other departments proceeded in freedom where they should have been restricted with care. Once again, the unfortunate M.M.D. must bear the brunt of criticism. The experience of the 1914-18 War had clearly shown that the shipping authorities occupied the pivotal point in the import system. As such, the Department should have foreseen the need for an extensive structure to coordinate the demands for shipping capacity, irrespective of whether that capacity was in short supply. It cannot have been unaware of the rudimentary nature of the supply departments' commodity control organisations. It should have foreseen that their incompleteness must inevitably throw the burden of coordination onto the shipping authorities. Yet it made only perfunctory attempts to establish an organisation for coordination. Not only did this allow the lack of a coordinated allocation of cargoes to ships to become one of the bottlenecks in the import system in wartime, but it delayed the development of satisfactory countermeasures by providing no suitable groundwork in peace. The unwillingness of the Department to accept its proper responsibilities in this area has been criticised already.

Clearly the Department's omissions were partly the result of the application of policy determined by central government. But that policy stated only a principle, that intervention should be kept to a minimum consistent with national security. Closer definition of that minimum was the responsibility of the departments, such as the M.M.D. This was the objective of the enquiry into the adequacy of shipping. This was where the Department failed. Had the Department not concluded that shipping would be adequate for the first year of war, the state would have been forced to accept a higher profile of involvement in the industry. The M.M.D., or the supply departments, would have been forced to develop adequate structures to ensure the coordination of ships and cargoes and to decide priorities among conflicting demands for the shipment of essential commodities. In short, the entire system of controls which had to be set up in 1940-1 would have been anticipated before the war. Even had the organisation itself progressed slowly, at least the departments involved would have anticipated the need, prepared more flexible policies and adopted a more responsible attitude to their demands upon shipping. The conclusions of the adequacy enquiry were not announced to the rest of the bureaucracy until the time of Munich. No preparations had been made before this, and it is doubtful whether more than the principles of the organisations required could have been decided before the war. But even this would have been an immense help to the Ministry of Shipping. Departments would have been more prepared to accept its early warnings concerning the adequacy of shipping. Its early attempts at restricting their excessive import programmes would have encountered less opposition. The intemperance in the use of shipping noticeable in the early months of war would not have occurred. Above all, the departments would have faced the war with a clearer idea of the problems the import system was likely to face, and it is to be hoped, with a greater readiness to accept individual hardship in the cause of resolving those problems. In short, a most significant constituent, perhaps the single most significant constituent, of the national war effort would have been better equipped to carry out its wartime task.

The official historian has noted that the Mercantile Marine Department failed to foresee 'only one of the immediate consequences of war, a shortage of shipping'.[59] True — but what an oversight.

[59] Behrens, 39.

5

THE INSURANCE OF BRITISH SHIPPING

The M.M.D.'s plans for the control of British shipping in the early stages of war were constructed on the assumption that the shipowners would continue to direct ships to employment as if normal conditions still prevailed. Without requisitioning, the continued employment of British shipping in wartime would therefore depend on the ability or willingness of the owners to continue to run their ships in the face of the vastly increased likelihood of their being sunk. There were two methods available to owners to safeguard themselves against the loss of a ship, by charging increased rates of freight on the cargoes they carried, or through insurance. Of these methods, the alteration of freight rates would be severely restricted by the government's intention to control freight rates in wartime, in order to prevent their inflation to levels at which they would restrict the flow of trade by making transport prohibitively expensive.[1] This left insurance as the essential precondition of all plans concerning the employment of merchant shipping in wartime. Broadly similar considerations also applied to the private owners of cargoes shipped by sea, since state control over retail prices would prevent them from covering their increased risks by raising the price of the articles concerned. Without adequate insurance facilities in wartime, ship and cargo owners would be encouraged or discouraged from trading as the difficulty or expense of obtaining insurance fell or rose. Thus, as the continued flow of trade to this country was vital, so the provision of adequate insurance facilities for it became vital.

Both ships and cargoes were naturally insured as a matter of course in peacetime, but the marine underwriters of the insurance companies and of Lloyd's made a distinction in their attitude between normal peacetime risks and the risks to be provided against in wartime.[2] In the inter-war period in the United Kingdom the insurance market, as commercially available facilities were known, confined its insurance of the vessels themselves (known as 'hulls' insurance), to cover against accidental loss or damage such as might be caused by the normal perils of marine navigation — force of

[1] See above, p. 112.

[2] For the general structure of the market, see the Report of the C.I.D. Sub-Committee on 'The Insurance of British Shipping in Time of War,' CAB.4/9, C.I.D.400-B, 27 February 1923.

weather, collision, stranding and so forth. Policies could be obtained on either an annual basis or for each individual voyage of the ship concerned, depending on the nature of the trade in which the ship was employed. Cargoes were insured on a similar basis.

Insurance of ships and goods against war risks was provided by the market, but on a separate basis. Under wartime conditions losses would be likely to increase, and the general level of claims would be markedly higher. Clearly, existing premiums, based on the level of peacetime claims, would be inadequate to provide the insurance companies with a fund sufficient to cover the demands for compensation made upon them. Thus the market, in general, included in its peacetime policies a provision securing their cancellation in the event of war. New policies could then be negotiated with due regard to the conditions of the time in the calculation of rates. This system had one major drawback from the point of view of the shipowners and cargo-owners. Certain vessels would inevitably be actually at sea, engaged upon voyages, at the time of the outbreak of war and of the cancellation of their normal peacetime insurance policies. They would therefore be subject to risks of a type specifically excluded from their peacetime policies, and at a time when they might in fact have no insurance at all, despite the fact that a premium had been paid for the period of the voyage in question.

To protect themselves against this hiatus, the shipowners had joined together to form War Risks Associations (or Clubs). These were confederations of owners which offered insurance in peacetime specifically against war risks, on an annual premium paying basis. Security against the level of claims exceeding the sums received in premium payments was provided by the pooling of the resources of the shipowners' companies. Any excess would be paid by the companies, in proportion to the value of the ships they had insured with that particular association. The Associations' policies provided insurance cover from the time of cancellation of the peacetime cover until a new policy could be negotiated with the market, whether the vessel concerned was at sea or in port. The Associations were not intended to, and in any case did not have sufficient financial strength to, replace the insurance market in providing insurance for voyages commenced after the outbreak of war.

Owing to the nature of commerce, no such associations could be formed to provide insurance for cargo, and war risk insurance could only be obtained for cargo in peacetime by the conclusion of a special policy. Policy conditions varied, but, as with hulls insurance, cargo was (at best) only covered against war risks for voyages actually in progress on the outbreak of war.

In wartime, the expense and difficulty of insuring in the open market rose. Underwriters could not hope to cover all the risks which were presented to them and still charge economical premiums. The greatest risks, which in a war between the United Kingdom and a continental enemy were those involving transportation to the U.K., would therefore be the most expensive to insure, if they could be insured at all. Thus the economics of the open market tended to discriminate against those services which were most vital to the nation. Similarly, the cover provided by the market fluctuated according to the incidence of losses. When losses were high premium levels rose to cover the expectation of an increase in claims, yet in this situation it was essential that trade should be encouraged, to overcome the general effect of the losses. Thus the facilities offered by the market decreased as the national need to encourage trade increased. Furthermore, owing to the rapid changes in conditions in wartime, the market refused to accept insurance on a long term basis, since premiums charged at the time of issue of the policy might be totally unrelated to the actual risks to be encountered after, say, three months. This was a crucial aspect. The international shipping markets functioned to a large extent on the basis of forward engagements — engagements made, frequently several months in advance, for the transportation of cargoes by ships. To obtain such contracts it was obviously necessary to be able to quote, and maintain, freight rates, but these rates depended in part on the cost of the insurance which would have to be borne by the shipowner, and in wartime conditions the insurance market would not, in general, quote rates for longer than a week in advance. This was simply not long enough to enable such forward engagements to be made.

Thus the general policy of the insurance market towards the war risk insurance of ships and cargoes was that, while it was prepared to cover the risk of an outbreak of war, it would not commit itself to the risks that would have to be run during war itself. It could confidently be expected that if insurance facilities in wartime were confined to those provided by the market, trade would cease in areas or in times of high risk, as a result of unacceptably high premium levels, or of a refusal to provide insurance at all. And as is so often the case, those services which were most at risk in wartime were frequently those services which were most vital to national survival.

This was by no means a new problem in this period, or this century. It was the one area of planning for merchant shipping which had received extensive investigation prior to the First World War, and for which plans had been formulated before 1914. These plans, produced by a Sub-Committee of the C.I.D. under Mr. Huth Jackson, were implemented on the outbreak of war, and remained the basis of state intervention during the conflict. The investigations which were conducted after the First World War were therefore based on a considerable amount of practical experience gained from the operation of the schemes in that war, and proceeded, for once, with the firm acceptance by all parties concerned that state intervention was not only necessary, but desirable.

Nonetheless, there was some doubt, particularly among the commercial representatives consulted, as to whether a new investigation was necessary, since the schemes which had proved satisfactory in the 1914-18 War were already available. However, the committee which investigated this question after the war, and which began its considerations in 1923, had anticipated this criticism.[3] The basis of Huth Jackson's scheme for hulls was that the War Risks Associations should undertake, in addition to their normal work, the permanent wartime insurance of merchant ships against war risks, at valuations ascertained with the state's approval. They should then re-insure 80 per cent of those risks with the state, which would receive a proportionate amount of the premiums charged. Premiums would not be charged for voyages current on the outbreak of war, and premiums for the subsequent voyages were to be laid down by the state, within maxima to be agreed in consultation with the Clubs. All the administration and administrative costs were to be the responsibility of the Associations.

This system remained in operation until August 1917, when it was undermined by events. In an attempt to keep traffic moving as freely as possible, the government had set its premium rates too low. Then, to take account of the effect of wartime inflation on the value of the vessels concerned, it had increased the insured valuation of the entered vessels (i.e., those registered with the Clubs).[4] Consequently, it found it was paying out greater sums in compensation for losses than it was obtaining in premium receipts. Additionally, the number of ships requisitioned by the state reached a level which undermined the financial basis of the Associations.

The schemes only applied to vessels running on private account, not to those requisitioned by the state.[5] Yet, to an extent which

[3]*Ibid.* For additional details concerning the First World War, see Fayle, *Shipping Industry,* Ch.IV.

[4]Valuations were increased by 20 per cent on 10 March 1915. and by a further 30 per cent on 3 January 1916. CAB.4/9, C.I.D.400-B, 27 February 1923, para. 34.

[5]For the position of requisitioned ships under the schemes, see MT.59/495, AT/RB 327, May 1940, and MT.9/2977, M.8311/38, correspondence with Mr. Todd of the North of England Protecting and Indemnity Association.

depended on the policy of the Club involved, the owners of ships which had been entered with the Clubs prior to requisitioning remained liable for calls made in respect of those ships, even after they had been requisitioned. (Calls were the contributions levied by the Clubs from the owners of registered vessels when the level of claims on the Clubs exceeded the receipts from the premium fund.) Requisitioned ships fell outside the state reinsurance scheme, so in these circumstances the owner of the requisitioned vessel found himself liable for the whole amount of any call made upon him, whereas the owner of a ship remaining inside the state scheme was re-insured by the government for 80 per cent of his liability for calls. Furthermore, the owner of a requisitioned ship was not at liberty to attempt to recoup any loss by variation of his freight rate, since the rate was fixed at the time of requisition. This rate had been set without reference to the fact that the government was charging uneconomic-ally low premiums for its insurance. The owner of a requisitioned ship was thereby subject to heavy calls from the Clubs, and was subsidising those owners who continued to operate ships on private account, and who only had to pay 20 per cent of the calls made upon them. This enabled the owners of such ships to make an unfair profit through providing them with artificially cheap insurance cover.

In response to this crisis the government assumed full respon-sibility for losses. The Associations were reduced to the administration through which the schemes were operated, receiving no premium, and subject to no liability.

In the atmosphere prevailing after the war it was inevitable that such a far reaching measure of state intervention should be viewed with distrust, and the 1923 Committee specifically rejected the idea of reintroducing the scheme as operated at the end of the First World War, ostensibly on the grounds that the scheme was merely an expedient and not a thoroughly considered measure. As, however, the schemes as originally operated in the war had the demonstrable defects which had led to their replacement during the conflict, it became obvious that some new scheme would have to be devised. On the recommendation of the 1923 Committee, a further committee was established to discharge this responsibility.[6]

The British Shipping War Risks Insurance Organising Committee, as it was known, was intended to determine the details of government intervention in this area. It was never its function to question the necessity for state intervention — that problem had been resolved by

[6]CAB.16/57, I.B.S., Minutes of 1st Meeting, 30 July 1924.

the 1923 Committee. The Organising Committee was not provided with any indication of the approved scope of government intervention, although the 1923 Committee had concluded that the objective should be to produce a scheme at the minimum cost to the community as a whole. The Huth Jackson schemes and the experience of the First World War provided a basic framework within which the main outlines of the scheme could be rapidly sketched, so the Organising Committee was mainly concerned with considering those areas of the earlier schemes which had proved contentious in the war years. In the main, therefore, it was concerned with relatively minor details of administration, which are only interesting to the degree to which they illuminate matters of principle.

As we have seen, the general attitude towards state intervention at this time was that it should be restricted to the absolute minimum necessary to achieve its objectives.[7] While recognising this policy in its recommendation that the schemes eventually produced should operate at the minimum cost to the government, the 1923 Committee had also recommended that the state should try to secure a monopoly of the marine insurance market in war. This was, in fact, likely to occur in any case, since the government schemes were to be run on a non-profit making basis, and premiums would thereby be lower than those offered by commercial companies which had to make a profit. However this may be, the divergence of view inherent in the 1923 Committee's report was one which was to cause some confusion within the deliberations of the Organising Committee.

This problem was particularly prominent in the Committee's considerations of the questions of the valuation of ships under the scheme, and of the types of risks against which the state should provide cover. The valuation question arose out of the details of the First World War schemes. In keeping with the original intention to restrict government liability to a minimum, the Huth Jackson Committee had devised a formula for the calculation of the current value of ships insured, which did not provide sufficient compensation in the event of loss to enable the shipowner to replace his vessel from these funds alone. It did however, allow a sufficient proportion of the cost of replacing the vessel to be insured with the state at cheap premiums, to enable the owner to bear the cost of insuring the remainder on the open market. Thus, while the state's financial liability was considerably restricted, it

[7] See the Defence Regulations, quoted above, p. 68.

nonetheless achieved its objective of ensuring that trade was not interrupted through reason of inability to find insurance.[8] These provisions came under attack both during and after the war, mainly from shipowners who resented having to pay large sums for insurance outside the state scheme.[9] These views were supported by some bureaucratic members of the Organising Committee who considered that a comprehensive scheme to insure the whole replacement value of the ship would be both more logical and simpler to administer.[10]

Similar arguments were aired over the question of the types of risks to which the scheme should apply. The intention in 1914 was to restrict the state's liability to the so-called 'King's Enemy Risks', which were less extensive than the war risks normally insured by the market. However, certain disputed cases had been taken before the House of Lords in post war years, and the decisions then given had broadened King's Enemy Risks to a level approximating to the standard market policies. Once again discussions took place within the Organising Committee as to whether the restriction of state liability involved in re-establishing the original intention of the schemes was worth the difficulty of obtaining commercial approval of such action.[11]

In some measure those who argued in favour of the extension of state liability — of the adoption of logically complete schemes — had missed the point. The only reason the government had entered the insurance field was because the commercial companies, carrying a wide range of liabilities, had been unable, thereby, to provide insurance at a sufficiently cheap rate to enable the continuation of trade under war conditions. Although the state schemes were to be run on a non-profit-making basis, they were intended to break even and to cover administrative costs, and thus could not ignore the value of liabilities accepted. If the state chose to expand the extent of its liabilities, it might, in order to avoid making a loss, find itself forced to charge rates which would discourage trade. It would thus frustrate its own objectives in introducing the schemes.

[8]On the objectives of state backing for the insurance market see Sir Norman Hill's arguments in MT.9/3094, M.9194/39., Memo. of 19 June 1939. On the success of this system in the First World War, see CAB.16/58, I.B.S.7, Memo. by Hill, 27 September 1930.

[9]CAB.4/9, C.I.D.400-B, 27 February 1923, para. 67.

[10]CAB.16/58, I.B.S. 8, Memo. by Hipwood, 14 October 1930.

[11]CAB.16/57, I.B.S., Minutes of 1st Meeting, 30 July 1924, CAB.16/57, I.B.S., Minutes of 10th Meeting, 14 June 1938; CAB.16/58, I.B.S. 15, Memo. by Joint Secretaries to Committee, 30 May 1938.

The essential object of the schemes was to keep traffic moving. If this were to be achieved, it was vital that insurance rates were kept low. The advantage of the fixed valuation as devised by the Huth Jackson Committee was that it provided the minimum degree of insurance cover sufficient to ensure the free movement of trade, by providing just sufficient cover to enable owners to accept the cost of insurance as a whole. Given the state's unwillingness to keep trade moving by accepting a substantial continuing loss in terms of compensation payments exceeding premium receipts,[12] the adoption of the full replacement valuation of the ship for the purposes of the state schemes would have resulted in the level of state premiums being forced up to the point at which they, too, discouraged trade. The objects of the scheme would thus have been frustrated. In short, it would have produced a return to the normal arrangements and consequent shortcomings of the market system, with the state merely acting as a large insurance company.

The most concise statement of these views was provided by Sir Norman Hill[13] when he wrote that,

> The purpose for which the scheme is framed is the maintenance of overseas trade in time of war, and the provision of insurance facilities for shipowners is only a means to the attainment of that purpose. It has never been the intention that the Government scheme should provide a full measure of reinsurance ...[14]

The Organising Committee's reaction to such arguments was mixed. In the case of the valuation question they accepted them and retained the 1914 system, while in the case of the definition of war risks their position was less consistent.

Initially, in 1926, they obtained agreement with the Clubs, to restrict government liability to a narrow definition of King's Enemy Risks.[15] The details of the schemes were then referred to the Board of Trade to be confirmed by legislation. This, however, had not been achieved by 1935, when the Abyssinian crisis forced the introduction of some form of war risks agreement. Under pressure of events the Clubs were able to obtain the government's acceptance of a commercial

[12]Between October 1916 and August 1917, the government insurance schemes lost £16 million in order to keep trade moving. CAB.4/9, C.I.D.400-B, para. 48.

[13]Sir Norman, a member of the Organising Committee, was a past Chairman of the Liverpool and London War Risks Association, had been a member of the Huth Jackson Committee, and Chairman of the Port and Transit Executive Committee. He was, as it were, the elder statesman of the Committee.

[14]MT.9/3094, M.9194/39, 19 June 1939.

[15]B.S.W.R.I.O.C. 2nd and 3rd Annual Reports; CAB.4/14, C.I.D.652-B, 21 December 1925 and CAB.4/15, C.I.D.736-B, 8 November 1926.

definition of war risks.[16] After the crisis had passed, the Organising Committee was reconvened and set to consider this problem again. This time it concluded that the advantages of having a single standardised definition of a war risk, based on commercial practice, far outweighed the disadvantage of any additional liabilities which the state might thereby incur.[17]

The incident itself was a relatively minor one. The liabilities involved can hardly have been significant when compared with the overall cost of the schemes. Nonetheless, it does raise the point of the extraordinary hiatus between the Committee's completion of its report and its embodiment in legislation. Sir Norman Hill was bitterly critical of the Board of Trade over this aspect, with, one feels, some justification.[18] So too the shipowners: Alfred Booth, for one, 'had confidently expected that this scheme [the 1928 agreement] would receive Parliamentary sanction without delay, but years went on and nothing was done'.[19]

By June 1928, the Organising Committee had drawn up a complete draft scheme, and had submitted the draft to the government for the approval of the Cabinet and of the other departments concerned. After amending its proposals in accordance with suggestions from other departments, the Committee sent the completed documents to the Board of Trade solicitor to ensure their legality. The documents languished there, as did the progress of the enquiry as a whole, until the Committee met again in April 1937. In the intervening years the Board of Trade had vetoed the draft scheme, but gave no indication of its reasons for doing so. The whole enquiry ground to a halt for seven years. It was only reopened as a result of the Abyssinian crisis, which had forced the Board of Trade to conclude an emergency agreement with the Associations. This agreement was in several respects less favourable to the state than either the 1914 scheme or the 1928 drafts, since in the crisis the government had had to accept terms which favoured the Clubs to achieve the speedy establishment of a scheme. In the remaining years before the war the Organising Committee continued its task with the added incentive that it was essential to replace the unfavourable provisions of the Emergency Agreement before hostilities actually broke out, and that

[16]MT.9/2977, M.8311/38. Meeting with representatives of War Risks Associations, 24 October 1935. CAB.16/58, I.B.S.16. Letter from Hill to Sir Julian Foley, June 1938.

[17]Final Report of Organising Committee, CAB.4/29, C.I.D.1511-B, 26 January 1939.

[18]CAB.16/58, I.B.S.12, Note by Hill, 27 April 1937.

[19]Quoted in *Fairplay,* 2 April 1936.

legislation was necessary to achieve this. The Committee succeeded. It presented the proposed drafts to the Cabinet on 16 January 1939, in time for them to be incorporated in the annual policies of the Clubs which were issued on 20 February each year.[20] However, the Committee never received an explanation of the strange hiatus between 1928 and 1937.

If the Board of Trade did not entirely discharge its responsibilities in these years, the Organising Committee — when it was in existence — certainly did. The structure of the Organising Committee as a standing body, well equipped with commercial representation, possessed several advantages from the government's point of view, not the least of which was that the Committee was continually in touch with developments in the insurance world. This undoubtedly simplified its resurrection in 1937.

From this narrative it may appear that the Organising Committee was mainly involved in negotiating minor points whose actual importance was relatively small compared with the overall extent of the import trade of this country. From the administrative point of view this is to a large extent true. The bases of the schemes were not greatly modified from those of the First World War. However, concentration on such factors does not allow a proper estimate of the importance of the Committee's functions to be achieved. The objective of the Committee's schemes, the maintenance of trade during a crisis, depended ultimately on a factor which could not be quantified — the confidence of the commercial world — and it is not entirely appropriate, therefore, to assess its performance solely in terms of the concrete problems dealt with. Like every body dealing with insurance or with finance generally the marine insurance market was extemely cautious in nature. It was all too ready, from the point of view of the state and of trade, to take fright and to restrict the facilities it provided. To a large extent therefore the Committee was concerned with maintaining the confidence of the market, even if this forced it into areas of investigation which, superficially, do not seem crucial. It should be remembered that, although the First World War schemes could presumably have been reintroduced had this been necessary, there were no arrangements with the Clubs actually in force during this period, until the necessary legislation passed Parliament in the beginning of 1939. Also, while the Organising Committee had delved deeply into the problem of providing hulls insurance it had not before 1938 made any arrangements for, or even discussed, the problem of providing insurance for cargo, except that actually at sea on the

[20]CAB.16/58, I.B.S.26, Note by Joint Secretaries, 2 March 1939.

outbreak of war.[21] The effects of this neglect, and the sensitivity of the market to changes in the international situation, are well demonstrated by the events of the crisis of September 1938.

In the face of the darkening situation the underwriters of Lloyd's and the Companies decided to withdraw from the war risks insurance market on 15 September 1938.[22] Existing contracts were terminated, and future contracts could only be obtained for individual voyages which had to start within seven days of the conclusion of the contract. Commercial bodies immediately began to lobby the Board of Trade concerning the effects of these provisions on trade, although they were slower than the Treasury, which had made enquiries the previous day.[23] A deputation from the U.K. Chamber of Shipping arrived on 16 September, and pressure for an announcement of state acceptance of liability for the war risks insurance of cargo continued until the end of September.[24] The main argument used was that the terms requiring the vessel to set sail within seven days were impossibly restrictive, particularly to the conclusion of forward engagements. Thus one letter stated that, 'in order to preserve the continuity of shipment of flour to this country, it is necessary to have reasonable war risk rates that can be accepted by the merchant at the time of purchase to cover the period of shipment whether that be prompt or deferred'.[25] Representatives of the timber and coal trades, who called at the Board of Trade on 21 September pointed out that they could not even load their ships during the seven days' period, let alone put to sea.[26]

Eventually, the Board capitulated to this pressure and produced a scheme. This was based on the formation of a pool of Lloyd's and Company underwriters which would accept insurance in respect of cargoes consigned to or from the United Kingdom. The state would reinsure all the liabilities of this pool for 100 per cent in the event of war. Policies would apply to vessels sailing within 30 days of the conclusion of the contracts.[27] This scheme received the approval of

[21] Provision had been made in the 1928 drafts, but no negotiations had taken place with the underwriters.

[22] MT.9/2981, M.12995/38.

[23] *Ibid.* The Treasury enquired through Mr. Twentyman on 14 September.

[24] *Ibid.*

[25] *Ibid.*, letter from Mr. Pillman of Pillman and Phillips, flour importers, 17 September 1938. MT.9/2981 contains ten other dockets composed of representations from commercial interests about the insurance of cargoes and ships against war risks, and the effect of the current situation on trade.

[26] MT.9/3155, M.16991/39. Statements of Mr. Meyer and Mr. Ratcliffe Steel at the meeting.

[27] MT.9/2981, M.13297/38. Draft of Scheme, 1 October 1938.

the Chancellor of the Exchequer on 30 September, and formed the basis of the permanent scheme introduced on 13 April 1939. This was to be superseded by a State Cargo Insurance Office offering policies on similar terms once war had been declared.[28]

It is not clear whether trade actually was hampered by the lack of such a scheme during the Munich crisis. Experts on the Committee stoutly maintained that it was not, though Mr. Lloyd of the Food (Defence Plans) Department of the Board of Trade produced evidence which would seem to be conclusive.[29] Whatever the true facts, there is no doubt that the operators themselves were genuine in their fears, and that this was the crucial factor. It was all very well for the M.M.D. to take the logical point of view in assessing the dangers of the crisis — they did not have to hazard their livelihood on the strength of their opinions. It was their function to provide facilities to enable others to do just this, and although such facilities were devised, and in a remarkably short time, it would surely have been better had they been available from the first.

This was in distinction to the general history of the relations of the Committee with the ship and cargo owners, and with the War Risks Clubs. For the most part relations proceeded in an atmosphere of the most cordial cooperation, and it was only on one or two of the most hotly disputed points that harsh words were ever exchanged, and even then this seems to have been as much a matter of personalities as of policies.[30] In some respects, the Committee may have been aided in this field by the fact that there was no centralised body putting forward a unified policy on behalf of the Clubs. The separate Associations were loosely organised on a regional basis, the largest in each area taking the dominant role. Apart from Associations dealing with specialised branches of the marine insurance market, such as the Association which specialised in insuring coasting vessels, there were three major groupings: the North East, which was represented by the North of England Protecting and Indemnity Association, based on Newcastle; the West Coast, represented by the Liverpool and London War Risks Association, and London and the South East,

[28]MT.59/2290, W.R.I.3124, Minute sheet (signature undecipherable), 9 April 1940.

[29]According to Lloyd, the making of contracts for cereals and oil seeds had come to a complete standstill, and grain and tea shipments were being held up through inability to find insurance. Letter to Griffiths of 29 September 1938, in MT.9/2981, M.12995/38.

[30]See the exchange between Mr. Todd (General Manager of the North of England Protecting and Indemnity Association) and Griffiths, MT.9/2875, M.7265/38, especially Griffiths to Foley of 8 June 1938: 'I think all I can do with Mr. Todd is to give up an afternoon to talk with him, and see who gets tired first.'

represented by the United Kingdom Mutual War Risk Association. Their views on the individual questions frequently varied.

The Committee's good relations with the Clubs may also be attributed to the policy of co-opting active members of the insurance world on to the Committee. There was thus a built-in safeguard against the Committee taking a stance over a particular issue which would lead to conflict with the Clubs. Where the Committee and the Clubs differed it was because a genuine difference of emphasis or attitude was involved, and not because of a simple misunderstanding. The expertise brought to the Committee by the commercial representatives also served to forestall the traditional criticism of state intervention — that the bureaucrats did not understand the problems they were attempting to solve.

As the government's schemes were intended to be operated in partnership with the Clubs, the maintenance of good relations should have been a primary objective of the Committee's policy. The wisdom of the policy of cooperation itself is a matter that requires more careful examination. There can be no doubt that the utilisation of existing commercial organisations, or as in the cargo scheme, of creating organisations in cooperation with commercial bodies, brought with it certain disadvantages. The government had to compromise with the Clubs' point of view over a number of factors, such as the question of King's Enemy Risks. But if the state's freedom of action was constrained in some respects, it derived advantages which more than counter-balanced this in other areas. In the first place, it saved the expense of creating an organisation to administer the schemes from scratch, and at the same time provided itself with a vast amount of practical experience and expertise. This allowed the practicability of the plans to be confirmed before they had to be tested in full operation, and enabled them to be designed so as to avoid their success being jeopardised by administrative problems. The full cooperation of the market brought all its experience into play in avoiding mistaken assumptions and in ensuring that the objectives of the schemes were safeguarded from the effects of sharp practice by the owners.

Such full cooperation was advantageous to the market as well. The commercial bodies concerned were able to become thoroughly familiar with the plans and to assure themselves that their interests were in no danger of being sacrificed to some inflexible bureaucratic ideal. Furthermore, the use of existing machinery reduced the disruptive effect of war, and this, with the prior knowledge of the plans, contributed greatly to achieving the confidence of the market in them. This was perhaps the most important precondition for their success. On the whole, the government seems to have received great benefits from cooperation with commercial bodies, far outweighing the minor inconveniences it had to accept. There was no conceivable way in which it could, alone, have put together an organisation to duplicate the experience of the insurance market, and even had this been achieved, it would have been far more difficult to obtain commercial confidence in it. Without doubt, the policy of cooperation with, and administration through, the commercial bodies already existing, was the correct one to ensure the achievement of the government's objective of reducing to a minimum the disruptive effects of war.

Compared with the problems faced by other branches of government attempting to plan for merchant shipping in this period, the British Shipping War Risks Insurance Organising Committee had a relatively easy time. The greater proportion of this advantage derived from the experience of the problems of war risks insurance of ships and cargoes obtained during the First World War. It cannot be too greatly stressed that, in contrast, say, with the M.M.D.'s investigations concerning the control of shipping, there was never any doubt as to the need for state intervention in the insurance market in wartime. The inability of commercial facilities to meet the requirements of war was accepted by officials and insurance specialists alike, and thus the Organising Committee never had to face the fundamental problem which played so large a part in other investigations — that of deciding whether state intervention was a necessary application of the state's powers, and, if so, of convincing the commercial bodies concerned that this was the case.

Similarly, experience of the First World War provided the Organising Committee with the broad outlines of suitable plans, and highlighted the areas which were most likely to prove troublesome in war. This enabled the Committee to restrict the scope of its investigations to a considerable extent, which simplified the preparation of plans. In short, compared with the other investigations carried out by the Board of Trade in this period, the parameters within which the Committee had to work were far more closely defined, and this simplified its task.

The success of the Organising Committee also reflected the fact that, for once, the instrument to which the task of planning was entrusted was ideally suited to the problem it had to investigate. Unlike certain other problems whose investigation was entrusted to committees in this period, the insurance problem, as presented to the Organising Committee, was sufficiently restricted in scope for it to be capable of complete solution by an expert bureaucratic body. The Organising Committee was never required to decide policy questions — not only was the principle of state intervention accepted, but it was accepted that it would be necessary even before the beginning of war. Thus the Organising Committee was only set to do what its name implied — to organise the details to bring this policy into operation. For this task, the Committee, as constituted with effective representation of commercial interests, was ideally suited, and thus its history demonstrates the great strength of the committee system of government. Complex and involved problems could be investigated and solutions proposed with speed and efficiency, and the commercial representation on the Committee ensured that such solutions would be both practicable and acceptable from the commercial point of view. The Organising Committee only met regularly for five years during this period, 1923 to 1927 and 1938-9, and only held thirteen meetings in all, yet this was sufficient to achieve its purposes twice — once with the 1928 drafts, and once in 1938-9. The efficiency of this system of detailed planning can hardly be in doubt.

This very efficiency occasionally led the Committee to concentrate on relatively unimportant points to the exclusion of the wider objective. The tendency to spend time considering minor adjustments of financial liability may be seen as an example of this, as may the attempts to produce a logically complete scheme of insurance by undertaking liability for the full replacement cost of the vessel. The tendency in an expert bureaucracy was to attempt to approach an ideal solution to the problem, but this was inappropriate in this field. The only crucial point was that a scheme should be introduced, and compared with this, the odd few million pounds of government expenditure, in wartime, was of little importance. In this respect the committee system showed the inherent inflexibility of a civil service trained to attempt to approach perfection, and it was indeed fortunate that the commercial representatives such as Sir Norman Hill were able to bring a countervailing breath of practicality into the Committee's affairs. This was not the least of the contributions they made to the success of the Organising Committee.

If the Organising Committee was in most respects better served than any contemporary investigation into merchant shipping in terms of overall direction and policy making at higher levels of government, there were still areas where guidance was unclear. The question of the desirability of achieving a state monopoly of war risks insurance at sea was one such question. The 1923 Committee had accepted this principle as regards hulls, but not for cargoes, yet this policy conflicted with the general policy of government during the inter-war years of restricting the scope of state intervention so far as was consistent with the achievement of its objects, and with the direction to the Organising Committee, that the schemes should be designed so as to reduce the financial liabilities incurred by the community as a whole. In this case the dispute also coincided with arguments concerning the proper extent of state intervention, and thus of the ultimate objectives which it was intended to achieve by such intervention. Thus, even in its severely restricted area of operations, the Organising Committee could not entirely avoid the fundamental problem which beset all areas of the M.M.D.'s planning — that of being set to determine the details of schemes when the principles which should guide the construction of them had not been clearly or consistently formulated.

Nonetheless, the Organising Committee did manage to produce suitable schemes in time, despite the effect of events during the peculiar hiatus in the early 1930s. Moreover, these schemes proved adequate in the test of war. Although the necessity for the insurance of hulls ceased as soon as the requisition of all deep sea cargo vessels was completed, insurance was still required for coasting vessels, fishing vessels, certain specialised ships not requisitioned, and all cargo which was not owned by the government.

But apart from these quantifiable contributions, the success of the Organising Committee in producing schemes had a much wider effect, both in terms of achieving the confidence of the insurance market, and in proving that it was possible for officials and commercial representatives to work harmoniously together and to produce compromise schemes acceptable to both. The problem of confidence was the crucial factor in the areas investigated by the Organising Committee and, as both the Abyssinian and Munich crises proved, the insurance market was peculiarly susceptible to crises of confidence. In dealing with these crises and in deducing results and conclusions from them, the M.M.D. was greatly aided by the close connections with the market which the commercial representatives on the Organising Committee enabled it to maintain. Furthermore, as a standing committee, the Organising Committee was able to act rapidly in response to changes in the situation, and in the cover or conditions offered by the market's policies. Thus, in conjunction with the expertise it derived from those representatives, and the confidence they inspired in commercial operators, the Committee was able to gain the acceptance of its schemes by the market which was essential if its primary object, to ensure that trade was not hampered by reason of inability to find insurance, was to be attained.

The Committee's success in achieving the confidence of the market and of shipowners was aided by the policy of entering into partnership with commercial bodies in order to obtain efficient administration without great expenditure of effort or money. This partnership did much to reduce the distrust of bureaucratic intervention which was noticeable in other areas of the M.M.D.'s investigations. The policy of utilising existing commercial methods and organisations wherever possible was a major factor in the success of the Organising Committee's plans. By ensuring that the schemes were run on lines familiar to all shipowners and masters, and by administering them through familiar personnel, the impact of the confusion inevitable on the outbreak of war was lessened, and the confidence of the insurees in the viability of the new schemes was increased.

There is thus good reason for attributing much of the eventual success of the Organising Committee to the wisdom of the policy of cooperating wholeheartedly with existing commercial organisations, and this factor, combined with its more restricted area of manoeuvre, goes far to explain the contrast between the achievement of the Organising Committee, and those of the other investigations into the problem of planning for the defence of merchant shipping conducted by the M.M.D.

The Organising Committee was undoubtedly favoured in these respects, but it was concerned with the one crucial factor without which ships would not sail at all or cargoes be brought for them to carry. It was thus the precondition upon which all other plans made by the M.M.D. were based. As such, it is perhaps fortunate that the Committee was so favoured.

6

THE AIR THREAT TO THE EAST COAST
PORTS AND PLANS FOR
THE DIVERSION OF SHIPPING

On 25 November 1932, the First Sea Lord, Frederick L. Field, submitted a memorandum to Sir Maurice Hankey entitled 'The Reception and Distribution of Imports into the United Kingdom in Time of War'.[1] This memorandum pointed out that the dependence of this country on seaborne imports had been increasing for some time, and had now reached the stage where a steady flow was a necessity. Field noted that,

> The Admiralty, in drawing up their plans for defence, are guided to a certain extent by statistical data of the normal flow of commodities in time of peace. But they are impressed by the extent to which changes in dispositions, and in the routeing organisation (which must be prepared and distributed in peacetime if it is to function in time to be of use in the early stages of a war) may be made necessary by various factors such as:
>
> The need for large supplies of war material
> The withdrawal of enemy sources of supply and shipping
> The requisitioning of merchant ships for war purposes
> The possible change of sources of supply in order to secure shorter voyages
> The requirements of charter tonnage
> The possible dislocation of certain ports due to air attack and finally by:
> The possibility of the reinforcement of surface by submarine attack, the cumulative effect of which might be to enforce the temporary abandonment of certain approach routes to this country.

Having summarised the extent of the trade involved, the First Sea Lord noted that information was not available as to the extent to which this trade could be 'diverted, interrupted or expanded, without serious consequences to the life of the country' should enemy attack on the trade itself or on the ports render this necessary.

> The measures that can be adopted for the defence of shipping against attack in Home Waters must therefore depend largely on the capability of certain ports to receive and distribute a volume of supplies greatly above their normal, and it is essential that the

[1]CAB.16/114, D.I.C. Paper No. 2.

Admiralty shall know to what extent and to which ports the traffic can be diverted without causing very serious congestion in other directions. It is also necessary to have a clear understanding as to our dependence or otherwise on coastwise traffic.

Hence,

... the Admiralty consider it necessary as a preliminary to the formulation of their plans for the protection of shipping, both overseas and coastal, that similar schemes for the reception and distribution of seaborne commodities in which the various interests are coordinated, should be in existence and ready for immediate adoption on the outbreak of war. The latter schemes should where necessary allow for the use by ships of ports other than those normally employed in handling the commodities they carry. They should deal with the possibility of the diversion of traffic on a large scale being necessary, and with such matters as the maximum bulk of commodities that can be handled at one time, in order to decide upon the composition and frequency of arrival of convoys at the terminal ports in the United Kingdom to which it may be decided that they can be diverted.

Field therefore suggested the establishment of a sub-committee of the C.I.D. to investigate the problem.

Concern about this problem was by no means new. As early as August 1912 it had been recognised that enemy action in the vicinity of the British Isles, particularly against the Channel and east coast routes, could disrupt Britain's import trade, and possibly force a large scale diversion of ships and cargoes from the ports to which they had originally been routed. In that event some organisation would be necessary to control the process of diversion, to ensure that it was carried out as efficiently as possible, and to keep confusion to a minimum.

However, the previous history of the question did not encourage a diversion of the kind Field had suggested. The 1912 investigation, conducted by a Sub-Committee of the C.I.D., recommended against diversion, except as a last resort, and suggested the establishment of a small permanent committee of representatives of all interested bodies, which became the Diversion of Shipping Committee of 1914.[2] This was purely advisory and possessed no executive powers. A similar omission hindered the efforts of a Board of Trade committee established early in the war under Lord Inchcape to advise on congestion in the docks. These two Committees were amalgamated into the Port and Transit Executive Committee in 1915, which remained responsible for plans to deal with diversion throughout the

[2]CAB.16/114, D.I.C.3, 14 February 1933. Report of Committee, 26 January 1914.

war.[3] Since large scale diversion never proved necessary, the P.T.E.C. was mainly concerned with problems resulting from simple inefficiency, rather than the effects of unusual pressure on certain ports.

However, further investigations into this possibility began in October 1917 with the appointment of the Traffic Diversion Committee. This Committee undertook the first detailed analysis of the problem. It produced two reports, one in January 1918 on diversion from London, and one in March 1918 on diversion from the east coast generally.[4] These reports concluded that Britain's inland transport facilities, at this time principally the railways, were unsuited to the carriage of imports from the west coast ports to London and the east. Complete diversion of food or raw materials normally consigned to the east coast would be impracticable. If trade to the east coast was cut off, that area would have to survive on accumulated stocks unless serious congestion and dislocation of the entire railway network was acceptable. Partial diversion (not exceeding 12,000 tons weekly) could, however, be undertaken without serious dislocation. The Committee concluded that: 'Complete diversion, necessitating the carriage across country to London of over 100,000 tons weekly, is impossible, without displacing existing railway services to an equal extent, and closing the Port of London to export as well as import trade.'[5]

Thus, investigations of the problem before 1920 were doubtful as to the practicability of diversion on a scale capable of achieving a marked reduction of imports through the eastern ports. Their views were neatly summarised in one of the concluding reports of the Port and Transit Executive Committee: 'In the opinion of the Committee the great bulk of the nation's overseas supplies of food and raw material must be landed in ports within the districts in which the supplies are to be used ...'[6]

The problems of port congestion did not disappear with the signing of the peace treaties, and the wartime organisation was retained until, in 1920, the functions of the P.T.E.C. were transferred to the newly created Ministry of Transport.[7]

[3]CAB.3/6, C.I.D.238-A, Interim Report of D.I.C., 21 July 1936, paras. 3-7, Fayle, *Shipping Industry,* 152.

[4]CAB.16/114, D.I.C. 25, 25 January 1935. Reports dated 1 January and 19 March, 1918.

[5]*Ibid.* Report of 19 March 1918.

[6]Report of P.T.E.C. to Cabinet, 16 February 1918. Quoted in Appendix to CAB.4/12, C.I.D. 557-B, 'Diversion of British Shipping in Time of War,' 5 January 1925.

[7]CAB.42(20), 27 July 1920. On post-war problems in the ports, see D. H. Aldcroft, *Studies in British Transport History 1870-1970,* 169-87.

When discussion of such problems resumed after the war, there was a new and extremely serious threat to the security of our ports and of the shipping travelling to them. It is little exaggeration to say that naval planning between the wars was dominated by controversy concerning the effectiveness of the aeroplane. Realisation of the increasing capabilities of air power forced reassessment of the question of diversion of shipping. In the 1920s Britain's most obvious potential enemy was France, then engaged in constructing a large air force and strenuously opposed to measures to limit the use of the new weapons of commerce destruction such as the submarine. In the event of war with France it was clear that her air force would be able to undertake a prolonged assault upon shipping movements and ports along the south and east coasts of Great Britain. This threat prompted demands for the investigation of all aspects of the problem.[8]

The resulting enquiries concluded in 1925. One investigation, conducted by a joint committee of the Admiralty and the Board of Trade, considered the feasibility of diversion from the military and ship-management angles. It specifically considered the diversion of trade arriving from east of Suez only, but was cautiously optimistic that diversion could be administered, fuel found for the merchantmen and escorts, and so on.[9] The other enquiry, a Board of Trade committee established to consider the supply of London in the event of the east coast ports being closed by enemy action, produced less clear-cut conclusions. The terms of reference for this Committee assumed that all ports between London and Southampton, inclusive, had been put out of action by the enemy. However, no indication was given as to the effects of such damage on railways and other inland transport facilities in the area, which, under the circumstances described, would be crucial to the supply of the local population. The Committee concluded that, unless the efficiency of the London docks area and the distributive network it contained remained at least 50 per cent of normal 'it was impossible to imagine how London or the larger London area could continue to be fed under any adaptation of the present system ...'.[10]

[8]CAB.4/8, C.I.D.352-B, Memo. by Secretary of State for Air (F. E. Guest), 30 June 1922. The C.I.D. Sub-Committee on National and Imperial Defence, (the 'Salisbury Committee'), recommended that a special investigation should take place into the diversion of shipping, CAB.24/162, C.P.461(23), Report of Committee, 15 November 1923, para. 16 and conclusion (t).

[9]CAB.4/12, C.I.D.596-B, 'Report of Sub-Committee on Diversion of Shipping from the Mediterranean and Channel' (undated). CAB.4/13, C.I.D.610-B, 7 May 1925, C.O.S. Report on C.I.D. 596-B.

[10]CAB.3/4, C.I.D.132-A, 'Report of Committee on Diversion of British Shipping in Time of War', 18 December 1924, para 27.

In order to supply London from the west, new railheads and distribution centres would be required, and difficulties would be experienced in distributing goods to consumers. London's coal imports could only come by sea. Finally, the Committee pointed out that its report was only introductory and that the hypothesis upon which it was based could hardly serve for any further examination. If the import capacity of the docks was reduced by enemy action, it was unlikely that the distributive networks would remain undamaged. Furthermore, the Committee had been unable to take account of the effect of the diversion of trade from London on the normal operation of those ports to which it was diverted. This question could only be investigated when a statistically useful definition of the extent to which the operation of London would be impaired had become available.

The import of these remarks was to condemn the findings of the investigation as useless to any serious consideration of the problem. Nonetheless, the Chiefs of Staff, concluding the enquiry, assessed the hypothesis on which it had been based, that of a war with France, as so unlikely that, in the circumstances, our measures could be considered well advanced, and that periodic review of existing plans to ensure their current relevance was all that was necessary.[11]

The significant fact concerning the conclusions of these enquiries was that they did not reject diversion on grounds of inability to cope with its organisational problems. The major argument against diversion was that it would cause wholesale congestion in the ports to which shipping was diverted. Some of the reasons for the development of port congestion have been touched on elsewhere. The simple fact of the existence of war brings its own problems to the ports, through the disruption it introduces in the normal operations of the shipping community as a whole. Delay of ships, or their diversion from traditional routes, affects the ports directly — ships fail to arrive at the expected date, leading to a strain on facilities when they eventually turn up. The departure of ships may be delayed, leading to congestion of berths when other ships come in. Certain ports may be closed to commercial shipping to enable their use for military purposes. In wartime the shipping community is subject to additional interference from many sources, the effects of which are not easily predictable. Convoy is particularly disruptive so far as the ports are concerned since the arrival of a convoy brings a large number of ships into a port at one time, thus creating an unusually heavy strain on its facilities. Thus wartime conditions, by their very nature, are likely to produce

[11]CAB.4/13, C.I.D. 610-B, 7 May 1925.

congestion, even before any measures such as the wholesale diversion of a substantial proportion of the nation's trade from the ports to which it is normally directed are considered.

In this respect the introduction of a measure of diversion acts rather like a declaration of war, only on a grander scale:- by introducing an unexpected element of confusion, all existing arrangements are rendered more or less inadequate, and the resulting inability to deal smoothly with ships and cargoes results in delays, leading to the cumulative process known as congestion. Beside such factors the administrative problems posed by diversion appeared comparatively insignificant.

No further consideration was given to such problems until, in 1932, the First Sea Lord revived the enquiry with the memorandum quoted above. The Naval Staff remained confident of the ability of the Royal Navy to deal with the traditional menaces to trade posed by submarines and surface raiders, but the increasing range of aircraft and the deliberations of the Air Raid Precautions Committee, which had suggested that French aircraft might be able to restrict the normal operation of the Port of London by 50 per cent, had stimulated fears of this new and as yet untried weapon of commerce warfare. Faced with the possibility of a considerable interruption to the trade entering this country through the Channel and North Sea ports, the C.I.D. constituted a Sub-Committee under the chairmanship of Lt. Col. Sir Cuthbert Headlam to:-

> review generally the question of the stocks, the reception and distribution of food, raw material and other imports to the United Kingdom in time of war, including particularly the capacity of the ports and the means of transport serving them to handle goods, whether for export or imported, which may have to be diverted from their usual ports in a war exigency.[12]

This concentration on the ports reflected current military opinion as to the effectiveness of aircraft as commerce raiders. Although in most matters regarding this question the Admiralty and Air Ministry were far from agreed, they both accepted that an enemy would be most likely to concentrate his attack on the ports and the approaches to them, where targets would be concentrated and less capable of evasive manoeuvres than when on the high seas. Additionally, any misses might damage port installations.[13]

The Distribution of Imports Committee, as it became known, held

[12]CAB.16/114, D.I.C.1, 14 February 1933.
[13]CAB.3/6, C.I.D.238-A, 21 July 1936, paras. 32-7.

a preliminary meeting on 9 February 1933, at which the Admiralty representative, Captain H.R. Moore, outlined the arguments summarised above. He stated that the Admiralty were now afraid that the Channel ports might have to be closed altogether. In these circumstances, he continued,

> The problem before the Admiralty was that they would have to divert their convoys from the usual ports of destination considerably more than was done in the last war, and they wished to know how much they would be able to divert shipping and how far the various ports would be able to compete with such a diversion.[14]

The task before the Committee was therefore one of assessing the import capacity of British ports, and the degree of flexibility which the system would accommodate, or which could be forced upon it.

The first action the Committee took was to review the previous attempts at this task, despite the Admiralty's dismissal of them as 'more or less unsatisfactory'.[15] This process provided a list of factors to be considered. In generalised terms these were: the number of ports which were within what came to be called the 'danger area', (that is to say the area which might be affected by enemy action); the degree to which they might be affected, and the degree and extent to which the coastwise trade might be affected. The Committee then had to obtain detailed information as to the facilities at the ports, and a detailed analysis of the coastwise trade. Having considered all these factors, they could then estimate the additional burden which could be placed on unaffected ports, and determine whether diversion to the extent apparently necessary would be feasible, and whether the inland transport facilities would be able to distribute the diverted goods.

At this point there was some controversy in the Committee as to the methods by which the enquiry should be conducted. The Admiralty suggested that the ability of the ports outside the danger area to handle traffic in excess of their normal levels should be calculated, so allowing an estimate to be made of the minimum trade which would have to be maintained through ports within the danger area. The Admiralty, being thus provided with statistics of the vital trade which it would have to protect inside the danger area, could then assess the degree of naval strength which it would require to maintain trade at that level. Headlam himself suggested that the Admiralty should quantify the degree to which it could protect trade in the danger area, and thus enable the Committee to arrive at a figure for the amount

[14]CAB.16/113, Minutes of Preliminary Meeting of D.I.C. 9 February 1933.
[15]CAB.16/114, D.I.C.9, 11 May 1933. Paper by Moore.

of trade which would have to be diverted. The Admiralty was unable to do this without some indication of how vital the individual constituents of the trade were.[16]

In actual fact, the Committee finally proceeded by making an estimate of the amount of damage to installations which would be caused by a hypothetical level of attack, and thus of the degree to which the normal operation of the ports would be impeded. From this figure they then estimated the percentage of traffic which would have to be diverted. This form of enquiry was the most hypothetical of the three suggested, and the least likely to result in an accurate conclusion, since its initial premise (the amount of damage to be expected from air attack by a hypothetical power with an air force of hypothetical strength on the ports of southern England) was a subject on which no practical experience existed at that time.

The foundation of the Committee's investigations was formed by estimates made by the Air Ministry which were communicated to it in two memoranda. The first, dated 8 June 1933, defined the area in which attack might be expected to be 'all ports south of a line from the Menai Straits to Robin Hood's Bay (Yorkshire)'.[17] There was no indication as to the severity of attack which might be experienced within this area, nor did the Committee receive any until March 1935, apart from the estimates of the Air Raid Precautions Committee which had been used as a basis for calculations concerning the defence of the civil population. These estimates consisted merely of figures of the weight of bombs which the Air Ministry had calculated might be dropped, they were not estimates of the damage that this tonnage might be expected to cause.[18]

At this stage, however, this was not a serious handicap to the Committee, since most of its time was spent in circularising the ports to obtain details of the existing situation on which it could base its estimates and investigations. During this period the Committee obtained statistics on the coastwise trade; on the reduction in the volume of trade which could be achieved by the banning of inessential imports, and on the increase to be expected from heavier importation of war materials. It also obtained a formidable array of statistics about the ports themselves by sending questionnaires to the Port Authorities.

Figures were collected on the number of ships using the ports; the quantity of imports passing through them, and the capacity of the

---

[16]*Ibid.* CAB.16/113, Minutes of First Meeting of D.I.C., 31 May 1933.

[17]CAB.16/114, D.I.C.10, 8 June 1933.

[18]CAB.16/114, D.I.C.11, 9 June 1933.

inland transport facilities serving the ports to move goods from them. In addition the authorities concerned were asked to estimate the maximum quantities of cargoes which could be moved by existing facilities. The physical process of considering which information to elicit; drafting and sending out the questionnaire to the ports, and receiving and codifying their replies, occupied the Committee until the end of 1934.

On 4 December 1934, the Committee took note of the recommendation of the Chiefs of Staff that future British war plans should be based on the possibility of a war with Germany in five years from 1934.[19] This decision made little difference to the work of the Committee at this stage, since it had not yet begun to consider the scale of enemy attack which would have to be faced.

To provide such a figure was, of course, the responsibility of the service departments, and they rapidly addressed themselves to assessing the implications of the Chiefs of Staff report. The Admiralty assessment reached the Committee on 15 March 1935.[20] They remained confident, noting that Germany possessed few effective naval forces. Therefore, they discounted the possibility of a serious interruption of our trade by German surface warships or submarines. Regarding aircraft, they did not believe that international opinion would allow the use of aircraft in unrestricted attacks on shipping. Therefore, they considered that the primary threat posed by German air power lay in the possibility of its use against London and shipping in or approaching the London docks. Hence they envisaged the necessity for a substantial measure of diversion of the trade normally flowing through London.

The Air Staff agreed that London would be a primary target, although they arrived at this conclusion on somewhat different grounds. They had therefore made a detailed assessment of the damage which they considered the German air force could cause to London. They began by assuming the worst possible case — that of Germany having overrun the Low Countries, and having made London a priority target. Bearing in mind the size the German air force might be expected to attain, they then assessed the weight of bombs it could drop. The Air Staff saw several factors which would tend to reduce the effect of air attack on the London docks area: the comparatively small targets presented by vital installations such as power houses, lock gates etc.; the fact that alternative entrances existed to most basins and that the docks extended for such a great

[19]CAB.16/114, D.I.C.21, 4 December 1934.
[20]CAB.16/114, D.I.C.27, 15 March 1935.

distance along the length of the river, and finally, the fact that some 80 per cent of the cargoes handled by the Port of London, and some 30 per cent of those handled by the docks themselves, were off-loaded into lighters, and therefore needed no dock facilities for their trans-shipment. The Air Staff were also confident that the vulnerability of the dock area could be much reduced by efficient passive defence measures (air raid precautions).

Taking all these factors into account, the Air Staff made the following recommendation: 'it would be reasonable to assess the operating efficiency of the Port of London as some 25 per cent of the normal. It is, however, desired to emphasise that this estimation is necessarily based upon a number of arbitrary factors which preclude close and accurate assessment.' They considered that the most vulnerable facilities would be storage accommodation and the distributive networks — warehouses and transit sheds; railways and roads. Furthermore, they envisaged that the shunting yards might be reduced to 50 per cent of their normal operating levels. As regards the other ports in the danger area, the Air Staff suggested that, although the scale of attack would be less than that on London, the targets would be smaller and more vulnerable, and so a proportionate amount of damage should be expected. The substance of their conclusion was, therefore, that all ports south-east of the line from the Tees to Southampton would, under German air attack, be unable to operate at more than 25 per cent of their normal peacetime efficiency.[21]

These two reports were considered at a meeting of the Committee on 20 March 1935.[22] The Committee accepted the Air Staff's estimates, noting that it was their duty to consider the worst possible situation, and that it might well be that the effects of air attack would be much less drastic than was then envisaged. They also noted that the hallmark of the organisation must be flexibility, and that it was unlikely that it would be necessary to consistently operate 75 per cent diversion throughout the war. The organisation they proposed to set up should aim to achieve the absolute minimum of diversion required by the situation. Having arrived at a measure of the problem they faced, the Committee proposed to deal with it in two sections, and divided itself into two Sub-Committees for that purpose. Sub-Committee A was to:

> . . .consider, in the event of a 75 per cent diversion of traffic from all ports lying between the Tees and Southampton inclusive, the

[21]CAB.16/114, D.I.C.29, March 1935.
[22]CAB.16/113, Minutes of Second Meeting of D.I.C.

facilities available at the remaining ports in the United Kingdom, and to report whether these and the rail and road transport facilities from these ports, were adequate to deal with the additional burden of traffic which would be laid upon them in consequence of the diversion, and further, in the light of any inadequacy coming to light, to make recommendations for improving the facilities.

Sub-Committee B was to:

... make recommendations regarding the constitution of the executive body necessary to control the diversion of shipping and redistribution of imports in the event of war, to make recommendations as regards the powers this body should hold and as to its functioning, and further, to consider what steps should be taken in advance in peacetime to ensure that such a body would be available and ready to operate immediately on the outbreak of hostilities.[23]

These Committees were shortly to be joined by a third, Sub-Committee C, whose field of enquiry was coastwise shipping.

The centre of activity thus shifted to the Sub-Committees. Early in 1936 this process was interrupted, by a request from the C.I.D. Sub-Committee on Food Supply in War for an interim report on the progress of the D.I.C. enquiry. A report was furnished in July 1936.[24] The conclusions of this report were not markedly different from those of the final report of the Committee. Sub-Committee A had completed its investigations, and was cautiously optimistic about the ability of the ports outside the danger area to handle a diversion on the scale anticipated. Sub-Committee B had not yet completed its plans for the organisation. In general conclusion the full Committee noted that it was evident that large scale diversion might be necessitated by air attack, though its extent and duration could not be foreseen. On the arbitrary assumption that such diversion would effect some 75 per cent of the normal east coast trade, the Committee considered that its deliberations had shown such diversion unlikely to prove a major problem, provided an organisation competent to deal with it had been set up before the crisis arose. The scheme should be based as far as possible on the normal organisation of the shipping industry and the ports, and should be controlled by a central executive body in day to day touch with the situation. This body should work on the principle of achieving the least possible diversion — the absolute minimum required by the day to day situation in the docks.

---

[23] *Ibid.*

[24] CAB.3/6, C.I.D.238-A, 21 July 1936.

The final reports did not substantially modify these optimistic conclusions. The first to be completed was that of Sub-Committee B, on 23 Jaunary 1937.[25]

Sub-Committee B's responsibility was the organisation to control the operation of the ports. The Sub-Committee based its investigation on the principle that there should be the minimum interference with the normal direction of the ports consistent with the achievement of its objectives. Therefore it proposed to use existing bodies as far as possible. Its plans envisaged a tripartite structure. In each port the organisation was to consist of a Port Emergency Committee, composed of government representatives, members of the existing port authority, and representatives of the major trades using the port, coastwise shipping, road and rail transport and associated bodies. These Committees were to be convened by the existing port authorities. This part of the organisation had already been discussed with commercial representatives and their approval obtained. Indeed, 45 Committees were already established at the major British ports when this final report was presented.

As the next level of the organisation, the Sub-Committee recommended an Area Organisation, to provide co-ordination between the P.E.C.s and the Headquarters Organisation; to supervise the efficient cooperation of the individual ports in its area, and to ensure the efficiency of the inland transport system serving them. The Area Organisations were to be based on a Government Representative, assisted by an Area Officer (preferably a retired service officer of known organising ability), and an Advisory Committee. Fourteen such organisations were envisaged.

For the Headquarters Organisation, the Sub-Committee suggested that an existing department should take over preparatory work, and should, on the arrival of an emergency, indicate to the government the measures it thought necessary. It considered the Ministry of Transport to be the most suitable body, and recommended no organisation as such, merely suggesting that the Ministry might set up a peacetime advisory committee composed of the members of Sub-Committees A and B. The proposal for a central body in executive control of the situation which had appeared in the Interim Report was dropped.

The Committee also produced a rough draft of the instructions which might be issued to this 'port and transit organisation' as a whole, defining the functions of the individual bodies and their place in the overall scheme. This stressed the need for flexibility and speedy decision. It also suggested that emergency powers might be required to

[25]CAB.3/6, C.I.D.246-A.

enforce decisions vital to the efficient operation of the organisation.

After the completion of this report, the D.I.C. met only once more, its sixth meeting, at which it was decided that any further elaboration of the organisation should be left to the Ministry of Transport, or any body it might set up.[26] The C.I.D., at its 287th Meeting on 28 January 1937, confirmed this decision and the arrangements which the Sub-Committee had recommended.[27]

Naturally, events did not stand still during the deliberations of the Committee, and as early as July 1936, before even the Interim Report was completed, the Air Ministry representative, Wing Commander Andrews, pointed out that the ports outside the danger area were by no means immune to attack thereby, and must expect some degree of damage.[28] It was this factor, the growth in the range of aircraft, which prompted the second report by Sub-Committee A.[29] The Sub-Committee now envisaged all ports between the Tyne and Southampton, inclusive, being subjected to heavy and prolonged attack. In actual fact, the only result of this change was to alter the statistical sections of the report. For the rest the Committee found no reason to alter its optimistic conclusions concerning the possibility of diversion.

So far as the report qualified this optimism, it was over the question of internal distribution. The Admiralty had always expressed serious doubts about the capacity of the inland transport network serving the west coast ports to deal with a diversion on the scale anticipated — their representative expressed this view no less than four times during the first meeting of the main Committee.[30] The statistical examinations of Sub-Committee A however, argued against this alarm. The railway companies expressed confidence in their ability to handle four and a half times as much traffic from the west coast ports as they had actually handled in 1927-9, the period on which the Committee based its calculations. As regards road transport, the Committee felt that any shortage could be made up by the transfer of under-utilised vehicles from the east coast. These assumptions were, of course, based on the existing network of roads and rail lines remaining undamaged. Thus, in the draft report it sent for discussion by the main Committee in May 1936, Sub-Committee A concluded that: 'it is undoubted that in the majority of cases the

[26]CAB.16/113, Minutes, 4 March 1937.

[27]CAB.16/116, D.I.C. 48, 18 February 1937. CAB.2/6, Minutes of 287th Meeting.

[28]CAB.16/113, Minutes of Fifth Meeting of D.I.C., 15 July 1936.

[29]CAB.3/6, C.I.D. 252-A, 24 March 1937.

[30]CAB. 16/113, Minutes of First Meeting, 31 May 1933.

railways alone can deal with the traffic without the assistance of motor lorries'.[31]

At the fifth meeting of the D.I.C., those representatives unhappy at the confidence with which the problems of internal distribution were viewed, made a serious assault on their opponents. Headlam, Hodsoll (Chairman of the Air Raid Precautions Committee), Andrews and the Admiralty representative, Phillips, all pointed out that they were less than satisfied, particularly as to the effect that air attack might have on reducing the efficiency of the roads and railways. They did not carry the day. The final report maintained that: 'In view of the great capacity and flexibility of the existing road and rail systems, difficulties are not expected, even in the contingency of spasmodic aerial bombardment.'[32]

This ignored the fact that in considering the effect of attack on the ports the Committee had accepted the possibility of a serious and prolonged, rather than merely spasmodic, aerial assault. This inconsistency passed unnoticed however, and the C.I.D. accepted the final report of Sub-Committee A on 29 April 1937.[33] It was at this point that the enquiry rested pending its transfer to the Ministry of Transport.

The Ministry assumed responsibility for plans concerning the diversion of shipping early in 1937, in accordance with the C.I.D. decision of 28 January. On 24 May, Sir Cyril Hurcomb wrote to Hankey setting out the organisation which the Ministry proposed to establish to discharge this responsibility.[34] The D.I.C. was to be replaced by two committees: the Port and Transit Advisory Committee, composed of the departmental representatives from the Headlam Committee and representatives of the commercial interests concerned, and the Port and Transit Standing Committee, composed of the departmental members of the Advisory Committee. The third D.I.C. Sub-Committee, on coastwise shipping, was to continue unchanged. This Ministry of Transport organisation was officially established in June 1937, with the following terms of reference:

> To prepare complete schemes for the reception in time of war at ports in the United Kingdom of all shipping (including shipping

[31]CAB.16/116, D.I.C.37, 21 May 1936.
[32]CAB.3/6, C.I.D. 252-A, 24 March 1937, para 9.
[33]CAB.2/6, 293rd Meeting.
[34]CAB.21/730. 'Distribution of Imports in Time of War'.

which may have to be diverted from its usual ports in a war exigency), the distribution of all commodities passing through ports and the evacuation of essential commodities stored at ports within the danger area.[35]

The broad outlines of the organisation proposed by the D.I.C. were retained by the Ministry of Transport. The twin Port and Transit Committees took over the functions of the headquarters organisation in peacetime, although the brunt of the work fell on the Port and Transit Standing Committee: the Advisory Committee only convened three times before the outbreak of war in 1939.

The enquiry did not receive an immediate stimulus from its transfer to the Ministry of Transport. The P.T.S.C. itself only met three times before the Munich crisis galvanised defence planning. In this period, its activities were almost entirely concerned with receiving and collating reports from the Port Emergency Committees. Following the example of the London P.E.C., which submitted a report in 1937,[36] the other Committees were instructed to prepare reports dealing with the powers they felt they would require to discharge their responsibilities, and with any specific factors raised by the local peculiarities of the port or the trade with which it customarily dealt. For example, certain cargoes, basically the bulk cargoes such as grain, required special handling facilities which all ports did not possess. It was clearly essential that the central organisation should have details of such factors in order to avoid diverting ships to ports which did not possess facilities to unload their cargoes.

Replies from the major ports were available by mid-1938, and were used by the Standing Committee in drafting a comprehensive set of instructions for all the P.E.C.s. Two documents were eventually produced, P.T.S.67 and P.T.S.87, the former being a general summary, suitable for publication in the event of an emergency, and the latter containing the detailed information required by the Committees. However, both followed the same general format.[37]

The P.E.C.s would be the representatives through which, in wartime, the Ministry of Transport would exercise its powers concerning Britain's ports. These powers were to be exercised so as to secure the most efficient operation of the ports as conditions varied from day to day, subject to the overriding consideration that the normal commercial operation of the ports should continue so far as

[35]MT.63/22, P.T.S.1, 9 July 1937.

[36]MT.63/25, Minutes of First Meeting of P.T.A.C., 23 September 1937.

[37]MT.63/23, P.T.S.67, July 1939. MT.63/24, P.T.S.87, 14 August 1939.

was consistent with the achievement of this objective. The Committees were to exercise their powers through the normal commercial authorities of the port, and were to give all possible assistance to such bodies in expediting the operations of the ports.

The primary objective of the organisation was to prevent congestion, both of ships using the port, and of goods landed, but not yet distributed. To encourage the removal of goods landed from ships, the P.E.C.s were given powers to impose penalty rents on the owners of goods not removed, and in extreme cases, to physically remove such goods at the owners' expense. These powers would not apply to commodities owned by government departments. In such cases, Committees could only apply to the local representative of the department concerned, or, if that failed, to the Minister of Transport. The necessity for close cooperation between the representatives of importing departments and the Committees was apparent, and was heavily stressed in these instructions. In all there were eleven departments involved, many with more than one local representative. Thus the Food (Defence Plans) Department appointed one Forwarding Officer for each major commodity, each of whom would have to be consulted by the P.E.C. concerning his speciality. The instructions, issued in proof in August 1939, specified that no action which would prejudicially affect the operations of another department was to be taken without that department's prior consent.

The P.E.C.s' second function was to inform the headquarters organisation whether the state of any of the ports required the diversion of shipping from them; and which of the other ports would be best able to accommodate such diverted traffic without causing serious congestion.

The headquarters organisation was to be formed by the two existing Committees, whose membership would be modified to include representatives of the wartime Ministries. The executive powers of the organisation were to be concentrated in the Standing Committee. This Committee would receive information concerning the necessity for diversion from a central clearing house for all relevant information, known as the Shipping (Diversion) Room.[38] Information would reach the Shipping (Diversion) Room from all parties interested in the arrival of a particular vessel and the cargo it carried. Most of this information would be collated by the Shipping Intelligence Section of the Ministry of Shipping, and would consist of details of the ship itself; of its cargo; of the owners of that cargo; of any

[38]MT.63/22, P.T.S.9, 5 December 1938 and P.T.S.21, 16 November 1938; MT.63/24, P.T.S.87, 14 August 1939.

government departments interested in, or owning, any of the cargo, and of any special wishes of either a department, the Admiralty, or the Customs authorities, concerning the destination of the ship.

. The nucleus of the staff of the Shipping (Diversion) Room would be provided by nine Port Officers, who were also to provide the link between the P.E.C.s and the central headquarters. These Officers would be appointed from the nine major commercial ports in the British Isles, and would be intimately acquainted with the situation, both in those major ports and in the smaller ports in their vicinity. In an emergency, the Committees would submit daily situation reports of the condition of their port and of the ships at present in it to the responsible Port Officer. This information, that provided by the Ministry of Shipping, and any information provided by the Admiralty as to whether the approaches to any port were regarded as impassible owing to enemy action, would be passed on to the Standing Committee which would then take the actual decision whether to introduce a measure of diversion. This Committee would normally meet daily, but its Chairman would, if necessary, be able to order diversion himself should it be impossible to call a meeting of the full Committee. The Committee would operate on the principle of keeping diversion to a minimum, since dislocation was inevitable, both in respect of arrangements for receiving the cargo, and in respect of the export cargo the ship would normally have collected after discharge.

Having ordered a diversion, the Standing Committee would also be responsible for directing the vessel to a new port, having regard to the state of the ports as presented in their daily returns. They would then inform the interested parties of the new destination, so that the necessary alterations in arrangements could be made. The Admiralty would inform the ship; the Ministry of Shipping would inform the departments concerned and the owners of the ship and cargo, while the Ministry of Transport would inform the ports. Ports were only to be informed of a change in the expected arrangements, since when no measure of diversion was in effect the normal commercial arrangements would continue without interference from the Port and Transit Organisation.

In broad terms this organisation was that proposed by the D.I.C. The contribution of the Ministry of Transport lay in refining the details of its operation. The main features of this structure were approved by the C.I.D. at its 353rd meeting.[39]

At that meeting, the Minister of Transport announced that a test diversion of shipping was planned for the near future. Although the

[39]CAB.2/8, C.I.D. 353rd Meeting, 20 April 1939.

test was to take place on paper only, the staff of the Shipping (Diversion) Room were to assemble and act as in a real emergency.[40] The exercise lasted a week and was an administrative success, the organisation functioning smoothly at all levels. The Port and Transit Organisation report concluded that

> ... if at the beginning of hostilities it was necessary to restrict the movement of vessels up Channel to London and the other East Coast ports, it would generally be possible to find alternative accommodation in other ports for the probable intake of vessels during the first week without causing undue congestion at those alternative ports ... During the second week the pressure in other ports would become severe (particularly in the case of ports equipped for handling the larger vessels) unless greater use could be made of London; abnormal discharge overside would probably be necessary.[41]

Only minor administrative changes, such as in the form of return from the ports to the Shipping (Diversion) Room, were made as a result of the exercise.

However, the Standing Committee was not unaware of the deficiencies in the structure of the test. Apart from the inevitable restrictions of a paper test, no vital damage to any port had been postulated. Furthermore, the problem of the inland distribution of commodities landed at the ports had been ignored. It had been assumed that inland transport facilities had remained undamaged throughout the duration of the test, unlikely though this was. Since the Shipping (Diversion) Room had been instructed not to send ships to ports which did not possess storage facilities for the type of cargoes they carried, problems of storage accommodation had been ignored. The report on the test pointed out these deficiencies, and it was intended to hold a further and more exhaustive test later in the year, but this test was to be provided by events, with the outbreak of war.[42]

The result of this paper exercise once again raised the general question of the feasibility of diversion of shipping on any scale. The Port and Transit Organisation, although not specifically required to do so by its terms of reference, could hardly develop an organisation to control diversion without formulating a policy on the extent to which it considered diversion to be practicable. The conclusions of the D.I.C. on this question had been, broadly speaking, optimistic. The Port and Transit Organisation was less sanguine.

[40]MT.63/23, P.T.S.68, Memo by Tolerton, 18 April 1939.

[41]MT.63/110, P.T.S.74, 22 June 1939.

[42]MT.63/24, P.T.S.89, 15 June 1939 and P.T.S.92, 10 August 1939.

There were two major reasons why the D.I.C. conclusions were suspect. In the first place, the reports were entirely statistical in content. The Committee had assembled a large amount of information on the facilities available at ports both inside and outside the danger area, and had then assessed the capacity of the west coast ports to handle 75 per cent of the trade of the east coast ports in addition to their own trade. These figures, however favourable, took no account of the effect of handling this extra trade on the vital factor of turn-round times. No port operating under normal commercial conditions could expect to handle twice as much trade as normal without taking longer to deal with the extra trade than if it had proceeded to an empty port. Furthermore, the generalisation of the figures implicitly assumed that there would be a steady flow of imports to the ports throughout the year, and that the transport facilities serving the port would each be able to work on removing the goods which had to be distributed in the manner and at the speed, most convenient to the characteristics of the various types of transport. It was, in fact, as if the whole of one year's imports had been dumped in the port at one time, and the inland transport facilities were free to remove them at their leisure, and in the most efficient manner. Wartime experience was to show, as the experience of the First World War had already shown, that there was a great deal of difference between a transport facility having the statistical capacity to move a certain quantity by weight of unspecified goods in a certain time, and that same transport facility being able to move a comparable weight of commodities when they had taken solid forms which might be unsuited to the equipment the facility possessed, and when they arrived at irregular and frequently inconvenient intervals. Delays would result, leading to congestion of the ports and that cumulative round of delay which had had such a serious effect in the First World War.

Furthermore, as the D.I.C. had realised, some of the statistical data it had produced did not support the contention that diversion on the scale presupposed was feasible. For example, the Committee had collected information on the length of quayage available at the west coast ports and the length of quayage which would be occupied by the diversion of 75 per cent of the trade of the east coast ports. The result of this enquiry was to expose what the Committee itself called a 'serious deficiency' on the west coast of quayage suitable for accommodating diverted ocean-going vessels. In addition, the Committee had taken no account of the demands of the export trade, which it dismissed as being much reduced. It did recognise that diversion would seriously dislocate the normal arrangements of commercial bodies for dealing with imports, but nonetheless remained confident that diversion was feasible.

The Port and Transit Organisation rejected this conclusion: 'any wholesale diversion from East to West will cause widespread dislocation not only to trade but to inland transport facilities'.[43] Its view was admirably summarised by S.S. Wilson in a letter written in March 1939:

> ... any large scale diversion would give rise to endless difficulties. There seems to be considerable misconception about the figure of seventy-five per cent. diversion; the Committee of Imperial Defence made certain assumptions based on that figure, but I cannot trace that the Committee ever said that diversion on such a scale was practicable and further investigation leads us to the definite conclusion that the facilities at the ports themselves and for distribution inland could not cope with that problem. The least we can assume is that all ports will be expected to function to the maximum of their capacity unless prevented by enemy action from so doing and that if one or more ports are wholly or partly out of action for a period the plans should be so elastic that diversion on a limited scale could be put in hand.[44]

Such a marked divergence of opinion was a serious matter and produced two unfortunate results. Apart from the widespread acceptance of an incorrectly optimistic assessment of the feasibility of diversion, there was considerable misunderstanding among other departments of government as to the actual results of the D.I.C. enquiry. It was commonly believed that the optimistic conclusion of the enquiry had resulted in the establishment of the figure of a 75 per cent diversion of trade from the east coast as the policy of the government. At least one Sub-Committee of the C.I.D. had prepared plans on this assumption, (that on the Supply of Coal in Time of War to Public Utility Undertakings), and had to be informed it was working on a mistaken basis.[45]

The general acceptance of the feasibility of diverting 75 per cent of the normal traffic of the east coast ports also led to a campaign by the Admiralty for the introduction of a measure of preventative diversion on the outbreak of war, rather than waiting for diversion to be forced on us by heavy losses.[46] In the discussions in the C.I.D. on this proposal it became clear that the Ministry of Transport advised against introducing any measure of diversion until absolutely necessary.

---

[43]CAB.21/1231, Brief for Minister of Transport by Tolerton, 2 March 1939.

[44]MT.63/38, P.T.96, Letter to Manisty, 28 March 1939.

[45]MT.63/94, P.T.141, Correspondence between Tolerton and Mr. Bevir (C.I.D.), August 1939.

[46]MT.63/22, P.T.S.25, Memo. by Garside, 9 September 1938.

As a result of these disclosures, the Minister was requested to submit a report to the Committee showing the progress of plans for diversion, and the extent to which it would be practicable to operate such a diversion on the outbreak of war.[47] This report was presented to the Committee on 13 April 1939.[48]

The report began by pointing out that the figure of 75 per cent diversion had never been intended to mean that this degree of diversion could be accepted regularly by the west coast ports for the duration of the war. It was merely a useful guide for estimating the capacity of the west coast to handle diversion. Furthermore, it was no longer possible to assume that the west coast would be immune from attack. For this reason the scheme concentrated on elasticity. It had been assumed that ports would stay in full operation until enemy action prevented them from doing so. The organisation was flexible enough to allow diversion of shipping from damaged ports with the utmost rapidity.

The report then outlined the organisation which had been established, and the way in which it was intended to work. It considered the practicability of diversion, and noted the divergence of opinion between its findings and those of the D.I.C. It noted that the D.I.C. had found a shortage of quayage on the west coast for diverted shipping, even without considering the requirements of the service departments, and also quoted a memorandum by the Food (Defence Plans) Department on the probable effects of diversion as far as food was concerned.[49] This investigation had assumed that the ports between the Tyne and Southampton would be completely unusable for food imports, and that no substantial movement of population would occur. It therefore considered the worst possible case, and concluded that the additional transport requirement for this food alone would be 982 million ton-miles per annum. Since the bulk of this would have to be transported from the west coast to the east by rail, and since the current gross ton-mileage of the railway network was 5.5 thousand million ton-miles per annum, this represented an additional burden of approximately one-sixth of the railways' normal capacity. This burden would be further concentrated on the connections radiating from the major west coast ports of Bristol, Manchester, Liverpool and Glasgow. The report expounded at considerable length on the disorganisation of the normal habits of trade which would result from any measure of diversion. Any such disorganisation would

[47]CAB.2/8, Minutes of 349th Meeting, 3 March 1939.

[48]CAB.3/8, C.I.D. 316-A.

[49]The memo. is in MT.63/2, P.T.13, in a letter from Lloyd to Duffield (B.O.T.), 6 July 1937.

produce delays and congestion, which would have a cumulative effect. Such confusion would particularly apply in the early days of a war, when trading conditions would be unsettled anyway.

As regards the Admiralty plans for wholesale diversion on the outbreak of war, Mr. Burgin's report was of the opinion that some confusion would result: 'under modern conditions wholesale diversion at the outset of war could not be undertaken without incurring a grave risk of creating serious congestion at the West Coast ports and on the lines of inland transport and of causing great confusion to trade.' Subsequently, as the situation stabilised itself and the enemy's objectives became known, the report saw no reason why a considerable measure of diversion could not be introduced, if the situation required it. This, however, would have to be confined to food and general cargo. There was no possibility of diverting raw material shipments. Equally, the report hoped that every effort would be made to continue to use London as far as possible, in order to relieve the strain on the inland transport system — to supply London's food requirements from the west coast would demand an additional 375 trains per week.

Thus the conclusions of the report were cautiously optimistic:

> That in view of difficulties and delays, both in discharge and distribution that must inevitably be caused by any substantial measure of diversion of overseas imports to ports other than their normal discharging ports, the general principle for dealing with such imports in time of war should be to make use to the greatest possible extent of normal facilities until prevented from doing so by enemy naval or air action, by congestion at the ports or inland or by supply conditions.[50]

In view of the possibility of immediate heavy air attack on London, the report was prepared to recommend that ocean-going ships bound for London should be diverted to west coast ports on the outset of war, or should be held in safe anchorages, but this process should be discontinued as soon as possible. The C.I.D. approved the report and its recommendations on 20 April 1939, and again at its 363rd meeting. This policy remained in force in September 1939.

---

[50]CAB.3/8, C.I.D.316-A, 13 April 1939, paras. 39 and 45.

7

DIVERTED SHIPPING AND PORT CONGESTION IN THE SECOND WORLD WAR

Diversion of shipping was introduced as a precautionary measure on 1 September 1939, but was eased off during the second week of that month when the expected air attacks did not materialise. Growing fear of air attack prompted its reintroduction in October 1939, and by the end of that month it was estimated that some 25 per cent of the ocean going shipping bound for east coast ports was being diverted. At this time the general disruption caused by war had reduced the total import trade of the United Kingdom to little more than half of normal peacetime levels. Thus in peacetime terms, only one-eighth of the trade of the east coast was being diverted, and the west coast ports were, even so, dealing with a smaller volume of trade than their normal peacetime level.[1] Nonetheless this additional traffic so strained the west coast ports that the Port and Transit Organisation was forced to request a return to normal working. Diversion was criticised from commercial sources as delays occurred, and the situation was deteriorating. As the P.T.O.'s report stated: 'A certain amount of pressure was felt at these ports, but it cannot be maintained that serious congestion occurred. Had diversion on a drastic scale continued, the pressure would have become acute, with the consequent threat of congestion.'[2] It is significant that what was termed 'drastic' diversion in 1939, was substantially less than one third of that which the D.I.C. had regarded as possible. This early experience of diversion was so discouraging that no more attempts to divert ships were made before the fall of France.

In the interim, however, another vital constituent of the import system, the railway network, began to show signs that pre-war estimates of its capacity had been optimistic. One of the major problems of diversion was expected to be the east coast coal trade between Northumberland and London, and the railways had been earmarked to supply London should the seaborne trade be interrupted. The early months of the war saw a spontaneous diversion of this coal traffic to the railways. A general shortage of suitable coasters, caused by requisition and the necessity to supply France with coal contributed to this process. But the major reason was that the

[1] Behrens, 80-81.

[2] MT.63/24, P.T.S. 99, 22 November 1939.

government, while artificially preventing a rise in railway freight rates, had allowed coaster rates to reflect market conditions. The increased cost of war risks insurance and the lowering of coaster earning power due to wartime delays, rapidly made it cheaper to send coal by the railways.

Nonetheless this traffic was well within the railways' estimates of their capacity. But in December 1939 and January 1940, unexpected severe weather combined with this increased traffic to bring coal shipments throughout the country to a standstill. Despite requisitioning of both coal and trains, the crisis persisted through February. Much of the blame for the crisis must be placed on the unexpectedly harsh winter, but the railways' performance did not encourage confidence. As the official historian of inland transport put it: 'if severe weather could disorganise the railways and threaten the war effort, what would happen when air raids started?'[3]

Serious air raids did not occur before September 1940. Although doubts about the efficiency of the ports and inland transport systems had been stimulated by the events described, the breathing space thus granted to British planners had not been well spent. An investigation into the ability of the railways to clear goods from the west coast ports had been undertaken, but its results were generally regarded as unsatisfactory. Matters were little further advanced than in March 1940, when the Minister of Transport had suggested that it was

> urgently necessary to look into the question of western diversion, since it appeared that, after six months of war, no practical steps had been taken to prepare for it, and we now found ourselves in the position that we might, at possibly only a few days' notice, be faced with the urgent need to implement it. Chaos would almost certainly result. A large mass of shipping would be rendered immovable and, owing to the absence of suitable transport, there would occur an extreme shortage of essential commodities.[4]

The first heavy air attack on the London docks occurred on 7 September 1940. On that night and the two following nights, 21,000 t.g. of shipping were lost, and another 48,000 damaged. On 10 September it was decided that no ship larger than 6,500 t.g. should enter the Humber or ports to the north, and that no ship larger than a coaster should proceed to ports south of the Humber.[5] Diversion had been introduced on the grand scale. Port operations began to feel the effects within a month. By October complaints were flooding into the

[3]C.I. Savage, *Inland Transport,* (London, 1957), 139.

[4]MT.63/137, P.T.199/2. Minutes of Meeting of P.T.O., 6 March 1940.

[5]Behrens, 126.

Ministry of Transport from all interested parties. There are few statistics available concerning the delays and congestion produced by diversion. There does not seem to have been time to collect them. Evidence as to the seriousness of the crisis can only be obtained from the reaction it produced at the time, and from the assessment of the official historian that, in the winter of 1940-1 'transport shortage came to be a limiting factor in the nation's war effort'.[6] Admittedly, congestion was never serious enough to cause the long queues of ships waiting for berths which had occurred in the First World War, but it has been estimated that, during the period of confusion, the United Kingdom was losing imports at a rate of at least 10 per cent of the total imports for 1941.[7]

Two points must be borne in mind when considering the performance of the ports and transport facilities during this period. The first of these concerns the total volume of imports arriving in the ships. Even at the height of the crisis the ports on the west coast were faced with a volume of trade that was, overall, only very marginally higher than that with which they had dealt successfully in boom years in peacetime. Furthermore, the trade of Liverpool during the six months October 1940 — March 1941 was in fact lower than that it had dealt with during the same period of the previous winter, while that of Bristol and South Wales could not be considered abnormal. Only in the case of the Clyde did total imports increase substantially during the period.[8] The problem facing the authorities was not one of trying to force a quart into a pint pot, nor was the sheer volume of goods being landed beyond the capacity of the port facilities themselves. The problem was of more complicated origin.

The second point is, that despite the breadth of its effects, the real crisis of import capacity in this period was extremely localised. It derived from the inability of the inland transport network to clear goods from the ports after they had been unloaded from the ships. As Behrens says, 'even so, the ship could usually 'beat the quay;' it was easier to get the cargoes out than to deal with them afterwards ...' This factor was obvious at the time. The Minister of Transport wrote on 31 October 1940:

> I am receiving constant complaints as to delays in the discharge
> of shipping at the ports, and I am very concerned at the position.
> Recent summaries of reports by the Port and Transit Organisa-
> tion on the state of the ports tend to show that these delays are

[6] Savage, 191.

[7] Behrens, 128, and Appendix XIX, 146. See above, pp. 38-9.

[8] Savage, 209.

mainly due to shortage of wagons, not only of bolster wagons, of which there appears a particular shortage for imports of iron and steel, but also of open wagons and covered vans.

One thing is clear. Ships in ports are progressively taking longer and longer to turn round, with the result that our national importing capacity is being seriously diminished. I have no doubt that there are many reasons contributing to these delays but, as a port is dependent for clearance mainly on the railways, I look first in that direction to see if and where movement can be accelerated.

The recurring — and increasing — note in all the summaries to which I have referred is shortage of rolling stock. The position has been aggravated by slow discharge of wagons on the part of consignees, and this state of affairs has been brought specially to the notice of the Minister of Supply. Nevertheless, when all allowances have been made, it is undeniable that there remains a heavy shortage of wagons of all kinds ... and that the discharge of vessels is being held up thereby at a time when circumstances demand that shipping should receive the quickest possible dispatch ... it is of vital importance to the war effort that nothing should be left undone which is likely to lead to an improvement.[9]

This area alone excepted, the organisation whose task it was to deal with the diversion of shipping functioned with a high degree of efficiency. The Shipping (Diversion) Room never failed to organise the diversion of a ship when circumstances dictated it. Similarly, the actual organisation for the allocation of ships to berths in the ports never broke down, although it was rendered less effective by the failure to clear the quays, leading to delays in discharge and the inability to clear berths which resulted. Up to the point at which the cargo landed on the quayside the organisation cannot be held responsible for any delays in the system. At that point however, the problems began. Wagons to move the cargo were frequently unavailable, port storage space became full. The only solution was to pile cargo on the quays, where it impeded the discharge of newly arrived ships.

At the time it did not prove difficult to isolate the causes of this congestion. There was no effective machinery for the coordination of demands for transport, and departments wishing to move goods had to compete fiercely with each other for the capacity available. In such circumstances the P.E.C.s, which could only issue advice to persons wishing to secure transport, but could do nothing to actually obtain transport, became almost superfluous. They could not even enforce

9*Ibid.*, 207-8.

clearance of port storage accommodation and the quays, since their power to levy penalty rents on consignees who refused, or were unable, to arrange transport, did not extend to government departments, which were, by now, in control of most cargoes reaching the west coast.[10] Above all there was the inability of the railways to deal with the volume of trade requiring shipment. The railways were crucial to the problem of transporting diverted goods to the east coast, but, in contrast to their pre-war estimates, they did not have the capacity to deal with the strain of diversion. It was not only a shortage of wagons. There were also the delays produced by air raids and wartime restrictions on train speeds. Essentially however, the crisis point in the railway network was in the inland junctions and marshalling yards between the ports and the destinations of the cargoes. Diverted goods had to be moved to their original destinations in a generally easterly direction, whereas the main lines were predominantly disposed in a north to south direction, radiating from London. This placed an unusual strain on junctions and marshalling yards. All imports for the English east coast landed on the Clyde had to pass through Carlisle, all goods landed in South Wales had to pass through the Severn tunnel, all goods landed in Liverpool had to pass through Crewe. Further inland, junctions such as Birmingham became congested with traffic moving in north or south-easterly directions. Trains could not get through. Wagons could not be sorted into trains, nor could empty wagons be sent back to the ports. Thus an apparent shortage of wagons developed because the lines and junctions did not possess the capacity to deal with the volume and direction of traffic forced on them by diversion.[11]

The extent of this disruption makes it difficult to accept that the possibility of congestion could have been overlooked before the war. The explanation of this oversight is to be found in the history of plans for the control of inland transport. Although the import crisis of the winter of 1940-1 was primarily caused by the inability of the railways to clear commodities landed at the ports, this failure cannot be explained solely by an examination of the railway preparations. The railways were only part of a network of services forming Britain's inland distribution system; their failure must be examined in the light of the performance of inland transport as a whole. It is now clear that the difficulties experienced with inland transport in the early years of war arose from a failure of pre-war planning at two levels — both on the detailed level of plans for the utilisation of the resources of

[10]Behrens, 81.

[11]Savage, 209-10.

individual transport facilities, and in terms of the organisations provided for the coordination of all facilities into a coherent framework of activity. (In effect from a failure to appreciate that inland distribution could only function effectively if it was regarded as a whole.)

Arrangements for the inland distribution of commodities landed at the ports became an area of fierce contention in the late 1930s. Hitherto, the tendency had been to regard such arrangements as the province of the organisation controlling the transport which would be involved. Thus the D.I.C. had envisaged an Area Organisation to control inland distribution as an essential part of the structure for administering diversion. The terms of reference of the P.T.O. included the phrase: 'To prepare complete schemes for ... the distribution of all commodities passing through the ports.'[12] This, however, proved to be in complete contradiction to the expectations of the departments controlling the commodities, who insisted that the internal distribution of commodities should be in the hands of the organisation best informed about the country's requirements for the commodity concerned, that is, the department specifically concerned with it.

The first outbreak of this dispute had occurred while the D.I.C. was still in existence in 1937, and a running controversy developed which continued until the circumstances of 1940-1 forced a resolution. The matter at issue was quite precise. The supply departments wished to arrange or control the provision of inland transport for the commodities with which they were concerned. The transport authorities, on the other hand, considered that the allocation of transport to particular commodities could only be made with regard to the national situation of inland transport. Only the transport authorities themselves would have the necessary information concerning the pressure on all aspects of the distribution system to be able to make such allocations in accordance with the best interests of the wartime economy as a whole.

Initially the transport authorities were triumphant. As the Minister of Transport, Mr. Hore Belisha put it, the Minister responsible for securing the transport should decide by what means the traffic was to be carried, and could 'with his ample powers under the Defence Regulations, arrange for the most appropriate form of transport and could allocate traffic to rail, road or canal'.[13] On 23 March 1937, in

[12]Above, p. 146 n. 35.

[13]CAB.3/6, C.I.D. 251-A, 'Report on Control of Rail and Road Transport Services in War', 12 March 1937.

response to this report, the C.I.D. concluded that 'in time of war or emergency the responsibility for the provision, allotment and coordination of transportation services should rest with the Minister of Transport'.[14]

By April of the following year it had become apparent that the Food (Defence Plans) Department at least, had not taken this policy to its heart, and the Chairman of the P.T.O. was forced to point out: 'It is recognised that the Minister of Transport will be the controlling and coordinating authority for all rail and road transport and that the Food Controller will look to the Minister of Transport to provide the necessary internal transport facilities in time of war.'[15] The F.(D.P.)D., however, proceeded undeterred, and at a meeting in August 1938 at which it, the P.T.O. and the Ministry of Transport were all represented, obtained vehicles for its exclusive use, none of which could be requisitioned by the Ministry of Transport without the approval of the food authorities.[16]

Hard on the heels of this decision, the D.I.C.'s proposals for an Area Organisation to coordinate the use of inland transport were discarded. Coordination was to be arranged within existing structures. A person wishing to arrange transport by rail, canal or coasting shipping would have to approach the appropriate representative on the P.E.C. If road transport was required, the Regional Transport Commissioner's staff would be responsible.[17]

Criticism of these proposals developed rapidly. The Manchester P.E.C. had already reported itself 'gravely handicapped by the lack of definition as to the organisation which is intended to control the forwarding of goods from the port, and more particularly their inland distribution and storage'.[18] Mr. Hynard suggested that the intention of the F.(D.P.)D. to make its own plans for the inland distribution of its commodities was the strongest argument for the establishment of an Area Organisation since the other supply departments would take similar measures, and their individual distribution agencies would be competing against each other for the use of inland transport.[19]

[14]CAB.2/6, Minutes of 291st Meeting, 23 March 1937.

[15]MT.63/2, P.T.13, Letter from A.T.V. Robinson to Lloyd, 27 April 1938.

[16]Ibid., Meeting of 15 August 1938.

[17]MT.63/22, P.T.S.24, Report of Liverpool P.E.C., 6 December 1938.

[18]Ibid., P.T.S.31, Report of Manchester P.E.C., 15 July 1938.

[19]MT.50/112, T.03188, Letter of 14 November 1938 to Robinson.

These complaints were ignored until, in June 1939, the First Lord of the Admiralty interested himself in the situation.[20] As a result, a number of papers were devoted to the question, of which the most important were contributed by two members of the P.T.S.C., Mr. Wilson and Mr. Hynard. Hynard's paper was essentially an expansion of the views noted above — that, with control of the provision of inland transport in the hands of the individual supply departments, coordination would be minimal and every department would be competing against the others to obtain transport. He argued that 'a much larger scale of diversion could be contemplated if planning could be continued on the basis that more executive powers and responsibilities would, if need be in war, be vested in a small body independent of existing Government departments.' This body would have full powers over every aspect of the import and distribution of commodities for Great Britain, and would come into operation when existing plans broke down. Hynard suggested that a separate Ministry might be established, and that preparations should be made at once.[21]

The most important aspect of these proposals was their insistence that the body concerned should have executive control over the provision of inland transport. This was a complete departure from the existing proposals, which were based on the retention of executive powers by the individual departments, which would implement policy decided by an advisory committee upon which they would be represented. Hynard was not prepared to trust in the strength of such arrangements if the crisis became as serious as he expected. He felt that the transport authority should have the power to enforce its decisions even where they conflicted with the needs of individual departments.

Wilson was also worried about the inadequacies of the current arrangements, and also saw a solution in the establishment of a body with executive control over all aspects of inland distribution. He noted that the existing policy was to allow departments owning commodities to compete for inland transport on the open market until transport facilities came under heavy pressure, when the state would intervene. He suggested that diversion would almost certainly prove necessary and that, in those circumstances, it could be accepted that pressure on the transport facilities of the west coast would be 'enormous, and on occasions impossible, with an overwhelming demand for rail facilities'. In this event, the transport representatives on the P.E.C.s were to meet to consider what advice to give to consignees regarding

[20]MT.63/59, P.T.125, Letter Stanhope to Euan Wallace, (Minister of Transport), 19 June 1939.

[21]MT.50/105, T.01904, Memo. of 17 July 1939.

transport. The crucial point was that the transport representatives could only give advice. They could neither arrange transport for consignees, nor could they prevent the use of transport in an inefficient manner or on inessential services. Wilson suggested that the only practicable solution to this problem — given the uncooperative attitude of the supply departments — was for the P.T.O. to appoint officers from headquarters to exercise control at ports where the situation was critical. These officers would be able to determine the allocation of commodities to the individual forms of transport available, and to ensure that all facilities were used in the most efficient manner.[22]

As a result of this pressure the P.T.S.C. reconsidered the question at its seventeenth meeting in July 1939.[23] Representatives of the F.(D.P.)D., and the Raw Materials and Petroleum Departments again argued that the distribution of their commodities could be efficiently achieved only if it remained under their own control and was determined by reference to the conditions in the industry concerned. The meeting decided to set up a headquarters organisation similar to those already in existence for particular transport facilities to decide questions of the provision of transport generally, and of priority to particular traffics, in the event of congestion in particular areas. The intention was to arrange rapid transfer of facilities to the congested area. It was subsequently decided in the P.T.O. that this organisation might be based on the Railway Communications Committee, or on one of its sub-committees, with the addition of representatives of the ports, roads, canals and coasting shipping. The functions of this body were seen as being 'to coordinate the supply and allocation of transport in the country as a whole — the object being to have a machine capable of sending additional transport to places or districts where the local organisations were unable to provide the facilities required'.[24]

It is not clear whether this committee was ever established. In wartime its functions seem to have been subsumed into the Transport Priority Sub-Committee of the Cabinet Priority Organisation. In any case, it is clear that its terms of reference restricted its effective ability to combat congestion, which could not automatically be solved by the provision of extra transport facilities, even if they were available

[22]MT.63/59, P.T.125, Memo. of 22 July 1939.

[23]MT.63/20, P.T.36/2, 25 July 1939.

[24]MT.63/59, P.T.125, Tolerton to Hill, 9 August 1939.

(which they were not in 1940-41).[25] On the outbreak of war the policy for inland transport still envisaged restricting the activities of the P.T.O. to the ports. Only the P.E.C.s would be concerned with the coordination of demands on inland transport through their appropriate representatives.

In war, the Ministry of Transport would assume control of all main railway lines, and would operate them through a Railway Executive Committee composed of the commercial General Managers. Below this Committee would be divisional and local organisations. Coordination among interested departments would be achieved at the appropriate level, or, failing this, by the Railway Communications Committee, a headquarters organisation on which all interested parties would be represented. As regards road transport the basic unit would be regional, under a Regional Transport Commissioner. Each region would be subdivided into districts, under District Transport Officers, and sub-districts, under Sub-District Managers. Goods vehicles would be organised into groups, the Group Organisers being appointed from the operators. The Sub-District Managers would coordinate the groups into the main organisation. Coasting shipping would be controlled by the Board of Trade, through the Coasting Shipping Area War Control Committees.

Coordination of the use of resources within the separate facilities would be arranged by these controlling structures. Coordination between the railways, canals and coasting shipping was to be achieved through their representatives on the P.E.C.s. The roads, however, remained outside this system. It must be emphasised that these coordination arrangements were only to operate if difficulties arose. Normally the owners or consignees of commodities requiring transport were expected to compete for transport on the open market as in peacetime and without higher coordination, despite the fact that many of them would be government departments trying to move essential commodities. [26]

Thus, although the overall control of the transport systems remained in the hands of the Ministry of Transport, in normal circumstances the Ministry would have little to do with the employment of its physical assets. As a result the Ministry had made little attempt to devise a coherent policy for the employment of inland

[25] For the origins of the Cabinet structure, based on a Ministerial Priority Committee, see CAB.4/16, C.I.D.806-B, 'Report of Priority Organisation Sub-Committee,' 17 June 1927, and CAB.2/5, Minutes of C.I.D. Meeting 229, 14 July 1927.

[26] MT.63/59, P.T.125, Wallace to Stanhope, 29 June 1939. MT.63/3, P.T.S.87, 14 August 1939. Also MT.50/77, GEN.Z1/75/1, 1939.

transport as a whole. This reflected the unsettled position concerning the responsibility for the arrangement of transport described earlier When the Ministry set up its divisional organisations to control the railways, roads, and canals, the allocation of commodities to transport was still the responsibility of the P.T.O., which could be relied upon to provide the overall view required. But the fragmentation of this responsibility among the individual supply departments prevented the P.T.O. from fulfilling this role. The individual transport divisions of the Ministry of Transport were not competent to take an overview. They had been designed solely to ensure that the Ministry maintained control over the distribution and upkeep of existing transport facilities. They would, so to say, be purveyors of transport, and would leave others to decide the use to which the facilities so provided should be put.

Alongside these structural factors, the Ministry of Transport's attitude was conditioned by misapprehension as to the adequacy of inland transport to meet the demands which would be made upon it in war. There was no centralised statistical investigation into the capacity of inland transport as a whole in the 1930s.[27] There was no individual department of government concerned with such problems and there were no statisticians in the bureaucracy capable of undertaking the necessary calculations. The closest approach to a comprehensive survey of the potential of inland transport was made during the D.I.C. investigations, but, in so far as the Committee considered statistical evidence, the figures were provided by commercial sources.

Thus the only statistical investigations of the capacity of inland transport made before the war were produced by those commercial associations normally involved in the collection of transport statistics. In effect this restricted such investigations to the railways. The road haulage industry possessed no facilities for monitoring the activities of the individual firms. Furthermore, one of the more obvious effects of war on inland transport would be the need to impose petrol rationing, which would seriously restrict the activities of the road haulage industry. Consequently there was a general intention to confine the use of road carriage to short haul traffic in wartime, and to use the railways for long distance journeys.[28] Hence the railways would have to bear the brunt of diversion. Fortuitously the major railway

[27] Such bureaucratic investigations as took place were conducted by individual departments independently of each other. Thus the F.(D.P.)D. investigated the capacity of the railways to move food diverted to the west coast ports, while the Mines Department, Board of Trade, considered the problem of moving coal by rail from Northumberland and Durham to London.

[28] MT.63/59, P.T.125, Wallace to Stanhope, 29 June 1939.

companies kept fairly extensive statistics of the traffic they handled. The D.I.C. had approached them for an estimate of the railways' capacity to deal with the strain of diversion of shipping. The railway companies then produced the estimate that their facilities could distribute four and a half times as much traffic as normal from the ports outside the danger area. The optimistic view of the capacity of the railway network as a whole which this calculation implied remained the official attitude of the railway companies until the events of war rendered it untenable.[29]

Despite the experience of the First World War, in which the railways had been very hard pressed indeed, and despite the conclusions of previous investigations into the problem, these estimates were accepted by the D.I.C., and later by the Ministry of Transport. Clearly, neither body was in a position to refute the figures produced by the railway companies. Neither possessed statisticians capable of the necessary calculations. In the absence of any independent statistical monitoring by the government, the only figures on which to base such calculations were those provided by the railway companies themselves, which were unlikely to contradict their authors' findings. The Ministry of Transport, in the report to the C.I.D. of March 1939, did express doubts concerning the accuracy of commercial estimates of railway capacity, but the companies remained confident. So confident were they that they refused to consider the provision of additional facilities at vital points. In the face of such confidence, the Ministry did nothing. It seems to have been uncertain of the strength of its arguments, which were admittedly based more on a commonsense approach in the light of previous experience, than on firm statistical ground. The Ministry's circumspection was doubly unfortunate in that, in a general sense, it had identified those areas which were to prove critical in producing congestion in 1940-41. The Minister noted,

> Exact quantification of the additional traffic which the railways would be called upon to handle at any given time is impracticable, but whatever the proportion, expressed in terms of total capacity, it would in fact be concentrated in overwhelming volume on the connections radiating from Plymouth, Bristol, the South Wales ports, Liverpool, Manchester and Glasgow. Doubts must be entertained of the practicability of adding a heavy burden of this character to the railways' capacity ...[30]

[29] See Sir Herbert Walker in CAB.3/6, C.I.D.251-A, 12 March 1937, para.5: 'the resources and reserves of railway carrying capacity in times of emergency would be found to be "immense" and certainly equal to any strain thrown upon them'.

[30] CAB.3/8, C.I.D.316-A, 13 April 1939, para. 30.

Although some works to improve the railways' capacity were put in hand after the outbreak of war, it was too late for much to be achieved. Of one million pounds allocated for such use only £178,000 had been spent by June 1940, and most of this was employed in relieving pressure on London rather than in preparing for the strain of diversion.[31]

And yet, the general level of confidence with which the capacity of the railway network was regarded was hopelessly misplaced. The most important factor in this overconfidence was the optimism of the railway companies' estimates of capacity. The railways' calculations proceeded from the initial assumption that their facilities were under-utilised in peacetime. This assumption was based on the fact that their total annual traffic in the 1930s was less than it had been in the years before the First World War. There was undoubtedly some truth in the view that there was a surplus of capacity before 1939. But the companies underestimated the effects of war, and in particular of the intention to confine road haulage to short distance trips. Road haulage was very important indeed in the distribution of goods from the ports. In the case of Liverpool, for example, under 12 per cent of imports were distributed by rail in the 1930s.[32] Even a small diversion from road transport would place a disproportionate load onto the railways. The railways also failed to foresee that, at a time when increasing demands would be made upon them, their normal working techniques would be disrupted by wartime conditions. Round the clock working of marshalling yards was severely hampered by air raid precautions involving restrictions on lighting at night, and the arrival of air raids naturally imposed a complete blackout and the cessation of all work. The failure to take account of such factors is all the more remarkable since the introduction of diversion presupposed air raids, and the Air Staff had suggested that raids might restrict the efficiency of shunting yards by as much as 50 per cent.[33]

Furthermore, however large the pre-war surplus of capacity actually was, it did not follow that it existed in those areas which would come under the greatest strain in wartime. Indeed diversion implied that the strain would fall on lines and junctions which had been of lesser importance in peace, and on which surplus capacity was less likely to exist. Britain's long distance railway network was primarily designed to distribute goods from London and the south east. By the time they reached the western ports the lines could not carry the same volume of traffic as they could when they left London.

[31] Savage, 107.

[32] Behrens, 13 n.2.

[33] CAB.16/114, D.I.C. 29, March 1935.

Nor was the system well equipped to distribute goods in the broadly west to east direction which was essential if the industrial areas east of the Pennines were to be supplied from ports such as Bristol, Liverpool and the Clyde. Under diversion, the normal flow of traffic across the railway network would have to be completely realigned. Unprecedented strain would be thrown on little-used cross country routes, and on the major junctions and marshalling yards near the west coast.

There is no doubt that some estimates of the effect of this realignment could have been made, had some indication of the quantities and types of goods to be moved under diversion, and their ultimate destinations, been available. Here, however, the railways were in the dark. The supply departments, whose responsibility it was to provide this sort of forecast, completely failed to make any such estimates available to any of the bodies concerned with transport problems at this time. As a result the railways had no means of knowing the types of wagons which would be needed to transport commodities diverted to the west coast. They had no means of estimating how many trains would be needed each day to clear each port, nor how far each train would have to travel before it became free for some other service. The estimates they did produce were based on extrapolations from the type of trade carried from the various ports in peace, but this was a very inexact approach.

The railway companies' estimates were therefore based on very insecure ground, and perhaps their greatest omission lies in not making this insecurity obvious to officials who were by no means expert in the field of transport statistics. Had evidence of the erroneous nature of the railway companies' conclusions been available earlier, it is possible that something might have been done to improve the situation. The air of infallibility with which these conclusions were imbued restricted criticism and prevented an accurate assessment of their value.

But at least some effort had been made with the railways. The position regarding road transport was far less advanced. Information from the licensing authorities revealed that there were some 465,000 goods vehicles in Great Britain operated by some 225,000 separate firms. Beyond this no information at all existed concerning the normal employment of the individual vehicles, or the types of services they provided. There was no centralised organisation for road haulage as a whole.[34] It was of course impossible to make any estimate of the capacity of the road haulage industry in wartime, and the Ministry of Transport confined its activities to devising an effective rationing

[34] Savage, 54 and 77.

scheme for petrol, and to producing an organisation for the general control of road transport by districts, which has been described above.

Coasting shipping was investigated in a far more professional manner, and a detailed organisation was devised for controlling the use of the ships. This involved a number of regional organisations known as the Coasting Shipping Area War Control Committees. In particular attention was directed to providing coasters to relieve the strain of diversion on the western ports, by the overside discharge of ocean-going ships in a number of emergency ports without shore facilities.[35] However, there was no statistical investigation of the capacity of coasting shipping to discharge these tasks, except in so far as the Board of Trade considered the problem in the light of its investigations into shipping capacity as a whole. Such investigation had little application to the problems of inland transport, but gave no indication of a scarcity of coasters, and so contributed to the general air of confidence.

Thus, in so far as the capacity of inland transport systems had been considered in the 1930s, the results were broadly optimistic. This confidence was reflected in the failure to produce a coherent overall strategy for the use of inland transport in wartime. Since no shortage of transport was anticipated, and since the accepted policy was to leave the allocation of transport to be decided by market factors, it was felt that a general strategy was unnecessary. The only general principle which the Ministry of Transport laid down before the war was that, to save petrol, there should be a general attempt to restrict the use of road transport to short hauls, and to send goods on long journeys by the railways.[36] Beyond this, no general guidance was issued concerning the objectives which inland transport was expected to achieve.

Similarly, the expectation of a surplus and the intention to leave the allocation of transport to market forces, reduced the need for any effective central organisation to coordinate the use of the transport facilities. It was assumed that normal commercial practice would allocate transport in the most efficient manner, and that the various advisory committees would prove adequate in the event of any local

[35] MT.63/9, P.T.25, Part I, 'Coasting Shipping War Control Organisation', Explanatory Memo., December 1938.

[36] There were other reasons for the emphasis on the railways. Under the terms of its agreement with the railway companies concerning the use of their facilities in wartime, the Treasury was to receive a share of the profits realised by the railway system, a factor which seems to have had some effect in determining transport policy. (Hammond, 137). It is clear that the determination of transport policy on such grounds can only have prejudiced the achievement of a satisfactory relationship between capacity and demand.

shortages which might arise. Thus not only did Britain enter the war without a coherent overall strategy for the employment of inland transport, but, as the official historian says,

> the Government's whole defence policy, as far as inland transport was concerned, had been built up round the acceptance of a belief which had no firm basis in reality and which previous wartime experience had flatly contradicted, namely that there would be no serious scarcity of transport in a future war.'[37]

As a result no structures had been devised to deal with a situation in which an overall scarcity of inland transport had developed. The advisory committee system proved adequate for dealing with local shortages by arranging the diversion of a surplus of transport from a more fortunate area, as was necessary on various occasions in the first year of war. But in a situation where transport as a whole was scarce, and where transport could only be provided for one essential commodity at the expense of refusing it to an equally essential commodity, a system based on the allocation of transport by authorities which possessed a vested interest in its use was bound to prove ineffective. The P.E.C.s' representatives could not enforce their recommendations upon departments whose immediate interests conflicted with them.[38] In cases of dispute, the only recourse beyond the P.E.C. system was the Ministerial coordination and priority machinery, which was neither the correct field for the adjudication of such detailed issues, nor swift enough in its operations to prevent delays occurring.

Over-optimistic assessments of the capacity of inland transport had allowed this situation to develop in the 1930s. An atmosphere of complacency characterised planning in this area, and vitiated efforts to create an adequate structure for controlling the allocation of transport in the light of the national situation and in the best interests of the wartime economy as a whole. The Ministry of Transport acquiesced in this inaction, but it is equally clear that the overall government policy of restricting intervention in economic affairs to a minimum provided the Ministry with ready justification for its policy. When war came, the initial lack of pressure on inland transport facilities provided no incentive to action. On 6 February 1940, Sir Julian Foley wrote:

> We are not satisfied that any scheme has been worked out for the best coordination of the use of road, rail and canal distribution in such an emergency as is contemplated ... The proper use of all

[37] Savage, 93.
[38] Behrens, 33-4, and above p. 146 n. 37.

> means of transport is one of the problems which has never been definitely tackled ... Our feeling is that there is much to be done.[39]

The situation had not altered to any appreciable extent when the German air raids began in September, with results which have been described.

To suggest that the crisis in the import system during 1940-41 could have been entirely solved by more efficient utilisation of inland transport would be to gloss over many deficiencies in other areas. Inland transport was but one area among many in which congestion developed. On the other hand, it was in many respects the most important area, and its failure demonstrates the operation of all the factors which contributed to the overall failure of pre-war plans for the import system. In this respect inland transport may be regarded as a microcosm of the import system as a whole. Certainly the measures adopted in 1941 to relieve the crisis in inland transport proved to have a more general application.

The narrative of the crisis in the ports was taken to the point at which, in November 1940, the true nature and extent of the problem were becoming evident. In many respects the organisation of inland transport at this time was more backward than that of any other aspect of the import system. Not only were there no effective structures for the coordination of the provision of transport with the demands made upon it, but the individual controls for the roads and the railways were proving incapable of the efficient control of the facilities themselves.[40] In contrast, the efforts being made to establish coordinated planning in other areas — for example in the relation of purchases of commodities abroad to the shipping capacity available for importing — however tentative, were at least proceeding in the right direction. The failure of arrangements for inland transport acted as a gap in the developing structure for the centralised control of imports. The effect of this gap was critical. Until the commodity left the docks it was subject to centralised control — of purchasing (and therefore of assessment of requirements and of its contribution to those requirements, at least in theory), of shipping and of unloading and passing through the port. Its journey was therefore dovetailed in with all the other demands for transport to ensure the most efficient use of all the various resources which contributed to the arrival of the commodity at the dock gates. Once there, however, its further progress was in the hands of chance. All departments with commodities requiring transport competed against one another and against commercial owners for

[39]MT.63/137, P.T.199/2, 6 March 1940.
[40]Savage, 241, 305, etc.

the facilities available for the inland movement of their goods, and as the Minister of Transport had stated before the war,

> Unless control is centralised in one Authority these competing demands [for inland transport in war] are certain to result in gravely uneconomical use and regional shortage of excess of road transport. The experience of shipping control in the late War shows that the natural anxiety of a particular service to move its own goods leads to desirable but unjustifiable margins [41]
> ...

There was no system for coordinating the available facilities with the demands being made upon them, or of adjudicating between conflicting demands for the same transport facility:

> there existed no inter-departmental committee where the needs of Government departments for transport services could be focussed and related to the ability of the various branches of the inland transport system to meet them. There was no ready link at the centre between the user Departments and the transport controls, and thus no means of estimating in a general way how scarce inland transport resources might become at any given time. Nor, as yet, had anyone studied ways and means of allocating inland transport. [42]

Inevitably some commodities were transported by specialised facilities which could more profitably have been employed elsewhere, while some commodities failed to get transport at all. The net result was uncertainty as to whether facilities would be available for the commodity in question. This removed all hope of accurate forward planning; consumers could never be sure of receiving deliveries on time as the port could not be sure that one ship-load would be cleared in time to allow the unloading of the next ship. Any attempt at predicting shortages in the hope of minimising their effect became illusory, in short all chance of running the economy with the degree of predictability essential in wartime was denied. Not only this, for congestion was an inevitable by-product; one which further reduced the performance of the import system, and contributed to its unpredictability. The whole process then entered a downward spiral since the system could not react to counter its reduced capacity with sufficient speed to stabilise itself, owing to the necessity for placing shipping contracts several months in advance.

Matters were taken in hand in November. Early in that month the War Cabinet received reports on the situation in the docks from both

41 CAB.3/6, C.I.D.251-A, 12 March 1937.
42 Savage, 271.

the Minister without Portfolio and from Sir Cecil Weir's Committee. The P.E.C.s were equipped with new transport sub-committees where all officials concerned with the provision of inland transport could meet and jointly plan the movement of all goods in the port. The reorganisation continued in December, when the Lord President's Committee established a central control over the provision of storage facilities.[43] Meanwhile the P.T.S.C. had met to consider the problem, but found itself unable to suggest any proposals which did not curtail or impede the authority and activities of government departments as they were exercised at present. 'The almost unanimous feeling of the Committee', according to the port authorities, 'was that there should be no interference with existing departmental policies and arrangements.'[44] Fortunately such obscurantist departmentalism was rapidly by-passed. On 19 December 1940, the Economic Policy Committee appointed a Ministerial Sub-Committee on Port Clearance to suggest a solution, and on 30 December, this Committee, in the absence of the Minister of Food, who continued to oppose any diminution of departmental independence in this matter, decided to appoint a Regional Port Director to each of the major west coast ports (Liverpool, Bristol and the Clyde).[45]

These Regional Port Directors were intended to assume full and sole responsibility for the day to day operation of the ports in their area and to coordinate all the activities involved in working them. They were to exercise all the functions concerning the ports which were within the authority of the Minister of Transport, and were to be responsible to him alone. Most important of all, the Regional Port Directors could force both individuals and government departments to accept arrangements and incur expenses which they might otherwise have wished to avoid — for the first time the disparate wishes of local authorities and government departments, including the service departments, could be overridden in the interests of the import system as a whole. In the last resort the Regional Port Directors could decide by which form of transport goods should be distributed from the ports. Although of the three Regional Port Directors appointed only the one on the Clyde proved an unqualified success, the measures introduced there enabled the port to operate without delay to shipping after just three months, i.e. by the end of March 1941 and, subsequently applied to the other ports, proved just as successful there. In fact, as

[43] Savage, 235-7.
[44] Quoted in Behrens, 129.
[45] *Ibid.*, 130-8.

Behrens says, 'in the United Kingdom the danger of port congestion never re-emerged after the spring of 1941'.[46]

By this time further reorganisation had taken place. The Economic Policy Committee had been replaced, and an Import Executive was now responsible for the entire import system. The name itself is a reflection of the changed emphasis with which the problem was now regarded. Later still, in April 1941, a Central Transport Committee was established to provide a meeting place for those organisations concerned with providing transport and those departments concerned in using it. For the first time the supply of inland transport and the prospective demands for it were considered together. The final stage in this process was the amalgamation of the Ministries of Shipping and Transport into one Ministry. The respective Ministers had been meeting fortnightly since November 1940, to consider port problems, and the amalgamation was an obvious step. The Minister of War Transport was appointed on 9 May 1941.[47]

It is clear that the problems experienced during the winter of 1940-41 had been solved before this new organisation was completed. The longer hours of daylight and better weather conditions of the spring brought some relaxation in the pressure on inland transport facilities. The capacity of the railways, and particularly the marshalling yards, badly hit by the restrictions of the blackout, began to return to a more normal level. Nonetheless, a substantial proportion of the credit for this improvement must be assigned to the concept of the Regional Port Directors, and to the new attitude towards import problems which their appointment reflected. This attitude may be described as a realisation of the necessity for a single executive authority to control the allocation of commodities to transport facilities, and of the need to determine that allocation by reference to the overall situation of the transport facilities themselves, rather than by reference to the commodity situation. The wartime structure which eventually proved equal to the problems of the import system therefore depended on the centralised allocation of transport by the authorities concerned with its provision. The freedom to arrange their own transport previously enjoyed by the supply departments was drastically curtailed.

There must have been many officials in the Port and Transit Organisation in 1941 who felt that such solutions could have been achieved before the outbreak of war had their advice only been adopted. Since pre-war planning took place on the departmental level, these remarks apply in the main to the solutions adopted below Ministerial level, although Hynard's proposal for a Ministry in charge of transport coordination should not be overlooked. At the lower level, the Regional Port Directors and the Transport Sub-Committees of the P.E.C.s discharged precisely the functions which the D.I.C. had assigned to its proposed Area Organisations. The D.I.C. had not envisaged the dictatorial powers (as they were termed in 1941) which the R.P.D.s possessed, but the objectives of the organisations were essentially similar. Furthermore, Mr. Wilson of the Ministry of Transport had, in July 1939, proposed what amounted to the appointment of R.P.D.s in all but name. He even justified his proposals by suggesting that existing arrangements for the provision of transport would break down because of the inability of advisory committees to enforce efficient allocation of transport.

It is clear, therefore, that the essential problem of dealing with the diversion of shipping had been accurately identified before the war, and that an effective solution had at least been proposed. Thus in so far as pre-war plans for diversion were inadequate, that inadequacy cannot be attributed to a complete failure of appreciation on the part of the officials concerned. Indeed, the organisations devised to deal with the diverted ships themselves functioned in an entirely satisfactory manner, and without structural alteration, throughout the periods of diversion. Herein lies the clue. The organisations concerned in the diversion of the ships — the Admiralty; the Ministry of Shipping; the P.T.O.; the ports; the shipowners — were accustomed to cooperating with each other. Each possessed well-defined executive powers to discharge its particular responsibilities. In particular, the P.T.O. possessed sole executive control over the actual decision to divert a ship, and over the decision as to where it should be diverted to. The necessity for state intervention to achieve diversion was self evident, and it involved no unusual decrease in the freedom of merchant ships in war, which was in any case restricted by the overall Admiralty and Ministry of Shipping controls. As there were no commercial organisations competent to direct the process of diversion, there was no opposition to the accurate definition of a prospective state organisation, nor to the precise description of its areas of responsibility.

In contrast, proposals for the control of diverted cargoes after they had been unloaded can only be described as chaotic. The origins of this situation may be traced to the decision in August 1938, that departments controlling commodities which required transport should be responsible for arranging it. The repercussions of this decision have been described. The policy itself was simply a logical extension of the general premise that the wartime economy would function most efficiently if state intervention was restricted to a minimum, and commercial processes were left to operate in as normal a manner as possible. The necessity for state control of the essential commodities for war production was never questioned, but when it came to arranging their transport from the ports it seemed most reasonable to allow the supply departments to act as if they were commercial owners of the goods, and compete for transport on the open market with comparable owners. Unlike the case of the diversion of the ships themselves, there appeared to be no reason why normal commercial processes should not be adequate to arrange the inland distribution of diverted cargoes. This doctrine of non-intervention by the state was buttressed by a series of over-optimistic assessments of the capacity of inland transport systems to withstand the strains imposed by war and by diversion. Thus an initially unfortunate misunderstanding of the correct nature of the relationship between the state and the transport system in wartime, was confirmed by mistaken assessments produced by both the bureaucracy and the commercial operators concerned. There appeared to be no overriding necessity to impose a single control over the movement of the commodity from the port, and consequently it was decided to allow the system to function with as close an approximation to peacetime conditions as possible.

If the policy itself was mistaken, the manner in which it was applied during the early months of war was simply profligate. Over-confidence in the capacity of inland transport induced the state to leave its allocation to cargoes to be determined by market forces. As the state took over control of an increasing proportion of all imports, the role of the supply departments' demands upon inland transport became more significant. These departments seem to have operated without regard for the essentially finite nature of all transport systems, whether internal or otherwise, and certainly seem to have made no attempts to economise on transport by more efficient use of facilities or interdepartmental coordination. Under war conditions such intense departmental autonomy can only be described as profligate. The supply departments were not prepared to make concessions of their individual convenience to relieve transport conditions as a whole, and ultimately, when the system proved incapable of withstanding the strain of diversion, found themselves forced to sacrifice their auto-nomous control of the provision of transport for their commodities. Their attitude towards the provision of inland transport for their commodities was exactly analogous to their attempt to retain control of ship chartering noted above, and produced the same unfortunate results. The wider attitude of these departments to all questions concerning the provision of transport exercised a consistently deleterious effect.

In essence, therefore, the failure of pre-war planning for the diversion of shipping consisted in a general failure to appreciate two factors. The first was that the strain of war, and particularly diversion of shipping, on Britain's inland transport system would be too great for it to function efficiently under conventional arrangements for the allocation of cargoes to transport. There would, additionally, be a scarcity of inland transport. To ensure the smooth operation of the wartime economy under such circumstances the state would have to step in and operate a system whereby cargoes were directed to appropriate transport in the light of the general availability of transport throughout the country. The state would require to exercise executive control over all forms of transport in order to be able to make arrangements for the most efficient use of the facilities available. Preparations for the achievement of such objectives were minimal. There were no plans for organisations to direct cargoes to transport, and the organisations for controlling the transport facilities themselves were in many respects deficient. The only problem which had been adequately provided for was that of arranging the physical diversion of ships should the need arise. There is no doubt that more extensive arrangements could have been provided and would have reduced the severity of the crisis when it arose.

The second factor, which in many respects induced the other failure, was a more general consideration. It took the form of an inability to comprehend the fundamental nature of the import system as a whole, and not simply of the inland transport sector, or of the problems posed by diversion of shipping. Indeed, it was essentially a failure to understand the nature of the wartime economy in a centralised industrial state, and hence of the type of relationship between the state and such an economy necessary for efficiency. As such it derived partly from the contemporary outlook regarding the propriety of state intervention in economic affairs, and partly from the structure of the bureaucracy within which the planning process occurred. And as such it raises questions of a more general relevance.

8

'ENDLESS COMMITTEES AND SUB-COMMITTEES' — A CONCLUSION

> the war has emphasised the difficulty of replacing, by departmental control, the free play of economic forces. One thing is certain, under any conditions, whether of State Control or unfettered private enterprise, the importance of 'turn-round', of the synchronization of shipping and railway movements, of close touch between those responsible for purchase, transport and distribution, and of maintaining a free flow of traffic through the ports, stands out as one of the most important, and perhaps one of the least appreciated lessons of the war.
>
> C.E. Fayle, *The War and the Shipping Industry*, 403.

Fayle's conclusion, written in the 1920s, was prophetic, in that it was in this 'least appreciated' area that the root cause of the problems of the import system in the Second World War lay. Yet it is evident from the narrative history recounted above that the experience of the First World War had not been totally squandered. There was, initially, a clear realisation, within the Civil Service if not among the shipowners, that the state would have to exercise some form of control over the activities of the import system in a future war. But this general intention did not prejudge the question of the extent to which the state should intervene, nor the form which this intervention should take, and it was on the answers to these questions that the success of the plans produced in the period came to depend.

It is impossible to isolate the character of the plans devised from the structure of the bodies concerned with their determination. Similarly, the structure of the bodies set to determine plans was itself influenced by the prevailing conception of the degree to which state intervention was necessary, since different structures would be required to administer different levels of intervention. The inter-relationship between such structural and policy factors operated at several levels throughout the planning process, and, as will be demonstrated below, was a significant factor in prejudicing the success of the plans eventually adopted. Such factors, were, however, subsidiary to the initial decision that some degree of state intervention would be necessary.

The importance of this decision lies in the fact that it ensured the steady development of planning throughout the years between the wars. Except in the immediate post-war period, consideration of the problems of the import system continued steadily, if intermittently, throughout the period. The War Risks Insurance enquiries began in 1923; the structure of the Naval Control Service and of the other Admiralty measures to control merchantmen were under more or less constant revision during these years. Enquiries into the diversion of shipping began in 1924, while the question of the control of shipping was raised as early as 1930. Clearly there was no last minute scramble to devise preparations in the later 1930s. In the field of economic preparations much had been achieved before 1935, and a solid groundwork for later developments had been laid.

A major factor in the steadiness of this process was unquestionably the clarity with which the experience of the First World War demonstrated the need for such preparations. The shipping crisis had assumed such proportions in 1916-18 that there was never any serious criticism of the necessity to plan against the possibility of such problems occurring again. The planning process, which was instituted by appropriate provisions in the departmental War Book, or by departmental initiative, proceeded unhampered by the need to justify itself which hindered other aspects of defence planning. The need to plan for the import system was a relatively uncontentious subject in these years, at least within the bureaucracy.

A further factor was influential in allowing the unhindered development of such plans. Planning for the wartime control of the import system was predominantly concerned with the elaboration of administrative structures which would not actually be established until the outbreak of war, when the problems they were designed to control had finally arrived. To a large extent therefore, it was concerned with the creation of paper establishments only, and with the earmarking of existing staff for future responsibilities. Consequently, little immediate financial expenditure was required, and planning could go ahead more or less in isolation from the periodic financial crises which did so much to hinder the maintenance of Britain's defences in an efficient condition in other areas. Even where expenditure was necessary, it was not possible to receive additional security from an increase in expenditure in peacetime — administrative arrangements cannot be stockpiled like guns or tanks, against a future emergency. Expenditure in this field was thus limited in a way that normal defence expenditure was not, and could be more easily justified thereby.

Significantly, in the one area of the defence of the import system where the provision of hardware was necessary (the defensive equipment of merchant ships) progress was held up by financial stringency. Here, the Treasury refused to allow expenditure until the last years before war, when the need for action was overwhelmingly evident. But even here it is difficult to argue that financial stringency played a specific part in hindering the achievement of security. As late as 1939 the Admiralty remained uncertain as to which types of weapons it wished to install in merchantmen, and as to what modifications would be necessary to fit existing equipment for such a role. Had the money been available it could not have been spent, nor was the necessary manufacturing capacity available to produce the weapons. There would have been little advantage in accelerating the stiffening programme yet further, if the weapons were not available for fitting. In the case of DEMS, it seems that the Admiralty's uncertainties were at least as crucial as the Treasury's stringency, in delaying the achievement of an adequate measure of security for the merchant marine.

While it is necessary to emphasise the gradual development of plans for this area, this does not imply that preparations were not stimulated by the darkening international situation in the later 1930s. It is merely to assert that these crises were not seminal in instituting consideration of these problems. It would be unrealistic to expect planning to continue without reference to events in the world at large.

While the development of renewed interest in the diversion of shipping in 1932 is to be attributed to developments in the range and striking power of aircraft, rather than to any stimulus imparted by the contemporary crisis in the Far East, there is clear evidence that the Abyssinian crisis stimulated a reappraisal of the War Risks Insurance arrangements. The government found that the hiatus since 1928 had left it without an agreement with the Clubs, and was forced to conclude an agreement under the stress of the crisis which was, in several respects, less favourable to the state than it had hoped. Revision followed. The same stimulus, accompanied by events in the Spanish Civil War can be seen behind the revival of investigations into the control of shipping, which took place shortly afterwards. Popular pressure for the convoy of merchantmen during the Spanish War was one of the reasons leading the Admiralty to reconsider the convoy system in 1938, and to introduce arrangements for it to begin immediately on the outbreak of war.[1] The Munich crisis stimulated the Port and Transit Organisation to activity.

But despite this history of acceleration in the last years before the war there is no evidence, with the exception of DEMS, that the success of any of these plans was prejudiced by their incompleteness at the outbreak of war, or by the effects of financial stringency in

[1] ADM. 1/9501, 19 February 1938.

earlier years. DEMS was, to a large extent, an isolated problem, uncharacteristic of the area with which we have been concerned. Clearly, the Admiralty's plans for the Naval Control Service, and the introduction of control over shipping movements, were in no way incomplete on the outbreak of war. The plans of the other departments were similarly complete, although this did not imply an intention to apply them all immediately, nor that they were all equally relevant to the problems they were designed to solve. It could be argued that a higher level of expenditure on planning in these years might have resulted, not in more complete plans, but in more apposite plans, but this is a proposition which I reject.

Where British plans for the import system proved inappropriate in wartime this failure is to be ascribed to the influence of the inter-relationship between policy and structure referred to above. Despite the readiness to accept the necessity for some degree of state intervention in the operations of the import system in wartime, it is clear that the philosophical outlook of the time — the intention to restrict state intervention to a minimum; the distrust of 'collectivist' planning in economic affairs — closely constrained the nature of the plans produced, and contributed to the (incorrect) general assessment current before the war that the problems of the import system were not serious enough to justify overriding such attitudes.

This approach was in direct contradiction to the experience of the First World War, and even to the bureaucracy's own analysis of that experience. Thus, in 1918, in perhaps the most concise summary of bureaucratic experience with the import system in wartime, the Port and Transit Executive Committee had concluded:

> Should an emergency such as that of 1914 again arise, some Body bearing the same general relation to the ports as has this Committee, would again be necessary, and the experience of this Committee should make the path more obvious. Buying control, shipping control, distributing control and rationing control imply a corresponding control of the port which links arrivals with distribution; unification, if adopted at all, must be continuous. The other main lesson to be learnt in the Committee's judgement is that along with this unity of control it is imperative, for success in working, that a proper relation be observed between all the successive stages of purchase, carriage, handling and distribution. Abundant ships and full cargoes are useless unless labour has been retained in proper force at the ports, and this again is in vain unless distribution by rail, coasting vessel, canal and road has been secured, and the inland destination of cargoes has been provided for.[2]

[2] Quoted in MT.50/105, T.01904, note of 26 February 1930 (signature indecipherable).

During the inter-war period, therefore, clear indications were available, both from within the bureaucracy and from independent analysts, of the central implications of wartime experience with the import system. Yet the early years of the Second World War saw a crisis in the import system and its resolution by trial and error methods directly comparable to that of the earlier war. Any attempt to explain this phenomenon raises broader issues, concerning both the attitudes of the governments of the day towards the economy, and the structure of bureaucratic control in the economic sphere. It is clear that a number of simple mistakes were made at all levels of government during the preparation of war plans for the import system in this period. Yet it is equally evident that to attribute the failures of the war years solely to such mistakes would be to overlook a number of more fundamental factors, whose influence was felt throughout the whole field of planning for the defence economy.

During the early years of the war, the phrase 'Business as Usual' was much in evidence. The phrase conveys exactly the general attitude of the governments and politicians of the period to the problems of organising a modern industrial state for war in the mid-twentieth century.[3] Every effort was to be made to limit the intrusion of war in normal life. The basic premise of the Defence Regulations was that the liberty of the individual should be infringed only to the minimum extent compatible with the achievement of national security. In the shipping sector, the policy was defined in the phrase 'the provision of tonnage will function most efficiently if left to market forces'.[4] The state's concern to limit the intrusion of war included an intention to restrict its own activities to a level as closely analagous to that of peacetime as possible.

This principle manifestly contradicted the advocacy of thorough control included in the final report of the P.T.E.C. Furthermore it did so less on the basis of a rational assessment of the requirements of the current situation, than on a vague, philosophical impression of the proper function of government, encapsulated in the phrase, 'he who governs least governs best.' As an official who served in the Food

---

[3]One of the clearest examples of the influence of this attitude is to be seen in the conduct of the rearmament programme of the late 1930s of which the official historians write: 'A parallel doctrine of economic practice, which may be called 'the doctrine of normal trade', was operating. . . to impede the mobilisation of economic resources in the war sector. Believing that 'industry ought not to be interfered with'', the Government was attempting to impose rearmament upon recovery within an uncontrolled economy' (Hancock and Gowing, 69.) For a discussion of the effects of this attitude of 'cooperation' on the achievements of rearmament — and its cost to the taxpayer — see Shay, *passim.*

[4]Above, p. 93 n. 20.

(Defence Plans) Department had written, referring to the earlier war, 'it is not surprising that the necessity for state intervention was only gradually admitted by Ministers who had spent the greater part of their careers in exploding the fallacies of Protectionism on the one hand, and Socialism on the other.'[5] These comments apply with equal force to the inter-war years.

This traditional view of the correct relationship between the state and the economy, even in war,was strengthened by various pressures from the commercial world. We have noted the way in which the ship-owners, equally traditionally, strongly opposed any governmental interference in their freedom to run the industry in their own way, even in wartime. In the words of the official historian of food,

> The political climate of Britain, in the years before 1939, was not propitious for the type of ruthless calculation that the prospect of modern war demands; the governing view of the time hated war and distrusted collectivist planning such as war must entail. It would be surprising if this attitude of mind had not spilled over into the way in which war plans were tackled.[6]

As a result of this attitude economic planning for war was accorded a low priority by the governments of the period. Resources were scarce, economic expertise was scarcer still, and the problems of the peacetime economy were pressing. But the failure to undertake an authoritative investigation of the defence economy allowed the unsuitability of the policy of minimum intervention to pass undetected.

To a degree, analysis was available to support the contention that the state would be able to restrict its intervention to a minimum in a future war. Such analysis depended on the assessment that the experience of the First World War was not applicable to the conditions of the 1930s. It stressed the difficulty of making accurate predictions of the nature of a future war. Such reasoning might have been used to support a higher level of preparations as easily as a lower, but it was not so applied at the time. In so far as the conditions of the period were seen to be different from those of the First World War, they had apparently altered to Britain's advantage. In the shipping sector there was the belief that the crisis of 1917-18 was caused by a number of factors which would not recur in a future war. The Admiralty was confident that the development of Asdic had neutralised the submarine menace; there was in general during the period no intention of employing large military forces overseas, and shipping would thus not be needed for their support; and, in a situation of worldwide shipping glut, it seemed unlikely that we should be required

[5]E.M.H. Lloyd, *Experiments in State Control,* (Oxford, 1924), 22.
[6]Hammond, I, 32.

to apply so substantial a proportion of our tonnage in support of our allies as in 1918. In so far as there were fears concerning the adequacy of British shipping, or indeed of any other transport facility, to discharge the services required of it in war, the primitive statistical enquiries of the time appeared to suggest that there was no cause to expect a serious crisis, and therefore no need to erect a costly and complex system of controls to deal with it.

Nor was the concept of minimum intervention challenged by official definitions of the nature of a future war, (to the extent that such definitions may be said to have existed). War with Japan, it was felt, would not necessitate extensive economic controls, and even when Germany was recognised as the major threat, after 1934, the contemporary concentration on the effects of bombing, and the difficulty of defence against it, encouraged the assumption that a future war would be settled in a matter of hours, rather than the years of 1914. In a short war there would be no need for close control over industry. By the time such views came to be discarded, little could be achieved, but, paradoxically, there appeared little need for haste, since a long war would afford ample opportunity to establish structures appropriate to the requirements of the time.

The difficulty of accurately predicting the nature of a future war, and therefore of the sort of control over the economy which would be necessary, was a common justification for restricting intervention. In other areas of defence planning a comparable lack of a clear definition of the wartime situation was cause for over-insurance — there was a generally accepted principle that defence investigations, (such as the Chiefs of Staff Annual Reports, and indeed, the D.I.C. enquiry), should plan on the basis of the worst possible combination of circumstances so far as Great Britain was concerned. But the general unwillingness to countenance interference with industry led to the abandonment of this principle in economic planning. It was felt that industry could best respond to the shock of war if it was not additionally hindered by the need to adjust to predetermined state regulation which could, at best, be only imperfectly tailored to the actual situation. Later, if conditions required it, controls specifically adapted to deal with contemporary problems could be introduced.

The ultimate foundation of this attitude was the belief that the economy could function best if left to respond to normal commercial stimuli, even in wartime. Experience was to show that this was a mistaken belief. But the shortcomings of this policy are less important than its effects on defence planning in the period.

Such a broadly defined policy offered little guidance to the departments of government charged with the preparation of detailed plans. It was, in fact, little more than a negative injunction to do as little as possible, and encouraged a tendency to approach problems from the point of view of defining an acceptable minimum of intervention, rather than in terms of seeking the most efficient solution, whether that involved intervention or not. The departments themselves were left to define the extent of the acceptable minimum intervention, but in doing so they received little guidance as to the conditions which might be encountered in a future war, or as to the nature of the effort Britain might be required to make. After 1934 there was a clear definition of the enemy, but the strategy — whether, for example, large military forces would be employed on the Continent of Europe — remained unclear for some time. There was thus little overall conception of the demands which the future conflict would make on the economy of this country, or thus, of the extent to which it would be necessary for the state to intervene in control of the economy. Lack of guidance from above had created a situation in which the departments had to define the acceptable minimum of state intervention without being provided with a yardstick by which to measure the necessity for that intervention.

But even had such a yardstick been provided, such a delegation of responsibility was a fundamentally mistaken policy. In omitting to assert a centralised coordinating control over all aspects of planning for the wartime economy, the governments of the period had assigned responsibility for the definition of policy in this area to organisations unsuited and ill-equipped to undertake it. Apart from the Food (Defence Plans) Department, and the Air Raid Precautions organisation, there were no departments of government in Britain at this time specifically concerned with economic war plans. The burden of planning was undertaken by ordinary departments in addition to their current administrative tasks. In the contemporary financial climate, this was natural, and reflected the low priority accorded to economic planning, but it brought with it serious impediments to the achievement of satisfactory results.

Initially it involved the assumption of another burden by staffs already overloaded by their current responsibilities. Furthermore, it was an unusual burden, for these staffs did not operate the import system themselves, but merely supervised the activities of the commercial organisations which did so. The bureaucracy had no practical experience of administering the import system, yet it was required to determine the extent to which wartime conditions would necessitate interference with the normal processes. The shortcomings of such an arrangement are obvious. But whatever their competence to administer the import system, it remains evident that the individual departments of government were not a suitable forum in which to define the degree of state intervention which would be necessary in a future war. Bureaucracies work by fragmenting problems into a series of simple constituents suitable for the attention of individual departments. They therefore tend to look to the specific and the particular at the expense of the overall view — a tendency frequently combined with a certain inflexibility and isolationism in outlook.

The deleterious effects of such factors are most obvious in the statistical sphere. Unable because of inexperience and the pressure of current administration to collect statistics for themselves, the departments turned to commercial sources, and attempted to produce a figure for the capacity of the import system as a whole by adding together the figures they thus obtained for the individual transport facilities. Such an approach was inherently misrepresentative, for it proved impossible to operate the transport facilities with the degree of segregation it implied. Even at the simplest level, the performance of one facility affected that of the others in so far as it influenced the extent of the total demand for transport.

Alongside such statistical errors, the departments created an administrative structure based on a similar allocation of a particular transport facility to an individual bureaucratic unit. Thus one department concerned itself with plans for the control of the railways, another with ships, a further with the ports and so on. This produced a logical and tidy administrative structure, which was reflected in the organisations established to control these facilities in wartime. But each facility was considered in isolation from its companions, its capacity was assessed in isolation from estimates of their performance, or of the overall demand on transport, and facilities for the coordination of its activities with those of its fellows were inadequate. The departments' lack of experience in the operation of the import system, and the technique of fragmenting problems along lines of administrative convenience rather than operational necessity, had obscured the fact that the import system was a closely integrated organism, whose totality could not be expressed as the sum of its constituents, either statistically, or in terms of the organisations controlling its various sections.

Such errors were encouraged by the policy of minimum intervention. The definition of the ideal level of intervention as the minimum invited departments to seek the most economical rather than the most efficient solutions. The current financial stringency was a complementary factor, but the concept of a minimum level beyond which it was not desirable to proceed was not conducive to the development of plans determined by the needs of the system rather than the determination of the Treasury to keep expenditure down. The deleterious effects of the Treasury's insistence on economy were not, however, restricted to the obvious constraints of its financial stringency. The emphasis produced a tendency in pre-war planning to concentrate on the financial details of schemes, rather than on consideration of the requirements of the physical resources themselves. Thus plans for the control of shipping largely reflected fears of the effects of a rise in freight rates in wartime, rather than fears about the adequacy of the marine to discharge its functions. Such approaches to the problems of the import system did not facilitate the production of the most pertinent proposals.

It was at this point that the inter-relation of structural and policy factors referred to above was instrumental in preventing the successful formulation of plans for the import system in wartime. The responsibility for determining the details of policy in this area had been thrust upon the departments for two reasons — the current pressure for financial economy made the creation of a new or specialised structure to investigate the problem unthinkable (the wartime structures, of course, had long since been demolished for similar reasons), and secondly, because, if intervention were to be restricted to a minimum, the question was not of the first importance anyway. The departments themselves, however, were incapable of discharging this responsibility adequately. The insistence on economy and the minimum of intervention encouraged the intrinsic tendency of hard-pressed departments to resist any further extension of their responsibilities. They therefore concentrated on the details of planning for their specific administrative concerns, which they discharged (with one or two exceptions) satisfactorily. Their restricted horizons and the fragmented approach inevitable in any specialised administrative structure prevented them from realising that this administrative achievement was not, in itself, a full discharge of their responsibility to determine policy concerning the scope of intervention. They devised their administrative structures with more regard to economy than to the efficiency of the system in wartime.

The departments themselves could never develop the wider view or overall competence necessary to identify their own inadequacy for policy making, or to expose the fallacy of their original instructions. Thus the attempt to define policy for the import system at the departmental level did not produce a single policy for the economy, but · a series of policies for individual sectors of it, conceived in isolation from each other, and from any conception of the economy as a whole, and provided with inadequate facilities for the coordination of their efforts — indeed, without a single coherent policy to guide those efforts. The fallacy of the policy of minimum intervention remained unexposed because departmental concentration on the particular, and the unwillingness of higher government to take initiative in the field, ensured that no investigation took place in these years with wide enough scope to demonstrate it.

Thus, although the departments performed satisfactorily in producing detailed plans, they failed to discharge the burden of policy formulation which the omission of higher government had thrust upon them. Essentially, they failed to overcome the problems of planning within a departmental structure for questions which transcended departmental boundaries. While this failure must be admitted, any criticism of departmental performance in this area must be tempered by the realisation that the initial delegation of responsibility for policy formulation to them was a mistake on the part of higher government. They were neither designed to undertake such tasks, nor accustomed to them.

The final result of the inability of the departments to discharge the tasks allocated to them by higher government was to confirm the incorrect analysis which had given rise to the situation. The inability of the departments to develop a wider view implicitly confirmed the contention that such a view was unnecessary.

While the reasons for the failure of the individual departments to expose the errors in policy in this field are easily identified, it is clear that such reasons cannot explain the similar failure of the inter-departmental coordinating committees. Such committees, composed of departmental representatives, were intended to overcome the inherent problem of a bureaucracy organised on departmental lines, by reconciling conflicting interests within the wider framework of the united effort. They should thus have transcended the effects of departmental separatism.

The very existence of an inter-departmental committee implied the need to restrict, in the national interest, the absolute freedom of the individual departments to regulate their affairs in the manner most convenient to themselves. But once again, the ability of the organisation to successfully discharge the functions expected of it was prejudiced by its structure. The committees of the period were explicitly advisory bodies, they had no executive powers of their own. The implementation of any decisions they might reach was achieved through the individual powers of the departmental representatives who composed the committee, and whose conflicts it was intended to reconcile. In such circumstances there were two contexts in which the committee could secure the adoption of its proposals.

The first was where those proposals could be shown to accord with an expressed policy determined at a higher level, or where the proposals were subsequently adopted as such a policy. In the present field there was no positive policy pre-existing inter-departmental investigations. Nor did the bureaucratic enquiries produce a strong enough case for the provision of such a policy.

The second context occurs in the absence of the first. It requires consent — the existence or creation of a consensus of opinion among the departments that the situation demands the sacrifice of their freedom of action in the interests of the greater good embodied in the policies of the committee. In the absence of a policy determined externally, an advisory committee can only function effectively on the basis of the mutual consent of its members that its recommendations are fair, reasonable, and above all, urgently necessary. The optimistic estimates of the capacity of the import system current in the 1930s prevented the growth of such a consensus among the departments.

Since neither of these two contexts existed in the period, it is not surprising that, even where an inter-departmental committee had succeeded in correctly identifying the fallacy of the policy of minimum intervention, and had devised a suitable replacement, (or, to put it another way, had accurately defined the level at which state intervention would be necessary for the efficient operation of the economy in wartime), its proposals came to nothing. An example is the experience of the P.T.S.C., which demonstrates the efficiency of departmental separatism in sabotaging the efforts of a committee. Contending that, as the owners of goods in wartime, the policy of minimum intervention implied that they should be free to find their own transport, the supply departments resisted the P.T.S.C.'s attempts to establish a centralised policy for the allocation of commodities to transport. As an advisory committee, the P.T.S.C. could not enforce its conceptions, and the optimism of the time seemed to justify departmental separatism. Once again, a decision had been taken on the basis of administrative convenience rather than efficiency.

In the optimistic mood of the 1930s, departments could see no necessity for the subordination of their own convenience to an inter-departmental structure,[7] nor could higher government see the need to

[7]Nor could they in the war years. Even in the grave conditions of December 1940, a senior official of the Ministry of Food could write: 'It occurs to me that somebody may think that the rather persistent enquiry in our Memorandum . . . about the intention of "these programmes" is purposeless or merely petulant. The point is, of course, that we

force them to do so. The efforts of inter-departmental committees to establish centralised coordinating structures, or policies for the determination of disputes in the demand for transport facilities in wartime, however feeble, were therefore unavailing. As Vansittart said: 'We have for years laboured under the burden of these endless committees and sub-committees, which spend nothing but time. The results are nearly always astonishingly futile ...'[8] Again, blame must rest with the shortsightedness of higher government. Where committees were provided with a clear definition of policy, they functioned effectively. The B.S.W.R.I.O.C., for example, was established to determine the organisational details of the accepted policy that a state war risks insurance scheme would be necessary to keep trade moving in wartime. Despite occasional contretemps, the committee achieved its objectives. The committee system had great strengths as an administrative technique, but it also had great weaknesses. Unfortunately, in the area of economic planning for defence in the 1930s, the restrictions of the committee system were not appreciated, and its weaknesses were accentuated by its being invested with undue responsibility. When required to formulate organisations to administer a policy determined elsewhere, the inter-departmental committee was a satisfactory institution. But when required to institute that policy, it could not, in the conditions of the day, overcome the forces of departmental separatism.

Essentially, the definition of policy was a function of higher government. The departments were provided to execute the details of that policy; the inter-departmental committee to coordinate departmental efforts within it. The failure of higher government in this period to determine a positive policy for the operation of the import system in wartime, embodied in the phrase 'minimum intervention', had thrown responsibility for the definition of such a policy onto organisations which were, by training, structure and experience, unsuited to undertake it. In the attempt to identify the real requirements of the wartime import system, the departments failed to overcome the inherent restrictions of their structure. In doing so, given the absence of higher backing and the optimism of the time, they nullified the efforts of those

---

are in practice entirely at the mercy of the Ministry of Shipping, which often means a more or less obscure official of the Ministry of Shipping, in regard to priorities; and it may well happen that a food cargo is delayed on merely shipping convenience grounds in favour of a cargo of steel or timber ... I think it unwise in the memorandum to bring out this point too clearly. I do not want to appear to be criticising the Ministry of Shipping. They do their best, no doubt, and anyhow we have got to work with them, and without their goodwill we shall undoubtedly suffer.' Such were the forces of departmental separatism. *Ibid.*, 162, n.2.

[8]Quoted in S.W. Roskill, *Hankey, Man of Secrets*, III, (London 1974), 110.

inter-departmental committees which had succeeded where they had failed. Consequently a fundamental flaw developed in planning for the import system in a future war. This may be described as the failure to appreciate the relevance of the 1918 conclusion of the P.T.E.C., that it would not be possible to operate the system efficiently without the most thorough unified central control.

Such control could only be established by higher government. Subject to the overriding control of the Cabinet, responsibility for planning for the defence economy rested with the C.I.D. until, in midsummer 1939, it passed to the Stamp Survey. In practice the Cabinet took no initiative in this field. There was little political appreciation of the economic rather than military aspects of defence, and little inclination on the part of politicians to involve themselves in so contentious an area as the problems of state interference in industry, even in wartime. As Eden was told, when complaining to Baldwin about Cabinet interference in drafting despatches, of his twenty colleagues 'there was probably not more than one who thought he should be Minister of Labour and nineteen who thought they should be Foreign Secretary.'[9] Thus although the Cabinet considered departmental conclusions concerning the import system, it did not possess the time, the interest or the expertise to genuinely relieve the C.I.D. of responsibility for decisions in this area. Even in the field of more conventional defence, a knowledgeable estimate has suggested that the C.I.D. effectively took 95 per cent of all decisions without reference to the Cabinet.[10] The Cabinet did not improve on this performance in the rather more arcane field of the defence economy.

But the C.I.D. in these years had little time available for the discussion of economic questions as a whole, let alone transport problems in particular. Like the Cabinet, it possessed little economic expertise, and it is evident that the problems of military planning were, in themselves, almost too extensive for the Committee to deal with satisfactorily. To expect it to undertake a wide-ranging concern with the economic activities of the nation at war as well, was to ask too much of an overburdened organisation. Indeed, in some ways, the C.I.D's responsibility for the import system was a hindrance to planning, since without it steps might have been taken to establish a body which could more effectively discharge the role of central coordination. There was a tendency to assume that the existence of the C.I.D. meant that something was being done: as the New Zealand

---

[9] Avon, *The Eden Memoirs, Facing the Dictators,* (London 1962), 319.

[10] This was the figure given by Ismay in his article 'The Machinery of the Committee of Imperial Defence', in the *Journal of the Royal United Services Institution,* LXXXIV, 1939, 241-57.

Naval Secretary wrote in 1938 'there seems to be a sort of hallucination that when a C.I.D. paper is written, all is well...'[11] In the last analysis, the C.I.D. was only the most senior and prestigious of the advisory committees, and suffered from the same disadvantages as its more lowly brethren. In itself, it could never have supplied the sort of leadership which the field of economic preparations for war lacked in the 1930s.

Thus, Britain entered the war without a comprehensive policy for the employment of the import system; indeed, without a coherent conception of the existence of an import system as such — of the essential interdependence of the transport facilities concerned. Confident that there would be no shortage of transport, policy for the import system rested on the assumption that the allocation of commodities to transport could be most efficiently arranged by normal commercial means. The fallacy of this assumption became rapidly apparent. Pre-war enquiries, which had suggested that transport facilities possessed the capacity to meet wartime demands, proved optimistic. In war a combination of state control of freight rates, intended to prevent profiteering, and unusual demands for transport, removed the flexibility by which the market system allocated surplus capacity to those goods able to bear the cost of carriage. Thus the policy of minimum intervention undermined the ability of the import system to function normally in wartime, for the one area of intervention regarded as necessary, the control of freight rates, destroyed the ability of the system to regulate itself. In normal circumstances, priority among goods was determined by price — by their ability to pay the cost of carriage. But in war, state control of freight rates ensured that purveyors of transport could make no financial distinction between goods competing for scarce facilities, and pre-war planning had omitted to provide any alternative criteria. The statistical inaccuracies of pre-war investigations played a vital role in spreading an unjustified complacency about the capacity of the import system, which so enfeebled further enquiries into the problem that an inadequate level of administrative preparation resulted. That this failure was largely unnecessary was implicitly admitted by the official historians when they concluded that:

> In summing up, it may be suggested that, if the pre-war estimates
> of shipping resources and the claims upon them had been less

[11]MT.40/6, T.01922, E.L. Tottenham, R.N., to W.G. Hynard, 19 September 1938. A similar tendency had been noted by Lloyd George, who described a 'readiness to assume that something resolved at a Committee was thereby an accomplished fact' in discussing the First World War. D. Lloyd George, *The War Memoirs of David Lloyd George*, (London, 1933-36), III, 1250.

optimistic, some of the difficulties of the first war winter might have been avoided. Still more might they have been avoided if administrative preparations had been pushed further forward before war began.[12]

Wartime conditions naturally proved a forcing ground for arrangements to administer the import system. Even so, it was not until the midsummer of 1941 that a satisfactory structure was attained; the higher level administrative organisations then established being retained broadly unaltered until the end of the war. The pattern which emerged was tripartite in nature, reflecting the three facets of activity concerned in managing the import system — administration, policy and information.

At the administrative level a rather ramshackle collection of structures had evolved to provide the necessary inter-departmental coordination. Together they constituted a system within which the needs of government departments for transport services could be focussed and related to the ability of the various facilities to discharge them, thus providing a central link between the user departments and the transport controls. The Ministries of Shipping and Transport had been amalgamated in April 1941 into the Ministry of War Transport, providing at last, a unified control over all transport facilities. The Regional Port Directors, Transport Sub-Committees of the P.E.C.s and the Shipping (Diversion) Room facilities established by the Ministry of Shipping, were joined by a Central Transport Committee and an Inland Transport War Council, to supervise the inland transport situation. Beyond the M.O.W.T. lay the Import Executive, established in December 1940 specifically to consider import priorities, and to secure coordination between the ports and inland transport. Its functions were gradually usurped by the M.O.W.T. and the Prime Ministerial Battle of the Atlantic Committee, which increasingly considered all aspects of the import problem. The Import Executive lapsed in May 1942, being partly replaced by a War Cabinet Shipping Committee, intended to take 'short term decisions necessitated by inadequate departmental planning'.[13]

In contrast to this rather haphazard structure of controls, policy determination was centralised in a single committee, chaired by the Lord President. Subject to the overriding authority of the War

[12]Hancock and Gowing, 134.

[13]*Ibid.*, 423. For a brief account of the Shipping Committee, see Sir Oliver Franks, *Central Planning and Control in War and Peace*, (London, 1947), 11. Perhaps the most concise account of wartime alterations in the central organisation of government is that of D.N. Chester. 'The Central Machinery for Economic Policy' in *Lessons of the British War Economy*, 5-14.

Cabinet, the Lord President's Committee, which consisted of the chairmen of the other civilian Cabinet Committees and the Chancellor, was the ultimate stage of appeal for problems which could not be resolved by the inter-departmental structures. It had no specific executive responsibilities of its own, and thus provided a central, representative and impartial authority with competence to take decisions in the national interest upon the conflicting claims of rival departments for transport. During 1941 the Lord President's Committee became 'the most important focus of civil government under the War Cabinet.'[14] handling many questions which would otherwise have drawn on the War Cabinet's time. In the import field, it came to occupy a position analogous to that of the Milner Committee in the First World War.

The final facet of this organisation was the provision of an efficient and impartial central statistical clearing house, which could accurately assess the needs of the wartime economy, and therefore the urgency of the conflicting demands for importing capacity. This was provided by the Central Statistical Office, whose figures were, by Prime Ministerial directive, to be accepted without question by the departments concerned.

This structure, while rather untidy, did make good the deficiencies of pre-war plans and provide accurate statistics, adequate facilities for inter-departmental coordination, and above all, a clear and comprehensive policy within which departmental activities could be coordinated. But however effective it proved, the fact remains that it took the best part of two years of war before it was established. The development of the administration of the import system in the Second World War closely paralleled the experience of the First — a series of ad hoc solutions modified in response to the actual experience of war, rather than in response to coherent policy as to the objectives to which the system was to be directed. It is an inescapable conclusion that this process could have been avoided if the lessons of the First World War had been adequately assimilated.

The logical response to the experience of the First World War would have been the creation of a single body responsible for preparing the import system as a whole for any future conflict. Although the exact nature of such a body is hypothetical, the dependence of so many sectors of the British economy on imports makes it evident that the wider the field over which it possessed responsibility, the nearer its preparations would approach adequacy.

[14]Hancock and Gowing, 220.

The inter-war years saw a number of schemes for centralising state activities concerning the economy, from the report of the Haldane Committee of Economic Enquiry of 1924, which proposed a sort of C.I.D. for economic affairs, to the various schemes mooted in the M.M.D. in the late 1930s, which were specifically concerned with the problems of the import system.[15] The details of these various proposals are less important than the fact that the need for some sort of general economic policy planning body was evident in these years, at least to some observers. Governments, however, seemed less conscious of such imperatives, and those attempts which were made to improve monitoring of the economy proved short-lived and ineffective — MacDonald's Economic Advisory Council of 1930 being a characteristic example. In any event, such general bodies would have found so much to occupy them in current economic problems that it is doubtful whether they could have devoted much time to the problems of controlling economic activity in wartime: a more specifically directed approach would have been required.

It is clear that the main reason why such an approach was not made lay in the general philosophical unwillingness on the part of business and most politicians in the period to countenance interference with the normal commercial operations of the economy in peace or war. It was argued that the establishment of an authority concerned with proposals for the control of the economy in wartime would merely prove a further and largely unnecessary complication in the already complex relationship between government and industry, and that its relationship to the C.I.D. would be difficult to define, giving rise to jurisdictional squabbles. There were also those who argued that the addition of yet another of Vansittart's 'endless committees' to the bureaucratic structure was no assurance that more satisfactory results would thereby accrue. These more practical objections carried some force, but there is no reason to suppose that they were insuperable, given careful definition of the structure and responsibilities of the body eventually established.

What is clear is that the facilities actually available for the overall consideration of the problems of the defence economy were so limited that there was an urgent need for some authority in which the wider problems of policy and strategy could receive adequate investigation. Whatever the structure of such an authority, the relevant consider-

[15] Above, 160-162. The most concise account of proposed alterations in the organisation for economic policy in the period is that in Daalder, esp. Chs. 13, 14 and 17. For a theoretical discussion of broadly analogous problems in the post-1945 situation, see Franks op. cit.

ation remains the degree to which it could have enhanced pre-war preparations. Although any bureaucratic investigation of the economy in those years would have been hampered by the statistical errors made by the departments and commercial organisations concerned, a centralised organisation, able to regard the import system as a whole, would have possessed significant advantages over existing arrangements.

A specialist authority concerned with the economy could have overcome the tendency of departments to regard the import system exclusively in terms of their individual compartmentalised concerns, and should have developed greater emphasis on the interdependence of departmental activities. The fundamental nature of the import system as an integrated and inter-related whole could have been identified and made the basis of preparations, so overcoming one of the major shortcomings of the plans actually produced. Better facilities for inter-departmental coordination would also accrue. Specific examples of confusion between departments, such as the case of the 25 per cent cut in food imports adopted by the M.M.D. as a result of its misunderstanding of the report of the Food Supply Committee, could have been remedied. The identification of such errors could only be beneficial. But the major argument for a centralised organisation remains that it could have developed a policy for the entire economy, rather than a series of policies for specific sections of it.

With adequate commercial as well as departmental membership, such an authority could have come to exert a degree of influence over the consideration of the problems of the wartime economy comparable to that which the C.I.D. exercised over more conventional defence matters. Its expert and influential membership, its specialist concern for economic problems, and the range and depth of the investigations it could have undertaken, would have enabled it to develop a monopoly of expertise concerning its responsibilities, which would have rendered its conclusions authoritative and difficult to reject. Whatever the actual composition or nature of the authority, a body with overall responsibility for economic planning for war should have been able to produce an adequate general policy, and to ensure the co-ordination of departmental efforts within it. An analysis of the objectives of the wartime economy in the widest sense would have enabled a clearer identification of the critical areas, and the preparation of more satisfactory detailed proposals to deal with them. Finally, the existence at the outbreak of war of a clearly defined plan and an experienced designated or skeleton staff, would have enabled a smoother transition to wartime conditions, and the speedier and more accurate analysis of the requirements of the particular struggle, so avoiding many of the inefficiencies consequent upon the uncoordinated and disjointed manner in which attempts to solve the problem of the import system were made in 1940-41.

In this context, it is instructive to note the one area of the defence economy where such circumstances obtained in 1939. The Ministry of Economic Warfare, established in 1938, was a purely advisory body, yet it succeeded in gaining the acceptance of an overall policy in its field, and was also able to coordinate the activities of such notoriously independent bodies as the Admiralty within that policy. Through its centralised control of policy and coordination, and its monopoly of expertise regarding the conduct of economic warfare, the Ministry managed to avoid the shambles of part-responsibilities overlapping with commercial bodies or other departments, which characterised the early years of the authorities concerned with the import system. In many respects, the Ministry of Economic Warfare represents a brilliant microcosm of what economic planning in the maritime sphere should have been before the Second World War. This judgement is in no way belittled by the fact that conditions in this field were peculiarly, indeed exceptionally, favourable to such a successful conclusion. Even so, the success of this organisation was hampered in the first months of war by a reluctance on the part of the government to fully deploy all the measures at its disposal, and to that extent, it failed to escape the dead hand of a government policy unwilling or unable to realise that total war demands total involvement by the state in economic affairs.

If the success of the M.O.E.W. derived largely from its ability to draw on the experience of the First World War, similar instruction was available to the bodies concerned with the import system. The official historians have concluded that:

> No doubt the experience of 1914-18 revealed, to those who in retrospect studied its meaning, the general type and pattern of a war economy under twentieth century conditions: but it could not reveal the actual weight and proportions and particulars of the war economy that Great Britain would be called upon to fashion twenty-one years after 1918.[16]

The statistical errors of the 1930s would have prejudiced the effectiveness of any detailed plans prepared at that time, but it remains clear that the most serious omission of planning in the period was precisely its failure to identify that 'general type and pattern' of the war economy referred to above. Had this been identified, and

[16] Hancock and Gowing, 53.

appropriate policy-making and coordinating structures been established, the 'actual weight and proportions and particulars' would have fallen into place, and the dismal record of the first two years of war would have been modified. The major factor in this failure was the unwillingness of inter-war governments to accept the need for thorough-going state intervention in the direction of all facets of the economic activity of the nation in wartime. In mitigation it must be admitted that this attitude was generally accepted at the time, but this made its effects no less deleterious.

Wartime cooperation between government trading departments and transport facilities is necessary on two levels — on the local day-to-day level, and centrally, in the form of an organisation through which the size and nature of all the larger government demands for transport can, wherever possible, be assessed in advance, and matched against the capacity available to meet them. Even with such machinery, supposing it can be made to function effectively, the uncertainties of war cannot be entirely foreseen; without such an organisation in wartime, congestion and waste of resources are inevitable.

The need for such arrangements had been clearly demonstrated by the experience of the First World War. The governments of the inter-war period possessed both the expertise and the ability to make adequate preparations for a future conflict. Their failure to do so, which I have attempted to explain, not only prejudiced Britain's security in the early years of the Second World War, but was a damaging restriction on her war effort in general. Both these consequences could have been avoided had those responsible for pre-war planning discharged their responsibility satisfactorily.

198

BIBLIOGRAPHY

For the most part, this book is based on primary source material, mainly the official records of the period. This bibliography therefore begins with a list of the classes of documents consulted, all of which are to be found in the Public Record Office, Ruskin Avenue, Kew, Surrey. The reference to these documents in the text includes both the P.R.O. classification number, in the classes given below, and the original official designation, where appropriate. The major published primary source relevant to the problems of shipping in this period is the trade journal, *Fairplay,* which may be consulted at the British Library Newspaper Library, Colindale.

Despite its importance, the subject of this book has attracted little historical attention. Secondary source material dealing specifically with it is restricted to the official histories, and some volumes of reminiscence by prominent figures, which therefore form the basis of this part of the bibliography. The problem of the general organisation of government for war forms a related field, and provides some references to the more specific topics with which this book is concerned. References to the problems of the import system in works on the naval history of the period are surprisingly few, and are almost exclusively limited to discussion of the defence of facilities against enemy attack. Nonetheless, the most important of such works have been included. The more general material on the history of the period is, of course, vast, and offers few relevant references. This section of the bibliography has therefore been treated very selectively, to include only those works actually cited, or those which I have found particularly informative in building up a background picture of the times. Most of them themselves contain substantial bibliographies.

PRIMARY SOURCE MATERIAL: THE OFFICIAL RECORDS

Committee of Imperial Defence Series

CAB 2:   Minutes of C.I.D. Meetings, 1902-1939

CAB 3:   C.I.D. Memoranda, Home Defence, 1901-1939
            (-A series)

CAB 4:   C.I.D. Memoranda, Miscellaneous, 1903-1939
            (-B series)

CAB 5:   C.I.D. Memoranda, Colonial Defence, 1902-1916;
            1919-1939 (-C series)

CAB 16: Ad Hoc Sub-Committees of Enquiry, 1905-1939 (B.S.W.R.I.O.C., D.I.C. etc.)

CAB 34: Standing Sub-Committee, 1921-1922

CAB 47: Advisory Committee on Trade Questions in Time of War, 1924-1939 (A.T.B. series)

CAB 53: Chiefs of Staff Committee

Cabinet Office Series

CAB 21: Registered Files, 1916-1939 (various subjects)

CAB 23: Cabinet Minutes, 1916-1939 (officially referred to as Conclusions)

CAB 24: Memoranda, 1915-1939 (C.P. series. Papers submitted for the consideration of the Cabinet)

Ministry of Transport Series

(The relevant Board of Trade material is contained in these classes)

M.T. 9: Marine Department, Correspondence and Papers (M.M.D. material, mainly relating to War Risks Insurance)

M.T. 40: Sea Transport Department, Correspondence and Papers

M.T. 48: Ports: Correspondence and Papers (peacetime operation only)

M.T. 50: Defence Planning (papers mainly relevant to the ports and the diversion of shipping)

M.T. 59: Shipping Control and Operation. Correspondence and Papers. 1938 onwards

M.T. 63: Port and Transit Organisation, Correspondence and Papers. 1937 onwards

Admiralty Series

ADM 1: Admiralty and Secretariat. Papers

ADM 116: Admiralty and Secretariat. Cases

ADM 167: Admiralty and Secretariat. Board Minutes and Memoranda

SECONDARY SOURCE MATERIAL

(Except where otherwise stated, the place of publication is London.)

Albion, R.G., *Naval and Maritime History: An Annotated Bibliography*, (Newton Abbot, 1973 edn.).

Aldcroft, D.H., *British Transport since 1914*, (Newton Abbot, 1975).

———— *Studies in British Transport History, 1870-1970*, (Newton Abbot, 1974).

———— *The Inter-War Economy: Britain, 1919-1939*, (1970).

Aldcroft, D.H. & Richardson, H.W., *The British Economy, 1870-1939*, (1969).

Alexandersson, G. & Norstrom, G., *World Shipping*, (New York, 1962).

Armitage, S., *The Politics of Decontrol of Industry: Britain and the United States*, (1969).

Ashworth, W., *An Economic History of England, 1870-1939*, (1972 edn.).

Avon, the Earl of, *The Eden Memoirs: Facing the Dictators*, (1962).

Barnett, C., *The Collapse of British Power*, (1972).

Beaverbrook, Lord, *Men and Power, 1917-1918*, (1956).

Beer, S.H., *Treasury Control: The Coordination of Financial and Economic Policy in Great Britain*, (Oxford, 1957).

Behrens, C.B.A., *Merchant Shipping and the Demands of War*, (1955).

Bell, A.C., *A History of the Blockade of Germany and of the Countries Associated with Her, 1914-1918*, (1961).

Beloff, M., 'The Whitehall Factor: The Role of the Higher Civil Service, 1919-1939', in: Cook, C. & Peele, G. (eds.), *The Politics of Reappraisal, 1918-1939*, (1975).

Bridges, Lord, 'Haldane and the Machinery of Government', *Public Administration*, XXXV, (1957).

(Central Statistical Office), *Statistical Digest of the War*, (1951).

Chester, D.N. (ed.), *Lessons of the British War Economy*, (Cambridge, 1951).

Chester, D.N., 'The Machinery of Government and Planning', in: Worswick, G.D.N. & Ady, P.H., *The British Economy*, (1952).

Churchill, W.S., *The Second World War*, 12 vols., (1964 edn.).

———— *The World Crisis*, 5 vols., (1923-1931).

Clark, J.J., 'Merchant Marine and the Navy: A Note on the Mahan Hypothesis', *Journal of the Royal United Services Institution*, CXII, (1967).

Colvin, I., *The Chamberlain Cabinet,* (1971).

Cooper, Duff, *Old Men Forget,* (1954).

Corbett, J.S., *Some Principles of Maritime Strategy,* (1911).

Corbett, J.S. & Newbolt, H., *History of the Great War: Naval Operations,* 5 vols., (1920-1931).

Cowling, M., *The Impact of Hitler: British Politics and British Policy, 1933-1940,* (1975).

Cresswell, Cmdr. J., 'The Self-Defence of Merchant Ships in War', *Journal of Royal United Services Institution,* LXXXIII, (1938).

Daalder, H., *Cabinet Reform in Britain, 1914-1963,* (1964).

Dilkes, D., *The Diaries of Sir Alexander Cadogan, 1938-1945,* (1971).

D'Ombrain, N., *War Machinery and High Policy: Defence Administration in Peacetime Britain, 1902-1914,* (1973).

Duckworth, Lt.-Cmdr., R.C.M., 'Blockade in the Great War', *Journal of Royal United Services Institution,* LXXXIV, (1939).

Dyos, H.J. & Aldcroft, D.H., *British Transport,* (Leicester, 1969).

Earle, E.M., (ed.), *Makers of Modern Strategy,* (Princeton, N.J., 1944).

Ehrman, J., *Cabinet Government and War, 1890-1940,* (Cambridge, 1958).

Elderton, W.P., *Shipping Problems, 1916-1921,* (1928).

Fayle, C.E., *History of the Great War: Seaborne Trade,* 3 vols., (1920-1924).

———— *The War and the Shipping Industry,* (Oxford, 1927).

Foley, E.J., 'The Board of Trade and the Fighting Services', *Journal of Royal United Services Institution,* LXXIV, (1929).

Franks, O., *Central Planning and Control in War and Peace,* (1947).

Gibbs, N.H., *The Origins of Imperial Defence,* (Oxford, 1955).

Gilbert, M., *The Roots of Appeasement,* (1966).

Hamilton, Sir H.P., 'Sir Warren Fisher and the Public Service', *Public Administration,* XXIX, (1951).

Hammond, R.J., *Food, I: The Growth of Policy,* (1951).

Hancock, W.K. & Gowing, M.M., *British War Economy,* (1949).

Hankey, Lord, *Government Control in War,* (Cambridge, 1955).

———— *The Supreme Command, 1914-1918,* 2 vols., (1961).

Hargreaves, E.L. & Gowing, M.M., *Civil Industry and Trade,* (1952).

Heckscher, E.F., *The Continental System, An Economic Interpretation,* (Oxford, 1922).

Higham, R., *Armed Forces in Peacetime: Britain 1918-1940, a Case*

  Study, (1962).

Hobsbawm, E.J., *Industry and Empire,* (1968).

Howard, M., *War in European History,* (1976).

Howson, S., *Domestic Monetary Management in Britain, 1919-1938,* (Cambridge, 1975).

Hurd, A., *History of the Great War: The Merchant Navy,* 3 vols., (1921).

_____ *A Merchant Fleet at War,* (1920).

_____ 'British Merchant Shipping Today', *Journal of Royal United Services Institution,* LXXXII, (1937).

Hurstfield, J., *The Control of Raw Materials,* (1953).

Hurwitz, S.J., *State Intervention in Great Britain, A Study of Economic Control and Social Response, 1914-1919,* (New York, 1949).

Ismay, H.L., 'The Machinery of the Committee of Imperial Defence', *Journal of Royal United Services Institution,* LXXXIV, (1939).

Jack, D.T., *Studies in Economic Warfare,* (1940).

Jellicoe, Viscount, *The Crisis of the Naval War,* (1920).

_____ *The Grand Fleet, 1914-1916,* (1919).

Johnson, F.A., *Defence by Committee: The British Committee of Imperial Defence, 1885-1959,* (1960).

Kennedy, P.M., *The Rise and Fall of British Naval Mastery,* (1976).

Kircaldy, A.W., *British Shipping,* (1914).

Leslie, Sir N., 'British Shipping — The Present Situation', *Journal of Royal United Services Institution,* LXXVII, (1932).

_____ 'The Mercantile Marine in a Future War', *Journal of Royal United Services Institution,* LXXIV, (1929).

Lloyd, E.M.H., *Experiments in State Control,* (Oxford, 1924).

Lloyd George, D., *The War Memoirs of David Lloyd George,* 6 vols., (1933-1936).

Lowe, R., 'The Erosion of State Intervention in Britain, 1917-1924', *Economic History Review,* XXXI (2), (1978).

Mahan, A.T., *The Influence of Sea Power upon History,* (1965 edn.).

Marder, A.J., *From the Dreadnought to Scapa Flow,* 5 vols., (1961-1970).

Matthews, Sir H., 'Food Supplies in Wartime', *Journal of Royal United Services Institution,* LXXXII, (1937).

Maurice, Sir F., *Governments and War,* (1926).

Medlicott, W.N., *British Foreign Policy since Versailles, 1919-1963,* (1968 edn.).

_____ *The Economic Blockade,* vol. I, (1952).

Middlemas, K., *The Diplomacy of Illusion: The British Government and Germany, 1937-1939*, (1972).

Middlemas, K., (ed.), *Thomas Jones, Whitehall Diary*, 3 vols., (1969-1971).

Middlemas, K. & Barnes, J., *Baldwin: A Biography*, (1969).

Milward, A.S., *The Economic Effects of the World Wars on Britain*, (1970).

Mitchell, B.R. & Deane, P., *Abstract of British Historical Statistics*, (Cambridge, 1962).

Mowat, C.L., *Britain Between the Wars*, (1955).

Moyse-Bartlett, H., *A History of the Merchant Navy*, (1937).

Norman-Jones, Cmdr. G., 'The Merchant Navy in War', *Journal of Royal United Services Institution*, LXXVI, (1931).

Northedge, F.S., *The Troubled Giant. Britain among the Great Powers, 1916-1939*, (1967).

O'Connell, D.P., *The Influence of Law on Sea Power*, (Manchester, 1975).

Olson, M., *The Economics of the Wartime Shortage*, (Durham, N.C., 1963).

Payton-Smith, D.J., *Oil*, (1971).

Pollard, S., *The Development of the British Economy, 1914-1950*, (1962).

Ranft, B. McL., 'The Naval Defence of British Seaborne Trade, 1860-1905', Unpublished D.Phil. thesis, Oxford, (1967).

Richmond, H., *Statesmen and Sea Power*, (Oxford, 1946).

Roskill, S.W., *Hankey, Man of Secrets*, 3 vols., (1970-1974).

_____ *A Merchant Fleet in War, 1939-1945*, (1962).

_____ *Naval Policy Between the Wars*, 2 vols., (1968, 1976).

_____ *The War at Sea, 1939-1945*, 3 vols., (1954-1961).

Russel-Smith, J., *The Influence of the Great War upon Shipping*, (New York, 1919).

Salter, J.A., *Allied Shipping Control*, (Oxford, 1921).

Savage, C.I., *Inland Transport*, (1957).

Schofield, B., *British Sea Power*, (1967).

Seton-Watson, R.W., *Britain and the Dictators*, (Cambridge, 1938).

Shay, R.P., *British Rearmament in the Thirties: Politics and Profits*, (Princeton, N.J., 1977).

Storey, Capt. F.E., 'The Defence of Merchant Ships in a Future War', *Journal of Royal United Services Institution*, LXX, (1925).

_____ 'The War Readiness of the Merchant Service', *Journal of Royal United Services Institution*, LXXI, (1926).

Sturmey, S.G., *British Shipping and World Competition*, (1962).

T. 124 (Capt. R. Grenfell), *Sea Power*, (1940).

Tawney, R.H., 'The Abolition of Economic Controls, 1918-1921', *Economic History Review,* XIII, (1943). Reprinted in an extended version in Winter, J.M., (ed.), *History and Society: Essays by R.H. Tawney,* (1978).

Taylor, A.J.P., *English History, 1914-1945,* (Oxford, 1965).

Thompson, Capt. F.J., 'The Merchant Ship in Convoy', *Journal of Royal United Services Institution,* LXXIX, (1934).

Thornton, R.H., *British Shipping,* (Cambridge, 1959).

Vansittart, R., *The Mist Procession,* (1958).

Watt, D.C.W., *Too Serious a Business,* (1975).

Webb, Vice-Adm., Sir R., 'Trade Defence in War', *Journal of Royal United Services Institution,* LXX, (1925).

Youngson, A.J., *Britain's Economic Growth, 1920-1966,* (1967).

DRAMATIS PERSONAE

This list includes the principal figures mentioned in the text. They are mainly officials, and I have included details of their departments, and, where possible, their positions at representative years. The details come from the Civil Service Yearbook.

Alcorn, A. (B.O.T.)	In 1935 Deputy Director, Sea Transport Branch, M.M.D. No subsequent details
Dorrell, W.J. (B.O.T.)	1935: Asst. Director, S.T.B., M.M.D. 1940: Dep. Director, Allocation of Tonnage Div., M.O.S.
Duffield, W.D. (M.T.)	1935: Principal, Secretarial Dept., M.T. 1940: Principal, Port and Transit Organisation
Elderton, W.P.	1938: Chairman, British Insurance Association 1940: Chief Statistical Adviser, M.O.S.
Faulkner, Sir A.E. (B.O.T.)	1925: Director, Sea Transport, M.M.D. Subsequently Under Secretary, Mines Dept. to 1940.
Foley, Sir Julian (B.O.T.)	1935: Under Secretary, M.M.D. 1940: Secretary, M.O.S.
Garside, F.R.	Captain, R.N. on Plans and Trade Divs. at various times
Glennie, P.G. (B.O.T.)	1935: Superintending Clerk, S.T.B., M.M.D. 1939: Senior Executive Officer, S.T.B.
Griffiths, F.A. (B.O.T.)	1935: Principal, B.O.T. 1940: Principal Asst. Sec., Allocation of Tonnage Div., M.O.S.
Haigh, D. (B.O.T.)	1940: Chief Executive Officer, War Risks Insurance Office, and Sec. to Committee of Management
Hargreaves, W.G.	A commercial insurance expert, who devised the cargo scheme in 1938. Member of the Committee of Management of W.R.I.O., 1940

Hill, Sir Norman		Member of B.S.W.R.I.O.C.
		Past Chairman of Liverpool and London War Risks Association and of P.T.E.C.
Hill, R.H. (M.T.)	1935:	Principal, M.T.
	1940:	Railway Control Officer, M.T.
Hipwood (B.O.T.)	1930:	Second Sec., B.O.T. Retired thereafter
Hurcomb, Cyril	1935:	Sec., M.T.
	1940:	Director-General, M.O.S.
Hynard, W.G. (B.O.T.)	1935:	Director, Sea Transport Branch, M.M.D.
	1940:	Director, Sea Transport Div., M.O.S.
Keenlyside, F.H. (B.O.T.)	1935:	Asst. Principal, Min. of Ag. and Fish
	1940:	Private Sec., Minister of Shipping
Lloyd, E.M.H. (B.O.T.)	1939:	Asst. Director, Food (Defence Plans) Dept.
	1940:	Principal Asst. Sec., Min. of Food
Manisty, Eldon	1940:	Paymaster Rear-Admiral, R.N., attached to Sea Transport Division
Meredith, A.P. (B.O.T.)	1935:	Executive Officer, S.T.B., M.M.D.
	1940:	Higher Grade Executive Officer, S.T.D., M.O.S.
Phillips, S.H.	1939-1940:	Principal Asst. Sec., Admiralty.
Picknett, B.F. (B.O.T.)	1935:	Chief Staff Officer, M.M.D.
	1940:	Principal, Commercial Services Div., M.O.S.
Robinson, A.T.V.	1935-1940:	Dep. Sec., M.T.
Rodgers, P.F. (M.O.S.)	1940:	Dep. Director, Allocation of Tonnage Div., M.O.S.
Thomson, F.V.	1940:	Principal Shipping Adviser to H.M.G. and Controller, Commercial Services Div., M.O.S.
Tolerton, R.H. (M.T.)	1935:	Asst. Sec. (Roads), M.T.
	1940:	Principal Asst. Sec., Port and Transit Org.

Weston, W.G. (B.O.T.)	1935: 1940:	Principal, M.M.D. Asst. Sec., Neutral Policy Div., M.O.S.
Wills, H.C. (B.O.T.)	1935: 1940:	Executive Officer, S.T.B., M.M.D. Higher Executive Officer, S.T.D., M.O.S.
Wilson, S.S. (M.T.)	1939: 1940:	Principal, (Roads), M.T. Asst. Sec., Port and Transit Organisation

INDEX

Other volumes in this series

Copies obtainable on order from
Swift Printers Ltd, 1-7 Albion Place, Britton Street, London EC1M 5RE